Fifth Edition

The Marketing Plan Handbook

Marian Burk Wood, M.B.A.

PEARSON

Boston   Columbus   Indianapolis   New York   San Francisco   Upper Saddle River
Amsterdam   Cape Town   Dubai   London   Madrid   Milan   Munich   Paris   Montréal   Toronto
Delhi   Mexico City   São Paulo   Sydney   Hong Kong   Seoul   Singapore   Taipei   Tokyo

Editor in Chief: Stephanie Wall
Senior Acquisitions Editor: Erin Gardner
Director of Editorial Services: Ashley Santora
Editorial Project Manager: Lynn M. Savino
Editorial Assistant: Jacob Garber
Director of Marketing: Maggie Moylan
Executive Marketing Manager: Anne Falhgren
Marketing Assistant: Gianna Sandri
Senior Managing Editor: Judy Leale
Production Manager: Thomas Benfatti
Creative Director: Jayne Conte
Cover Designer: Brice Kenselaar
Cover Art: © CLIPAREA.com
Full-Service Project Management: Sudip Sinha/PreMediaGlobal
Composition: PreMediaGlobal
Printer/Binder: STP/RRD/Harrisonburg
Cover Printer: STP/RRD/Harrisonburg
Text Font: Times

Credits and acknowledgments borrowed from other sources and reproduced, with permission, in this textbook appear on the appropriate page within text.

Library of Congress Cataloging-in-Publication Data

Wood, Marian Burk.
    The marketing plan handbook / Marian Burk Wood, M.B.A.—Fifth Edition.
        pages cm
    Includes index.
    ISBN-13: 978-0-13-307835-0
    ISBN-10: 0-13-307835-3
    1. Marketing—Management—Handbooks, manuals, etc.   I. Title.
    HF5415.13.W66 2012
    658.8'02—dc23

                                                                                    2012036309

10 9 8 7 6 5 4 3 2 1

ISBN 10: 0-13-307835-3
ISBN 13: 978-0-13-307835-0

BRIEF CONTENTS

CHAPTER CHECKLISTS

CONTENTS

PREFACE

WHAT'S NEW IN THIS EDITION?

- *New Sample Marketing Plan.* The new sample marketing plan for PretzL Elegance, a fictional start-up, serves as a model for summarizing the current marketing situation, planning for marketing-mix activities, and preparing to measure results.

- *New Examples of Marketing Plans in Action.* Reflecting real-world decisions and challenges, this edition includes dozens of new examples of consumer and business-to-business (B2B) marketing, goods and services marketing, traditional and digital marketing, U.S. and global marketing, not-for-profit marketing, and marketing by governmental agencies.

- *New Coverage of Contemporary Concepts, Trends, and Technologies.* This edition includes new coverage of cocreation, key performance indicators, group buying, mobile marketing, multichannel marketing, neuromarketing, showrooming, social gifting, social media, and other important new marketing developments and trends.

- *New QR Codes to Showcase Online Marketing.* Every chapter includes at least five QR codes, scannable by smartphone app, leading to the home pages of companies, nonprofits, and government agencies. By following the QR codes or entering the URLs provided in the text, you'll see how marketers present themselves online and take a peek at a few key sites that marketers should know.

- *Newly Revised Checklists.* Every chapter contains a newly revised checklist that focuses attention on the most critical aspects of marketing planning, from the situation analysis to the marketing audit. Answer the checklist questions to step through the details of preparing a marketing plan.

- *New PowerPoint Presentation.* For classroom use, the PowerPoint presentation has been thoroughly updated to detail all the steps in the marketing process, with special emphasis on the latest marketing concepts and techniques.

Whether you're marketing a new product, a special service, or *yourself*, a creative, well-researched, and practical marketing plan can make a real difference to your success. Although marketing textbooks often discuss the general use of a marketing plan or contain a brief outline of one, they don't explain exactly how to develop an effective plan—yet that's what marketers, marketing students, and entrepreneurs really need.

The Marketing Plan Handbook fills this gap by taking you through the entire planning process, one step at a time. The emphasis is on applying basic concepts of marketing strategy, tactics, and metrics to develop a marketing plan that is both practical and adaptable. Chapter by chapter, you'll learn how to formulate a good plan and gain valuable insights from reading about the marketing-plan successes (and occasional missteps) of organizations around the world. At the same time, this updated edition will give you a good overview of the latest marketing principles, trends, and technologies.

YOUR MARKETING PLAN, STEP BY STEP

Don't know where to start or how to approach all the decisions you face in preparing a marketing plan? Each chapter concludes with a special "Your Marketing Plan, Step by Step" feature that takes you through every step in the planning process. By answering the questions in these features and following up on the suggested data sources, you'll have a head start in gathering information and analyzing alternatives for your plan. You'll also find fresh perspectives on the practical application of key marketing concepts. No matter what kind of marketing plan you're creating, these features can help you generate ideas and think about critical issues.

REAL-WORLD VIEW OF MARKETING PLANNING

How did Movie Tavern use marketing plans to build its brand as one of the pioneers of the food-and-film industry (see Chapter 2)? What did LEGO do behind the scenes to plan for introducing new toys for girls (Chapter 3)? How does IBM plan its mix of business goods and services to achieve its marketing objectives (Chapter 5)? Why would McDonald's put its popular McRib sandwich on the menu for only a few weeks every year (Chapter 6)? What's the marketing story behind the Metropolitan Opera's highly successful HD Live program (Chapter 8)? How did Chobani use smart marketing to become a major player in the yogurt industry (Chapter 9)?

From a marketing perspective, what market leaders like LEGO, IBM, McDonald's, and Chobani have in common with niche firms like Movie Tavern and nonprofits like the Metropolitan Opera is their use of structured plans to identify appropriate target markets, guide the development of marketing strategy, coordinate marketing programs, and prepare to measure performance. *The Marketing Plan Handbook* includes these and many other examples from consumer and business markets, large and small companies, traditional and online businesses, U.S. and international firms, and not-for-profit organizations. In response to instructors' suggestions, the real-world examples go into some detail to illustrate the diverse challenges and opportunities that marketers face in preparing and implementing a successful plan.

SPECIAL FEATURES HELP YOU LEARN TO PLAN

The Marketing Plan Handbook provides a series of special features to support the hands-on development of creative yet practical and actionable marketing plans.

New Sample Marketing Plan: PretzL Elegance

What does a marketing plan look like? The appendix presents a new sample plan for PretzL Elegance, a fictional start-up company about to introduce its first two chocolate-covered pretzel snacks. This abbreviated sample plan, based on current conditions in the snack and chocolate markets, gives you an idea of how a typical marketing plan is organized and presented. In particular, the plan demonstrates how a company might analyze market needs and trends, examine environmental factors, look at the competitive situation, and set objectives to be achieved. It also touches on segmentation, targeting, and positioning; the variety of marketing strategies and programs needed to launch a new product; and some of the metrics used in evaluating marketing performance. A second sample marketing plan on the book's companion website www.pearsonhighered.com /wood/ shows the marketing decisions a high-tech company might make to prepare for launching a new smartphone.

Model of the Marketing Planning Process Connects the Steps

So much goes into the making of a marketing plan … yet it's not always easy to see the big picture when you're working on the details. The marketing planning model, introduced in Chapter 1, guides you through the process and is repeated in all 10 chapters, serving as a "you are here" organizing figure for the book. Use this model to visualize the connections between the steps and to focus on the three key outcomes of any marketing plan: to provide value, build relationships, and make a difference to stakeholders.

Helpful Checklists

How can you be sure your plan covers all the basics? Checklists in every chapter summarize key areas to be examined during the planning process. As you answer the questions in these ten checklists, you'll get good ideas for creating a realistic marketing plan, gain insights into the complexities of the planning process, and identify specific details for follow-up later in the process.

Practical Planning Tips

What important points and pitfalls should you keep in mind as you construct a marketing plan? Each chapter includes a number of special tips, shown in the margin, to help you make the transition from theory to application. These tips emphasize various practical aspects of planning and mention specific issues or questions to consider at each step in the process.

Powerful PowerPoint Presentation

Created by John Newbold of Sam Houston University, the updated PowerPoint presentation is a powerful supplement to *The Marketing Plan Handbook*. Expanded content and eye-catching graphics make this a high-impact presentation package for instructors to download.

Exclusive Online Features

Visit this book's website, www.prenhall.com/wood, for access to a variety of additional materials: a complete glossary, an outline showing the main sections of a marketing plan, a second sample marketing plan, hotlinks to selected online marketing resources, discussion questions for each chapter, and faculty materials, including the updated PowerPoint presentation.

ACKNOWLEDGMENTS

My sincere gratitude to the knowledgeable faculty reviewers who provided insightful comments and suggestions over the years: Mel Albin, University of Maryland University College; David Andrus, Kansas State University; Ismet Anitsal, Tennessee Tech University; Tim Becker, University of San Diego, University of Phoenix, Webster University; Cathleen Behan, Northern Virginia Community College; Normand Bergeron, Bristol Community College; Robert Blanchard, Salem State College; Brian Bourdeau, Auburn University; Cynthia Brooks, Cleveland State Community College; Michaelle Cameron, St. Edwards University; Ravi Chinta, American University of Sharjah; Yun Chu, Frostburg State University; Patricia Clarke, Boston College; Earl Clay, Bristol Community College; Greg Combs, Methodist College; Mary Conran, Temple University; John Crawford, University of North Texas; Larry Crowson, University of Central Florida; Brent Cunningham, Jackson State University; Don Eckrich, Ithaca College; Valerie Ellis, Santa Barbara City College; William Fillner, Hiram College; Douglas Friedman, Penn State Harrisburg; Ralph M. Gaedeke, California State University, Sacramento; Dennis E. Garrett, Marquette University; B. Christine Green, University of Texas at Austin; Tom Gruen, University of Colorado at Colorado Springs; James Hansen, University of Akron, John Carroll University; Harry Harmon, Central Missouri State University; Betty Jean Hebel, Madonna

University; Jeffrey Heilbrunn, Columbia College of Missouri; David Hennessey, Babson College; James Hess, Ivy Tech Community College; Stacey Hills, Utah State University; Mahmood Hussain, San Francisco State University; Lynn Jahn, University of Iowa; Michelle Jones, NC State University College of Textiles; Kathleen Krentler, San Diego State University; Michelle Kunz, Morehead State University; Ron Lennon, Barry University; Ada Leung, University of Nebraska at Kearney; Nancy Lowd, Boston University; Terry Lowe, Heartland Community College; William Machanic, University of New Hampshire; Gordon McClung, Jacksonville University; Byron Menides, Worcester Polytechnic Institute; Margaret Mi, University of Mary Washington; Chip Miller, Drake University; Peter Mooney, Embry-Riddle Aeronautical University; Charlene Moser, Keller Graduate School of Management; Michael K. Mulford, Des Moines Area Community College; Keith Nickoloff, Rochester Institute of Technology; Ralitza Nikolaeva, University of Wisconsin–Milwaukee; Bernadette Njoku, College of Saint Rose; Margaret O'Connor, Penn State Berks Campus; Carol Osborne, University of South Florida; Peggy Osborne, Morehead State University; Talai Osmonbekov, Northern Arizona University; Joseph Ouellette, Bryant University; Jeff Periatt, Auburn University; Henry O. Pruden, Golden Gate University; Elizabeth Purinton, Marist College; Michelle Rai, Pacific Union College; Ruby Remley, Cabrini College; Torsten Ringberg, University of Wisconsin, Milwaukee; Scott D. Roberts, Northern Arizona University; Mark Rosenbaum, University of Hawaii, Northern Illinois University; Bennett Rudolph, Grand Valley State University; David Saliba, Duquesne University; John Schibrowsky, University of Nevada, Las Vegas; Gary R. Schornack, University of Colorado, Denver; Camille Schuster, California State University San Marcos; Chris Shao, Midwestern State University; Annette Singleton, Florida A&M University; J. Alexander Smith, Oklahoma City University; Allen Smith, Florida Atlantic University; Jim Stephens, Emporia State University; Bala Subramanian, Morgan State University; Michael J. Swenson, Brigham Young University; Ronald Thomas, Oakton Community College; Scott Thorne, Southeast Missouri State University; Deb Utter, Boston University; Beverly Venable, Columbus State University; Ven Venkatesan, University of Rhode Island; Bob Veryzer, Rensselaer Polytechnic Institute; Edward Volchok, Stevens Institute of Technology; Kathleen Williamson, University of Houston–Clear Lake; Katherine Wilson, Johns Hopkins University; Wendy Wysocki, Monroe County Community College; and Mark Young, Winona State University.

Let me say thank you, from my heart, to my knowledgeable Senior Acquisitions Editor, Erin Gardner, and to the many talented professionals at Pearson Prentice Hall whose expertise and commitment have made this book so successful: Kierra Bloom, Senior Editorial Project Manager; Anne Fahlgren, Executive Marketing Manager; Maggie Moylan, Director of Marketing; and Stephanie Wall, Editor in Chief. I'm especially grateful to Lynn M. Savino for carefully shepherding my manuscript through the long and winding road of production with grace and good humor.

I want to dedicate this book to my beloved husband, Wally Wood, and my dearest sister, Isabel Burk, for their inspiration and loving support. Also, this new edition is dedicated to the memory of my grandparents, Theodore Schwartz, Hermina Farkas Schwartz, Isaac Burk, and Henrietta Mahler Burk, and to all who came before them in the branches of our shared family tree.

—*Marian Burk Wood*
marketinghandbook@hotmail.com
http://marketinghandbook.blogspot.com

ABOUT THE AUTHOR

Marian Burk Wood has held vice presidential–level positions in corporate and not-for-profit marketing with Citibank, JP Morgan Chase, and the National Retail Federation, as well as management positions with national retail chains. In addition to *The Marketing Plan Handbook*, she is the author of *Essential Guide to Marketing Planning* and *Marketing Planning: Principles into Practice*, both geared to the European market.

Wood holds an MBA in marketing from Long Island University in New York and a BA from the City University of New York. She has extensive practical experience in marketing planning, having formulated and implemented many marketing plans for a variety of goods and services. She has also developed numerous chapters, cases, sample plans, exercises, and print and digital supplements for college textbooks in marketing, advertising, and related business disciplines. Her special interests in marketing include social media, ethics, segmentation, retailing, and B2B marketing.

Please visit her marketing blog at **http://marketinghandbook.blogspot.com**.

Marketing Planning: New Pace, New Possibilities

In this chapter:

PREVIEW

Every day brings new changes and new challenges to the world of marketing. Goods and services that didn't even exist a few years ago (like the Kindle, iPad, and Instagram) have reshaped entire industries (publishing, computers, and photography) within a short time. New technologies and economic realities have pushed once-dominant market leaders such as Kodak into bankruptcy and have prompted consumers to rethink their brand and media preferences.[1]

As you know from your own experience, the rise of social media has allowed people to stay in almost constant contact, both verbally and visually, with each other and with favorite brands, companies, and events. Facebook and Twitter are the top two social media sites, but new sites emerge often. Pinterest, a virtual bulletin board where consumers and businesses "pin" images to share with others, became the third-largest social media site less than two years after it went live, attracting millions of users who like posting images, viewing images posted by others, and joining the online conversation.[2]

As the global marketplace continues to evolve in dramatic and sometimes surprising directions, businesses and nonprofits are picking up the pace of their marketing planning to explore practical, creative possibilities for success in this dynamic environment. In the first part of this chapter, you'll learn about marketing, value, the purpose of marketing planning, and the contents of a marketing plan. Next, you'll be introduced to the basic steps in developing a marketing plan. The chapter closes with a look at how to prepare for marketing planning.

APPLYING YOUR KNOWLEDGE

Completing the questions in the "Your Marketing Plan, Step by Step" feature at the end of each chapter will help you (1) think through the information you'll need for your marketing plan, (2) generate alternatives to consider, and (3) take a realistic approach to your marketing plan. Before you document your ideas in a written marketing plan, be sure to look at this chapter's summary checklist of key issues, which offers questions to help you gain a perspective on the big picture for marketing planning.

CHAPTER 1 CHECKLIST   The Big Picture for Marketing Planning

As you begin the marketing planning process, prepare yourself for the big picture:

✓ Who are my customers, and what value can I offer them, now and in the long term?
✓ What sources of information will help me uncover, follow, and anticipate major developments affecting my customers, my markets, and my competitors?
✓ What political, economic, social, technological, legal, ecological, and competitive changes are likely to affect my markets and my customers in the coming years?
✓ What lessons can I learn from existing products, campaigns, media, competitors, and other organizations that will help my marketing plan?
✓ Which stakeholders are most important to the success of my marketing plan, and why?
✓ How can I use marketing to make a difference to my customers, my organization, and my stakeholders?
✓ How can I generate new ideas and build on my resources and experience to better plan for marketing?

MARKETING PLANNING TODAY

Every hour of every day, marketing is all around us—at home, at work, at play, in the streets, in stores and restaurants, and in all the media we see and hear. Although marketing aspires to be informative and even entertaining, it can also be inescapable, irritating, or intrusive at times. Given the intense competition for customers' attention, businesses and products must plan carefully to engage customers, demonstrate the value they provide, gain customers' trust, and—ideally—win long-term loyalty.

A good product, brand, commercial, price, website, app, Facebook page, or store display is simply not good enough today. Customers have better information, more choices, higher expectations, better market access, and more purchasing power than at any time in the past. Increasingly, customers are getting involved in marketing by suggesting products or creating brand-related materials that are meaningful to them. For instance, Doritos has engaged its customer base through

the popular "Crash the Super Bowl" contest, which offers cash prizes for the best consumer-created commercials featuring the snack brand.[3] (Scan the QR code to see the Doritos brand page, or visit www.doritos.com.)

Another major trend affecting marketing is the public's demand for *transparency,* insisting that organizations be open and honest about their decisions and actions, including pricing, sponsorship, and other aspects of marketing. In part, this is a backlash against techniques that have been considered *stealth marketing,* such as a company arranging for blog posts or product reviews that appear to be initiated by consumers but are actually initiated by the marketer.[4] It's also a reaction to concerns about marketers invading the privacy of consumers by tracking their online behavior and sharing mailing lists, among other activities.[5]

In recent years, customers, employees, and others have been particularly interested in what organizations aim to achieve beyond making a profit (for instance, improving quality of life for local communities or contributing to society at large). "People want to know who is the company behind the brands," explains the head of marketing for Procter & Gamble, the parent company behind blockbuster brands such as Tide and Gillette. "What are the values? Are they interested in more than making money? What is its purpose?"[6] A company with a larger purpose and strong values can really stand out, especially when competition is fierce and brands are fighting for attention and loyalty.

This is where reputation counts: Customers (and distributors) prefer to buy brands that have a positive image and support organizations that are transparent and trustworthy. Of course, building a great reputation requires meticulous planning and constant vigilance, because both compliments and criticism can ricochet around the world in an instant through tweets, texts, e-mails, and blogs. Consider Warby Parker's plan for building its "buy one, donate one" eyeglass business and establishing its reputation for social responsibility.

Warby Parker. Founded in 2010 by four business-school friends, Warby Parker offers fashionable, affordable prescription eyeglasses and sunglasses with the promise of donating one pair of glasses for every pair purchased. Although Warby Parker has a handful of showrooms inside big-city fashion boutiques and in its New York City headquarters, it operates mainly online, selling directly to customers to keep its prices affordable. Another way the firm differentiates itself from big competitors such as Lenscrafters is by designing its own frames rather than licensing branded frames—which also keeps costs down and prices reasonable. Customers can use the company's virtual "try-on" tool to see how frames would look and can request up to five lens-free frames for in-home trial before making a final decision on which frames to purchase. Warby Parker makes transactions convenient and risk-free by paying shipping costs both ways and offering a money-back customer satisfaction guarantee.

The company's marketing plan calls for emphasizing social responsibility as well as the value that its glasses represent. Every time a customer buys a pair of glasses, Warby Parker gives one pair away to someone in need via nonprofit groups such as VisionSpring. To date, more than 100,000 pairs have been donated. The founders are committed to transparency and use Facebook, Twitter, and other social media to encourage dialogue with customers and to respond quickly to comments. "If you're claiming to be having a positive impact and not being transparent, you'll be found out, and it will be company-destroying," says cofounder Neil Blumenthal. "It will hurt your ability to build relationships with customers, and impede your ability to recruit and retain talent."[7]

Marketing and Value

Warby Parker could not have survived its start-up years without effective marketing. **Marketing**, as defined by the American Marketing Association, is "the activity, set of institutions, and processes for creating, communicating, delivering, and exchanging offerings that have value for customers, clients, partners, and society at large." This definition emphasizes the importance of **value**, the difference between the perceived benefits a customer receives (to satisfy a want or need) and the perceived total price the customer pays. Warby Parker is growing because it satisfies the need for well-made prescription eyeglasses and creates value by offering stylish frames at affordable prices. The company also creates value for society by donating thousands of eyeglasses to people in need.

Thus, marketing covers everything the company is and does to consistently provide competitively-superior value in order to win customers and earn their ongoing loyalty. Businesses such as Warby Parker, which are primarily Internet based, have the added challenges of developing, updating, and maintaining an attractive, functional website; handling customer service; and managing order fulfillment as they work on all the other elements of marketing strategy. Mobile marketing is another focus for many companies and nonprofit organizations. As an example, some local Goodwill groups now offer an app for locating used merchandise on the nonprofit's Amazon storefronts and eBay pages.[8] This appeals to the growing number of consumers who appreciate "vintage" merchandise or who are avid bargain-hunters.

The Purpose of Marketing Planning

Marketing planning is the structured process of determining how to provide value to customers, the organization, and key stakeholders by researching and analyzing the current situation, including markets and customers; developing and documenting marketing's objectives, strategies, and programs; and implementing, evaluating, and controlling marketing activities to achieve the objectives. The outcome of this process is the **marketing plan**, a document covering a particular period that summarizes what the marketer has learned about the marketplace, what will be accomplished through marketing, and how.

Exhibit 1.1 illustrates the overall process for marketing planning. As the exhibit indicates, the marketing plan resulting from this process should explain how the company will provide value, build relationships, and make a difference to its stakeholders. This exhibit also serves as an organizing figure for this handbook's coverage of how to develop a viable marketing plan.

The purpose of marketing planning is to provide a disciplined yet flexible framework for guiding the company toward its value and relationship objectives. Because marketing managers are accountable for achieving results on time and within budget, the process must include milestones for tracking progress toward results and control mechanisms for adjusting tactics or timing without abandoning sound long-term strategy. In fact, when the marketing environment is particularly challenging, "clarity of strategy becomes even more important," emphasizes strategy expert Michael Porter of Harvard.[9]

Clearly, companies have to engage their customers and plan marketing efforts in line with their customers' interests, concerns, behavior, attitudes, and feelings. Auto manufacturers are doing this as they battle for share in China, the world's largest market for cars, where purchases are accelerating at an unprecedented rate.

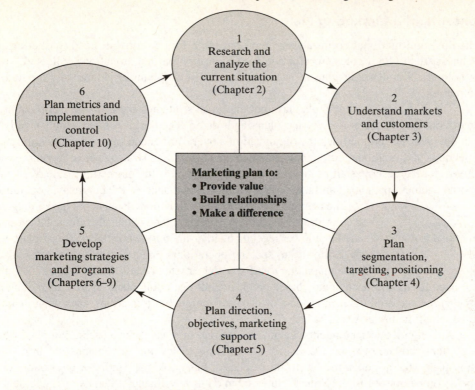

EXHIBIT 1.1   The Marketing Planning Process

Automakers in China. More than 18 million cars are sold in China every year as middle- and upper-income consumers seek out global brands, in particular, to convey status and individuality. Eyeing this fast-growing and lucrative opportunity, BMW, General Motors (GM), Honda, Peugeot, Toyota, and Volkswagen are among the automakers that have opened research and design facilities in China to study consumers' needs and to create new models attuned to their tastes. GM's made-in-China Buick Excelle is the country's top-selling car, but luxury vehicles are increasingly the focus for international automakers. Premium models already account for nearly 8% of Chinese car purchases, and sales are growing at a double-digit pace.

Culturally connected marketing has helped many automakers make inroads in China. For the Year of the Dragon, Rolls Royce created a limited-edition Phantom luxury model complete with custom exterior paint and custom embroidery on the seats. The price: an eye-popping $1.2 million—and every car was sold in a matter of weeks. Aston Martin produced only 88 of its special Dragon88 cars, with exclusive colors and 24-carat-gold accessories, as well as dragon-themed touches and high-end audio equipment. Demand was high, despite the $800,000 price tag. Detroit-based GM is also planning to boost sales of its upscale Cadillac in China. Its goal is to sell as many Cadillacs in China as it does in the United States within a few years. "Successful global automotive companies must have a luxury brand that competes around the world," says GM's CEO.[10]

Even the most successful automaker must prove itself month after month, year after year, car after car, market after market, in order to remain profitable and competitive. As a result, every marketing plan must be updated and adapted as the market and customers' needs evolve and as the organization's situation, priorities, and performance change.

Contents of a Marketing Plan

Start-ups, multinational corporations, and charitable foundations all need marketing plans to chart paths to their goals (whether defined by profits earned, donations collected, or people helped). A marketing plan is one of several official planning documents created by a company.

The company's strategic plan lays out the broad strategies for all its units, divisions, and departments over a three- to five-year planning horizon. The business plan, which usually covers a one-year period, outlines the organization's overall financial objectives, including profit projections and funding requirements, and explains the overall strategy for achieving those objectives. It also describes all products and services, explains the marketing strategy, identifies key management personnel and their qualifications, and discusses the company's operations.

PLANNING TIP

Get a fresh perspective by creating a new plan every year rather than adapting last year's plan.

The marketing plan contains much more detail about the coming year's marketing strategy and implementation than is included in the business plan. Created at a lower level than either the business or the strategic plan, it provides shorter-term, specific operational direction for how the organization will use marketing to achieve the targeted results. Often, a marketing plan is developed for the entire company; based on the overall marketing plan, separate marketing plans may then be prepared for each product or line, new product introductions, each geographic area served, one-time projects, and so on.

Although the exact contents, length, and format may vary, most marketing plans contain the sections shown in Exhibit 1.2. For ideas about how to develop and document your own marketing plan, take a look at the brief sample plan in this book's appendix or the sample on this book's companion website. (Note: Neither sample has any financial details or implementation schedules.)

In any marketing plan, the executive summary is actually the final section to be written, because it serves as a brief overview of the main points. The other sections are generally drafted in the order in which they appear in the plan, with each successive section building on the previous one. Managers can't prepare marketing budgets and schedules, for example, until their objectives, strategies, and action programs have been set. Note that when a company changes one part of the plan, it may have to change other parts as well (such as programs and budgets), because of the interrelated nature of the sections.

In the past, the marketing plan often was sequestered in the marketing department until it was reviewed by upper management, revised, and then distributed to sales and other departments. These days, however, the creation of a marketing plan involves organization-wide input and collaboration—sometimes including partners, suppliers, and customers.

Larger organizations such as Yum Brands frequently require a marketing plan for each unit (e.g., individual stores or divisions) as well as for each product or brand. KFC, Pizza Hut, and Taco Bell are among the well-known fast-food brands in Yum's global empire, each following a different marketing plan for profitability. Taco Bell has introduced breakfast items to attract consumers throughout the day, and has launched unique products such as Doritos Locos Tacos with social media marketing. Yum also has a separate plan for each restaurant chain in China, where KFC has been operating since 1987 and where Pizza Hut is the leading casual dining brand, as well as for India, where the company is experiencing an astonishing 34% annual sales growth.[11]

The success of a marketing plan depends on a complex web of internal and external relationships as well as on uncontrollable environmental factors such as technological

EXHIBIT 1.2   Main Sections of a Marketing Plan

Section	Description
Executive summary	Reviews the plan's highlights and objectives, linking the marketing effort to higher-level strategies and goals.
Current marketing situation	Analyzes events and trends in the environment that can affect the organization, its marketing, and its stakeholders: • Internal situation (mission, resources, offerings, previous results, business relationships) • External situation (political-legal, economic, social-cultural, technological, and ecological forces) • Competitive situation (current and emerging/potential competitors, competitive strategies and advantages) • Market situation (market definition, market share, customer needs and behavior) • SWOT analysis (internal strengths and weaknesses, external opportunities and threats)
Target market, customer analysis, positioning	Explains the segmentation, targeting, and positioning decisions. Also discusses the segments to be targeted, with an overview of customers' and prospects' needs, wants, behaviors, attitudes, loyalty, and purchasing patterns.
Objectives and issues	Outlines specific objectives, in three categories, to be achieved through the plan, and identifies any issues that may affect the organization's ability to achieve them: • Financial objectives • Marketing objectives • Societal objectives
Marketing strategy	Summarizes the overall strategy for achieving objectives by creating, communicating, and delivering value to the target market(s). Also indicates how marketing will affect other stakeholders.
Marketing programs	Lays out the programs supporting the marketing strategy, including specific activities, schedules, and responsibilities for the following: • Product • Pricing • Place (channels and distribution) • Promotion (marketing communications and influence) • Service • Internal marketing
Financial and operational plans	Financial and operational requirements and results related to marketing programs: • Expected revenues and profits • Projected budgets • Schedules and responsibilities • Additional information or resources needed for planning and implementation
Metrics and implementation control	Indicates how the plan will be implemented and evaluated, including metrics for performance measurement. Shows how and when adjustments will be made to keep plan on track toward objectives. Includes contingency plans as needed.

breakthroughs, competitive moves, and economic pressures. That's why marketing plans should be reexamined regularly in accordance with changes in competition, customers' needs and attitudes, product or company performance, and other factors, as Green Mountain Coffee Roasters recently discovered.

Green Mountain. Riding high on the huge success of its K-Cup coffee pods and the Keurig single-serve coffee/espresso brewing machines, Vermont-based Green Mountain enjoyed years of rapid growth and market leadership. Then the cost of coffee beans soared and one of the company's biggest K-Cup customers, Starbucks, announced its own single-serve coffee machine. At the same time, some key patents on K-Cup technology were expiring, and Green Mountain faced sharply higher competition from companies producing their own versions of K-Cup pods.

The result was lower-than-anticipated demand for K-Cups, slower revenue growth, and a smaller profit margin. In response, Green Mountain reexamined its marketing plan and redoubled efforts to forecast sales and revenue more accurately. Even as it took steps to reduce K-Cup inventory, the company focused on the launch of its new Vue espresso makers, on developing new coffee products, and on market tests of V-Cup pods in Dunkin' Donuts and other retailers.[12]

DEVELOPING A MARKETING PLAN

Marketing plans generally cover a full year, although some (especially those covering new-product introductions) may project activities and anticipate results further into the future. The marketing planning process starts several months before the marketing plan is scheduled to go into operation; this allows sufficient time for thorough research and analysis, management review and revision, and coordination of resources among departments and business units.

Coordination is even more critical for plans that involve multiple marketers and others affected by the planned activities. When the Palm Springs Convention and Visitors Authority wanted to boost long-term tourism in California's Coachella Valley, it sought help from a firm experienced in destination marketing. The firm spent months speaking with current and potential visitors, local hotels and restaurants, and city officials; it also analyzed a mountain of tourism data and reviewed feedback from previous campaigns. "What's been critical to our process is taking the time to not only get to know the community and the stakeholders," says the head of the Convention and Visitors Authority, "but to understand past successes and failures." The result was a new marketing plan that served as an umbrella for marketing the area to vacationers and convention planners and that brought brand cohesion to marketing efforts by individual travel partners such as hotels.[13]

For long-term success, marketers need to analyze connections with customers as well as suppliers, channel members, partners, and other key **stakeholders** (people and organizations that are influenced by or that can influence company performance). In the Palm Springs example, stakeholders included travelers plus hotels, restaurants, city officials, and tourism officials. Traditionally, companies kept up a monologue by sending information to stakeholders through advertisements and other promotion techniques. With a dialogue, however, information flows both ways—from the firm to its stakeholders and from stakeholders to the firm. Such a dialogue provides clues to what customers and other stakeholders think, feel, need, want, expect, and value—input that marketers need in order to adjust current programs and launch new programs based on a creative, practical, and adaptable marketing plan.

Should competitors be considered stakeholders? In general, the answer is yes: What each company does with marketing can (directly or indirectly) affect its rivals' performance and the overall situation in the industry and specific markets. Some companies create marketing plans to overtake particular competitors or to attain overall market leadership, closely monitoring what rivals do so they can adjust their marketing if and when competitors change course. Although U.S. law forbids competitors from discussing or coordinating price decisions, marketers do watch competitors' pricing moves and sometimes match or beat their prices, as in the airline industry and the supermarket industry. And at times, competitors will work together on industrywide initiatives such as the Eco Index, a measure of the environmental impact of apparel products offered by Target, Timberland, and other marketers.[14]

Thus, when you're developing a marketing plan, it's important to consider how competitors and other stakeholders can potentially influence your marketing performance and how your decisions might influence their performance. Exhibit 1.3 shows the main stakeholders that the retail chain Target should take into account during marketing planning.

The following sections introduce each of the six marketing planning steps shown in Exhibit 1.1, providing an overview for the remainder of this handbook.

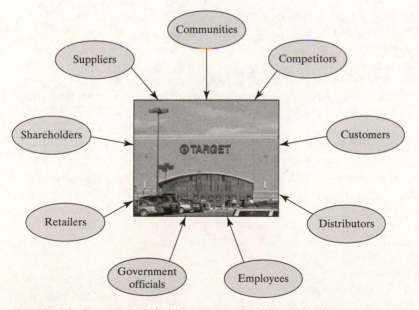

EXHIBIT 1.3 Target's Stakeholders Target should consider these main stakeholder groups when preparing marketing plans for the company, specific divisions, and specific stores.

Research and Analyze the Current Situation

PLANNING TIP

This analysis helps you identify influences on your objectives, strategies, and performance.

The first step is to study the current situation before charting the organization's marketing course for the coming year. Externally, marketers study environmental trends to detect political-legal, economic, social-cultural, technological, or ecological changes that can affect marketing decisions, performance opportunities and threats, and potential profits. Demographic shifts revealed by U.S. Census data will be part of the social-cultural analysis (see Exhibit 1.4). Marketing managers also assess the company's capabilities and the strategies of competitors so they can build on internal strengths while exploiting rivals' weaknesses and making the most of emerging opportunities.

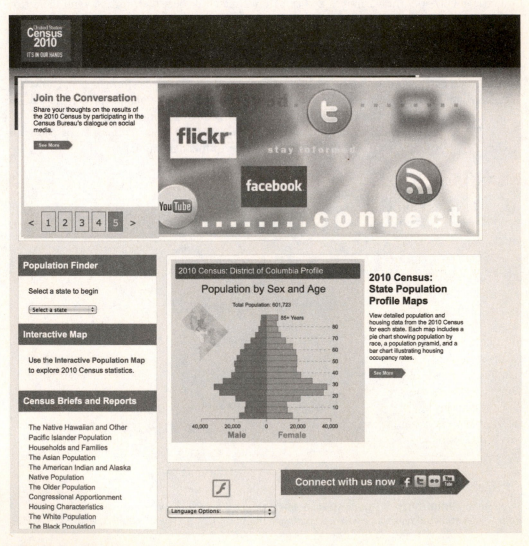

EXHIBIT 1.4   U.S. Census 2010 Website

Here's how Merlin Entertainments Group analyzes the current situation when planning to market its LEGOLAND theme parks around the world. (Follow the QR code to see the LEGOLAND Malaysia home page or go to www.legoland.com.my/.)

Merlin's LEGOLAND. Merlin Entertainments has a long-term marketing plan for each of its six theme parks on three continents. Licensing the LEGO brand, Merlin operates LEGOLAND parks in its home country of the United Kingdom as well as in Germany, Denmark, and Malaysia, plus California and Florida. Even when local and regional economic conditions aren't ideal, family-friendly LEGOLAND parks enjoy strong attendance because their rides are scaled to fit youngsters 12 and under and their LEGO sculptures appeal to parents and children alike.

Years in advance of a park opening or expansion, Merlin scouts locations, examines transportation and hotel availability, checks out competing attractions, estimates costs and revenue, and determines the likely return on investment. Following a carefully-crafted marketing plan, Merlin publicizes every major milestone in a LEGOLAND's progression from concept to construction to completion, building enthusiasm and demand along the way. Well before LEGOLAND Malaysia opened in 2012, Merlin introduced itself and its park to local officials, travel and tourism groups, and potential visitors. Thanks to its advance marketing efforts, LEGOLAND Malaysia had already sold more than 35,000 annual passes five months before the grand opening. As opening day approached, Merlin was planning tours and transportation to accommodate the 1 million visitors expected during the park's first year.[15]

Chapter 2 contains more details on gathering and analyzing data to examine the organization's current situation and the specific issues and opportunities it may face.

Understand Markets and Customers

The second step in marketing planning is to analyze markets and customers (whether consumers or businesses) by researching market-share trends, product demand, and customer characteristics such as buying habits, needs, wants, attitudes, behaviors, and satisfaction. Unilever, Procter & Gamble, and other major marketers are exploring the applications of **neuromarketing**, using technologies such as functional magnetic resonance imaging (fMRI) or eyetracking to measure consumers' physiological reactions to products and marketing. Although neuromarketing is not yet mainstream—and not within reach of the vast majority of marketers—large companies see potential advantages in understanding unconscious reactions so they can test marketing programs that could influence consumers' attitudes and behavior.[16]

When any marketer studies customers and markets, the goal is to answer questions such as: Who is doing the buying, when, why, and how? Are buying patterns changing—and why? What products and categories are or will be in demand? How do purchases and preferences change over time, and what do each market's customers want and need? McDonald's marketers, for example, are experts at analyzing and responding to differences in regional preferences. Instead of a Big Mac hamburger in India, the fast-food chain serves a Chicken Maharaja-Mac sandwich. In France, the chain offers table service, and the menu includes freshly baked baguettes and pastries. During the recession, when many customers were sensitive to prices, McDonald's maintained sales momentum by expanding its value-priced menus in Europe and Australia.[17]

With cutting-edge technology, marketing managers can examine detailed customer buying behavior based on sales by product, by time and place, and by other factors. Target digs deeper to look at the combinations of products that shoppers buy on individual shopping trips. This analysis helps it create marketing programs such as customer-specific couponing to stimulate future purchasing of related items.[18] Another key issue is measuring customer engagement with brands and marketing campaigns. The credit-card company Visa, for instance, measures how many views its YouTube videos achieve, the number of Facebook likes its brand page attracts, and—most important—the engagement of its customers, based on the content they upload and the brand content they share. These *metrics,* numerical measures of specific performance outcomes, relate to brand awareness and customer relationships. Other metrics that Visa tracks, such as the number and size of credit transactions, reveal card-usage patterns and spending trends, indicators of how its marketing activities are affecting customer behavior.[19] See Chapter 3 for more information about analyzing markets and customers.

Plan Segmentation, Targeting, and Positioning

Because organizations can never be all things to all people, marketers have to apply their knowledge of the market and customers to select groups within the market, known as **segments**, for marketing attention. In the past, this meant dividing the overall market into separate groupings of customers, based on broad characteristics such as age, gender, geography, needs, behavior, or other variables. With today's technology, however, some companies can now identify and serve very specific segments, based on what they know (or can find out) about that consumer or business. Target, for instance, gathers considerable data about each shopper's purchases over time, which it can then use to target segments such as new mothers.

PLANNING TIP

Use segmentation and targeting to focus on opportunities; then use positioning for competitive advantage.

The purpose of segmentation is to group customers with similar needs, wants, behaviors, attitudes, or other characteristics that affect their demand for or usage of the good or service being marketed. Once the market has been segmented, the next set of decisions centers on **targeting**, including whether to market to one segment, several segments, or the entire market and how to cover those segments. Segmentation and targeting are vital both in consumer markets and in **business-to-business (B2B) marketing**. For instance, the San Francisco tech firm Aria Systems creates marketing content geared to the decision-making role of each executive who is involved in influencing purchases of technology services at customer companies, rather than targeting only the top decision-maker.[20]

Next, the organization formulates suitable **positioning**, using marketing to create a competitively distinctive place (position) for the brand or product in the mind of targeted customers. This positioning sets the product apart from competing products in a way that's meaningful to customers. For example, the European discount airline EasyJet promotes cheap fares to communicate its differentiation. To be effective in creating a particular image among targeted customers, companies must convey the positioning through every aspect of marketing. This is why EasyJet's website emphasizes ticket price rather than in-flight service. Chapter 4 discusses segmentation, targeting, and positioning in detail.

Plan Direction, Objectives, and Marketing Support

Marketing managers are responsible for setting the direction of the organization's marketing activities, based on goals and objectives. **Goals** are long-term performance targets, whereas **objectives** are short-term targets that support the achievement of the goals. Setting and achieving shorter-term marketing, financial, and societal objectives will, over time, move the organization toward its overall goals, whatever they may be and however they may be expressed. Your marketing plan should include specific profit objectives, projected sales and revenues, expected expenses, and expected income.

Most businesses use their marketing plans to support growth strategies through different combinations of product innovation and market penetration. To illustrate, Boeing has developed new products (like the fuel-efficient 787 Dreamliner jet) for its existing market of air carriers, including Air India and Japan Airlines, and for new airline customers. In addition, it develops new configurations of established products (like the best-selling 737 commercial jet) for new and existing markets.[21] Some companies choose to grow through diversification, innovating entirely new products or adding entirely new markets. No matter what direction and objectives a company pursues, its marketing plan must include resources and programs for marketing support, as discussed in later chapters.

PLANNING TIP

Be sure your objectives fit with the organization's overall mission and goals.

Many organizations are adopting **sustainable marketing**, "the process of creating, communicating, and delivering value to customers in such a way that both natural and human capital are preserved or enhanced throughout."[22] Preserving natural capital (natural resources and ecosystems) and human capital (talent and other resources provided by people) now and into the future requires balancing long-term company and societal interests with short-term financial realities.

The Anglo-Dutch consumer products giant Unilever is a leader in embracing sustainable marketing. Many of its new products are environmentally safe or help consumers live green lifestyles. By 2020, Unilever aims to slash its products' overall carbon footprint by 50% while increasing worldwide sales by 100%.[23] (See more about Unilever at www.unilever.com/ or by scanning the QR code.)

Chapter 5 provides more detail about planning direction and objectives.

Develop Marketing Strategies and Programs

The next step is to formulate strategies for providing value using the basic marketing-mix tools of product, place, price, and promotion, enhanced by service, to build stronger customer relationships and internal marketing to bolster support within the organization. Note that some companies can profit by developing a marketing mix for segments of one. Both Boeing and Airbus do this by adjusting the configuration of their jets, their product pricing, their delivery schedules, and their sales approach to the needs and buying cycle of each airline customer. Jets cost tens of millions of dollars, which makes very targeted marketing worthwhile for these competing aircraft manufacturers.

Multinational firms often implement different marketing mixes for different countries and products. Look at how Oreo cookies are marketed in different countries.

Oreos. Oreos are such an American icon that U.S. consumers take for granted the "twist, lick, dunk" enjoyment of these black-and-white sandwich cookies. The 100-year-old brand has more than 26 million Facebook likes, and the cookies also pop up as ingredients in other U.S. products, including ice cream. Oreos are now sweeping the global marketplace, thanks to reformulations that suit local consumers' taste preferences. In China, for example, Oreos are made with green tea or mango filling and are smaller, less sweet, and rectangular or cylindrical rather than round. These changes have made them the best-selling cookies in the country. In Indonesia, Oreos combine chocolate wafers with peanut-flavored filling. In Argentina, Oreos come in a banana–dulce de leche flavor combination. And in India, Oreos are marketed under the Cadbury brand, which is well known for chocolates and other desserts. No wonder annual worldwide sales of Oreos top $1 billion![24]

Social Community	Social Publishing
Building brand/Consumer relationships Promoting a presence Marketing research	Blogging Sharing branded content Advertising/PR Re-sharing
Social Commerce	Social Entertainment
Buying and selling Servicing Managing Converting to transactions	Enabling play Branded entertainment

Social Media Marketing *(center)*

EXHIBIT 1.5   Social Media Zones

Source: Tracy L. Tuten and Michael R. Solomon, *Social Media Marketing* (Upper Saddle River, NJ: Pearson Education, 2013), Figure 1-5, p. 16.

External marketing strategies are used to build relationships with suppliers, partners, and channel partners. Given the proliferation of social media, it's not surprising that many firms are putting special emphasis on *social media marketing,* the use of social media to facilitate value creation, communication, delivery, and exchange among marketing participants. Exhibit 1.5 shows that marketers plan for social media marketing within four broad zones of activity. Increasingly, marketers are leveraging three screens (TV, cell phone, and computer or tablet) in their marketing communications. *Mobile marketing* covers not just coupons sent to cell phones but also apps that help shoppers search out merchandise and compare prices.

In addition, an internal marketing strategy is needed to build support among employees and managers, demonstrate marketing's value and importance to the organization, ensure proper staffing to carry out marketing programs, and motivate the proper level of customer service. Chapter 5 contains a section on internal marketing and customer service; Chapter 6 covers product and brand strategy; Chapter 7 covers pricing strategy; Chapter 8 explores channel and logistics strategy; and Chapter 9 examines strategies for marketing communications and influence.

Plan Metrics and Implementation Control

PLANNING TIP

Use specific, realistic metrics to measure progress toward objectives.

To know whether a marketing plan has been successful, you must plan to track progress toward the desired outcomes. The first step is to identify **key performance indicators (KPIs)**, indicators that are vital (key) to effective performance in achieving the organization's strategic goals and marketing plan objectives. Next, you'll use *metrics* to measure whether your marketing activities are helping you reach KPI performance levels. The time to think about metrics is before the plan has been finalized, because you need to select the measures and the timetable for measures that you will employ during implementation. By planning for metrics to compare actual outcomes against yearly, quarterly, monthly, weekly, daily, or even hourly projections of expected results, you will be able to see where results are ahead or behind and where adjustments are needed in order to return to the right path. Just as important, your metrics will help you determine where to invest marketing money and emphasis and when to switch gears. Game retailer Gamestop briefly operated a

Facebook storefront. However, "We just didn't get the return on investment we needed from the Facebook market, so we shut it down pretty quickly," explains the vice president of marketing.[25]

Many companies use specific financial measures to evaluate marketing outcomes; these may include return on marketing investment, return on sales, market share, and cost per customer acquired.[26] Metrics are also applied to nonfinancial results, such as brand performance and customer loyalty, which support financial results over time. Amazon.com makes customer-oriented metrics its top priority.

Amazon.com. Since this online retail pioneer was founded in 1995, its priority has been to provide a customer-centric experience that builds and reinforces long-term loyalty. Today the company has 164 million customers and sells more than $48 billion worth of consumer and business goods and services every year. It tracks its marketing performance with dozens of metrics that measure such customer-critical areas as shipping on time, having sufficient inventory to meet demand, and speedy response.

During the very busy December selling season, when retailers go all out to attract customers and meet their gift-buying needs, Amazon pays special attention to on-time delivery. It publicizes the cutoff date for receiving orders before Christmas and does everything it can to deliver every shipment as promised. During one recent year, when the retailer got 99.99% of its shipments to their destinations before Christmas, founder Jeff Bezos commented, "We're not satisfied until it's 100%." Amazon's marketers immediately began planning to improve delivery performance during the following year.[27]

A B2B marketer would want to set goals for sales leads and track how many come from each direct mail campaign, e-mail newsletter, and other communications, for example. Why? Because closing a sale starts with generating a lead, and if the actual number of leads falls short of expectations, changes will be needed to keep sales performance on track.[28] Marketers that target consumers would want to see how each marketing element performs. The Gap, Old Navy, and Banana Republic measure how many people open their text messages and redeem their mobile coupons so they can determine the most effective content and timing for their mobile marketing efforts.[29] Etsy.com, the online craft marketplace, tracks metrics (such as size of transactions and number of log-ins) every 10 minutes so it can quickly identify and resolve any technical glitches.[30]

Your plan must also show how implementation will be controlled. In the **marketing control** process, marketers measure interim performance of the planned programs against metrics, diagnose the results, and then take corrective action if results fail to measure up to expectations (see Exhibit 1.6). Chapter 10 covers in more detail the topics of establishing metrics and planning for implementation control.

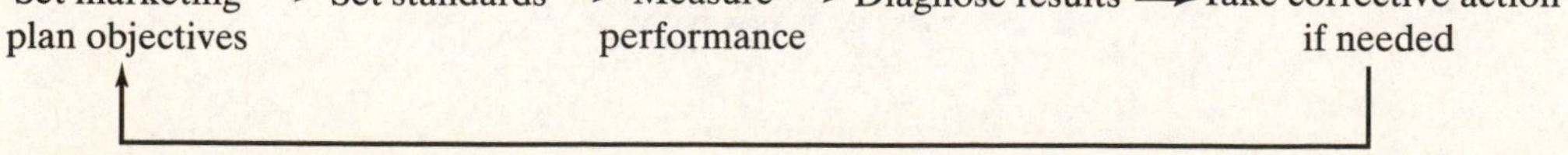

Set marketing ⟶ Set standards ⟶ Measure ⟶ Diagnose results ⟶ Take corrective action
plan objectives   performance   if needed

EXHIBIT 1.6   **Marketing Control**

PREPARING FOR MARKETING PLANNING

Considering the new urgency and the new possibilities for marketing planning, marketers need to understand and be ready to use any and all of the primary marketing tools, often called the marketing mix (or the four *P*s). They must also be prepared to support the marketing mix with both service and internal marketing.

Primary Marketing Tools

Every marketing plan uses the four marketing-mix tools of product, pricing, place (channel), and promotion to create a unique blueprint for providing value, building relationships, and making a difference. Exhibit 1.7 shows a selection of the new and traditional marketing-mix elements that may be used in a marketing plan. Based on your marketing plan's objectives and marketing strategies, you will select specific elements and combine them to create a unique marketing mix for each product, brand, market, or customer segment.

PRODUCT OFFERING   Although the product can be either a tangible good or an intangible service, many are actually a combination of tangibles and intangibles. Fast-food chains such as McDonald's compete on the basis of their menu items—tangible—and counter or drive-through service—intangible.

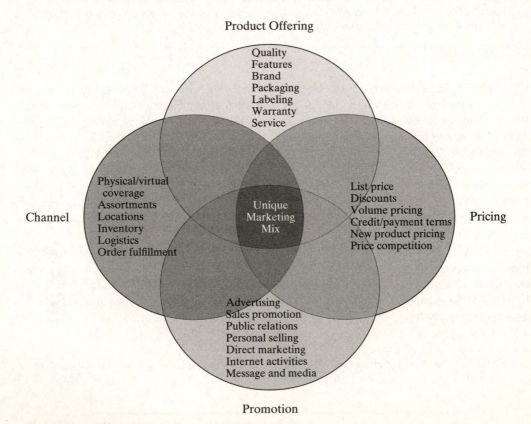

EXHIBIT 1.7   Combining Tools in the Marketing Mix

Branding is such an important aspect of the product offering that marketing plans must spell out how the company will support and evaluate brand performance. In addition to manufacturers' national brands, many large retailers now market products under their own brands: Costco has its Kirkland brand, and Target has several private brands, including Archer Farms and Market Pantry. These brands differentiate the retailers and provide choices at different levels of quality and pricing. Often, private brands carry higher profit margins, as well.[31]

PRICING   What should the organization charge for its product offering? Pricing decisions are based on a number of factors, including how customers perceive the value of the offering; how the organization positions the product; what the product's development, production, and distribution costs are; the competitive structure of the market; and the value that the organization expects to gain. Technology is bringing new possibilities and new flexibility to pricing, even as it increases customers' ability to compare prices online or with an app. Retailers with physical stores are concerned about price comparisons because of the rise in *showrooming,* which occurs when shoppers examine a product in a local store and then, after checking prices, buy from an online retailer that sells the item for less.[32]

Higher pricing can support an upscale image or better quality, but it also carries the risk that customers may perceive the price as too high relative to the product's perceived benefits. A low-price strategy can attract new customers, boost market share, and fend off rivals; however, it requires a careful balance between building relationships and building profits. At times, one competitor's pricing can upend an industry's pricing.

CHANNEL   Channel (place) strategy involves decisions about how, when, and where to make goods and services available to customers. Many consumer products pass through one or more layers of wholesalers and retailers in the course of reaching buyers. Moreover, many consumers like a choice of channels, sometimes buying from a firm online and at other times buying in its stores or by phone, which means firms should prepare for **multichannel marketing**. Transportation, inventory management, and other logistics issues should also be included in the channel strategy part of your marketing plan and should be carefully tracked to ensure control.

PROMOTION   Promotion covers all the tools used to communicate with and exert influence on the target market, including advertising, public relations, sales promotion, personal selling, and direct marketing techniques such as catalogs, text messages, and e-mail. Because of media proliferation and audience fragmentation, some firms are putting less emphasis on mass media like network television and are increasing their use of online marketing, mobile marketing, and social media. L.L. Bean, for example, doesn't just mail catalogs to customers—it also maintains a comprehensive retail website, a mobile website, a Facebook brand page, a Twitter account, a YouTube channel, and a number of Pinterest boards featuring its products and catalog covers. It has also planned specialty promotions such as driving a Bootmobile (a vehicle in the shape of the famous L.L. Bean boot) across the United States to publicize the firm's 100th anniversary.[33] (Scan the QR code to see L.L. Bean's home page or visit www.llbean.com.) The key to messages and media is to choose carefully, pace the timing, and integrate all content so the entire campaign achieves its communication and sales objectives.

Supporting the Marketing Mix

No marketing plan is complete without support strategies for customer service and internal marketing. Customer service reinforces positive perceptions of a brand, product, and company—and customers expect it (or even demand it). And, as you know from your own experience, good service can clearly differentiate a company from competitors, attract new customers, and retain current customers. Poor or inconsistent customer service simply will not satisfy customers; even worse, dissatisfied customers are likely to tell others about their bad experience, generating negative *word-of-mouth communication*. According to an American Express survey, consumers who use social media will alert 53 people about a bad-service experience (but tell only 42 people about a good-service experience).[34]

At the very least, your marketing plan should allow for handling customer inquiries and complaints; you may also need to cover installation (e.g., for appliances, floor coverings, or giant turbines), technical support (e.g., for computer products), and training (e.g., for software). Web-based FAQs and help indexes, e-mail, live text chat, live online telephony, blog and Twitter posts, and/or toll-free telephone contact are common customer service tactics. Firms in all types of industries, from banking to bakeries, use Twitter to address customer service questions quickly. A Wells Fargo Bank executive explains, "We use Twitter to engage customers, listen to our customers, and help them get to the right place for the answers they need." Wells Fargo, Bank of America, and other financial institutions that tweet take privacy very seriously. "We never disclose or ask our customers to disclose any confidential information during our interactions using Twitter," says a Bank of America official.[35]

The internal marketing strategy focuses all employees on serving customers and builds support for the marketing plan. Internal marketing can explain the marketing plan and its objectives, unify the organization's implementation efforts, and help employees understand their role in ensuring customer satisfaction (and service). For instance, Rentokil Initial, a U.K.–based business services firm with operations in 58 nations, uses special events to bring far-flung employees together in a positive and purposeful setting. "Getting things right for the customers is important, but you need to ensure your colleagues know where the business is heading and what it stands for too," explains the head of corporate communications. "Well-run internal events can really help get your messages across."[36]

Guiding Principles

Supplementing the marketing tools and support discussed earlier, you should apply four guiding principles for a marketing plan that will provide value, build relationships, and make a difference: (1) anticipate change, (2) engage everyone, (3) seek alliances, and (4) make marketing meaningful. These guiding principles, summarized in Exhibit 1.8, are explored in the following sections.

ANTICIPATE CHANGE   With geographical distance less of an obstacle than ever before, marketers can easily enter new markets hundreds or thousands of miles away and connect with the best suppliers, partners, and resellers anywhere—as can their competitors. As a result, marketers need to actively anticipate change by being alert for early warning signs of new trends that suggest potential opportunities and threats. They must also anticipate changes in resources and internal capabilities that will affect their ability to exploit new possibilities and effectively manage marketing plan implementation. For your marketing plan, this means thinking creatively about the practical consequences of the changes you see emerging. That's what McDonald's did

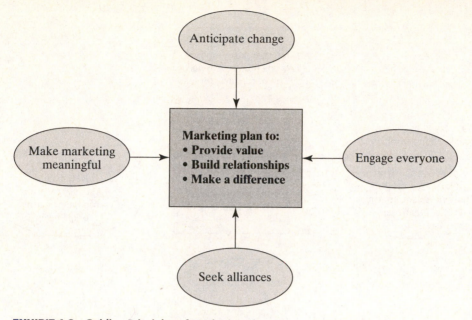

EXHIBIT 1.8 Guiding Principles of Marketing Planning

when it realized that many customers worried about economic uncertainty while others, with a bit more money to spend, were seeking upscale, unusual flavor combinations. McDonald's therefore expanded its Dollar Menu and, at the other end of the spectrum, added limited-time premium dishes and seasonal beverages to bring customers back again and again.[37]

ENGAGE EVERYONE   At one time, marketing and sales personnel were the only people responsible for an organization's marketing functions. Now, all employees must be engaged in marketing, and all contact points must be seen as opportunities to add value and strengthen customer relationships. Everything about the company sends a signal, so companies must project the right impression and meet customers' expectations through more than marketing. To keep employees actively engaged, they must be informed about products, promotions, and whatever else they need to know in order to satisfy customers. Many firms circulate printed or electronic newsletters, post news on internal websites or blogs, or send updates via e-mail or text messaging to keep employees informed. Keep this in mind as you prepare your marketing plan.

Organizations of all kinds are also paying special attention to customer engagement in their marketing plans. The online retailer Amazon.com was a pioneer in allowing customers to post product reviews, both good and bad, and now this is a common practice in retailing and beyond. Businesses such as Dell and Marriott engage customers through blogs and other social media. Dell aggressively seeks out online conversations that mention its brands and responds to as many comments as possible. It also started IdeaStorm.com (see QR code) for *crowdsourcing,* inviting customers to suggest new product ideas that Dell can test and ultimately implement via its marketing plans.[38]

SEEK ALLIANCES   Successful marketers plan to work through a network of alliances with carefully chosen suppliers, channel members, partners, customers, and community leaders (see Exhibit 1.9).

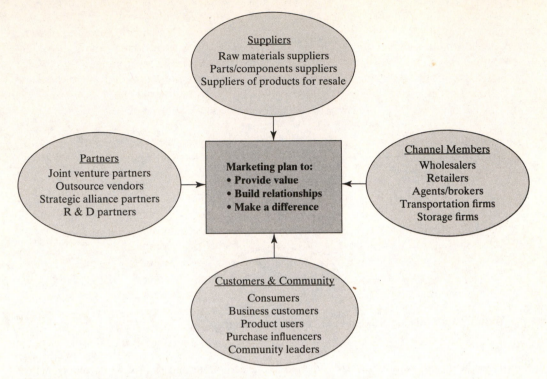

EXHIBIT 1.9   Alliances and the Marketing Plan

The purpose is to provide the mutual support, capabilities, and innovations that participants need to satisfy their customers, meet their objectives, and be competitive. In essence, the company's network of alliances is in competition with the networks that rivals have assembled.

- *Suppliers* not only provide raw materials, parts, and other inputs, they can offer insights regarding the external environment. Increasingly, companies are connecting with suppliers to lower costs and exchange data for mutual profitability. These alliances are critical because the quality of a product depends, in large part, on the quality of suppliers' materials.
- *Channel members* such as wholesalers and retailers have daily contact with customers and can provide vital feedback about buying patterns and preferences. Channel choices are critical because customers associate the firm's brand and value with the quality and convenience of their shopping experience. Consumer products giant Procter & Gamble (P&G) stays in touch with channel members to learn about new consumer-buying trends, to solve distribution problems, and to develop packaging variations for mutual profit.
- *Partners* in joint ventures, outsourcing, or other arrangements contribute their core competencies and market knowledge. Linking with a partner that has complementary capabilities and strengths gives both firms more marketing power. Fiat and Tata Motors have long had a joint venture to manufacture and market cars in India, combining their automotive know-how and customer insights. Recently, the two changed the arrangement to allow Fiat to establish its own branded dealerships in India for differentiation while continuing the production partnership for efficiency.[39]

- *Customers* can be excellent partners because they are eager for innovative, practical goods or services that meet their needs or, in the case of businesses, that help them better serve their own customers. Crowdsourcing ideas for products is a start; **cocreation** goes even further, involving customers more deeply in collaboration with the company for product innovation and development. As an example, the *Ladies Home Journal* now devotes many printed pages to reader-generated articles, professionally edited and checked for accuracy by the magazine. "Usually content creation begins with an editor," says the editor-in-chief. "We have content creation that begins with a reader."[40]

- *Community* leaders from civic groups, charities, school groups, and other parts of the community can contribute feedback about the organization's image and activities. They can also inform management thinking about social issues, local concerns, and environmental priorities.

MAKE MARKETING MEANINGFUL   By definition, marketing has meaning because it satisfies customer needs. Yet certain types of advertising, among other marketing activities, are sometimes perceived as excessive, intrusive, or frivolous. Knowing that today's customers have many choices, companies are increasingly formulating marketing plans that reflect their organizational values and that use marketing to make a difference to society. By serving a larger purpose—such as protecting the environment, helping the community, or saving endangered habitats—companies can counter negative perceptions, build a positive reputation, and earn the admiration of customers and other stakeholders.

PLANNING TIP

Think creatively about how your marketing plan can make a difference.

Other companies are making marketing meaningful in their own ways, by aligning themselves with worthy causes such as raising awareness of health threats, providing volunteers for community cleanups, or donating products and money to fight world hunger. The online search company Google promotes science and math education; outdoor apparel company Timberland supports environmental sustainability. Michael Porter and Mark Kramer believe that businesses should go further, because "societal needs, not just conventional economic needs, define markets."[41] In their view, putting society's needs at the center of the business equation can open new markets, lead to profits, and improve operations. Therefore, as you prepare your marketing plan, think about how you can make marketing more meaningful for others as well as for your organization.

Summary

Marketing planning is the structured process of determining how to provide value to customers, the organization, and key stakeholders by researching and analyzing the current situation; developing and documenting marketing's objectives, strategies, and programs; and then implementing, evaluating, and controlling marketing activities to achieve the objectives. The purpose of marketing planning is to provide a disciplined yet flexible framework for guiding the company toward its value and relationship objectives.

The marketing plan documents the results of the marketing planning process and explains strategies and programs for providing value, building relationships, and making a difference. It also serves an important coordination function and allows for accountability by showing how results will be measured and adjustments made if needed. The marketing plan provides direction for employees and managers; encourages collaboration; outlines resource allocation; and delineates the tasks, schedules, and responsibilities planned to accomplish objectives.

The six broad steps in marketing planning are (1) research and analyze the current situation; (2) understand markets and customers; (3) plan segmentation, targeting, and positioning; (4) plan direction, objectives, and marketing support; (5) develop marketing strategies and programs; and (6) plan metrics and implementation control. Every marketing plan uses the four marketing-mix tools of product, pricing, place (channel), and promotion, supported by customer service and internal marketing, to create a unique blueprint for providing value, building relationships, and making a difference. Four guiding principles for marketing planning are to anticipate change, engage everyone, seek alliances, and make marketing meaningful.

Your Marketing Plan, Step by Step

Answer the following questions to take the first steps in preparing your marketing plan.

1. What good or service will you focus on in your marketing plan? If you are preparing a plan based on a real offering, choose one specific brand and good or service, such as Oreo cookies or Zipcar's car rental service. Another option is to focus on a real company that offers one type of good or service, such as Etsy.com, the online crafts marketplace. If you are working on a marketing plan for your business or for a local business—or preparing a plan based on a hypothetical product—make your offer concrete by briefly describing the good or service, benefits, competition, and intended customers.

2. What background information is publicly available about your chosen product or product category? Refer to Exhibit 1.2 as you consider whether you will be able to gather sufficient research about competitors, customers, communications, pricing, and other details that a good marketing plan should cover. If a business has asked you to do a marketing plan for one or more products, ask to see historical data on sales, profit margin, pricing, distribution, results of promotions, and other relevant marketing details. (Bear in mind that firms may consider some information to be proprietary and may not make these details available to you.)

3. What sources will you use to gather information about your chosen product or category? List publications, associations, websites, and authoritative blogs that cover this industry; add any knowledgeable experts you might consult; and include your personal experience with this or similar goods or services. Watch for news stories, ad campaigns, social media efforts, and anything else that might spark interesting ideas as you begin formulating your marketing plan. Conduct an Internet search and bookmark sites with reliable sources of up-to-date facts and figures about the marketing situation for this product or company. Check the listing of marketing hotlinks at http://marketinghandbook.blogspot.com for more resources.

4. For idea starters, browse the sample marketing plan in this book's appendix and the sample plan on the book's website before you dive into writing your own marketing plan.

Endnotes

1. John Kotter, "Barriers to Change: The Real Reason Behind the Kodak Downfall," *Forbes*, May 2, 2012, www.forbes.com.

2. Jon Swartz, "Pinterest Growth Curve Levels Off," *USA Today*, April 26, 2012, www.usatoday.com.

3. Diane Tennant, "Virginia Beach Man Wins $1M for Super Bowl Doritos Ad," *Virginian-Pilot*, February 7, 2012, http://hamptonroads.com.

4. Minoru Matsutani, "Caveat Emptor: Not All 'Word of Mouth' Blogs Unpaid," *Japan*

Times, March 6, 2012, www.japantimes .co.jp.

5. Natasha Singer, "Following the Breadcrumbs on the Data-Sharing Trail," *New York Times,* April 28, 2012, www.nytimes.com.

6. Gideon Spanier, "Gillette Man Must Avoid Close Shave with Olympics," *London Evening Standard,* April 11, 2012, www.thisislondon .co.uk.

7. Christina Scotti, "Warby Parker's New Line of Sight," *Fox Business,* August 24, 2012, http://smallbusiness.foxbusiness.com; Shira Lazar, "Warby Parker's Grand Vision," *Entrepreneur,* April 10, 2012, www.en-trepreneur.com; David Zax, "How Warby Parker's Cofounders Disrupted the Eyewear Industry and Stayed Friends," *Fast Company,* February 22, 2012, www.fastcompany.com.

8. John Kelly, "Thrift the Web: Goodwill Goes Mobile," *Washington Post,* May 7, 2012, www.washingtonpost.com.

9. "Sound Long-Term Strategy Is Key, Particularly in a Crisis: Harvard's Michael Porter," *INSEAD Knowledge,* October 2008, http://knowledge.insead.edu.

10. Dan Neil, "The Ferrari with the Dragon Tattoo," *Wall Street Journal,* May 5, 2012, www.wsj.com; Viknesh Vijayenthiran, "Rolls-Royce Year of the Dragon Phantom Sells Out in Two Months," *Motor Authority,* January 30, 2012, www.motorauthority .com; "Beijing Auto Show: Luxury Brands Eye China, But Some See Trouble Ahead," *Reuters,* April 24, 2012, www .reuters.com; "Beijing Auto Show 2012: Luxury Automakers Unveil China-Focused Editions," *Jing Daily,* April 24, 2012, www .jingdaily.com.

11. Alicia Kelso, "Taco Bell's Comeback Clear in Yum! Brand's Q1," *QSR Web,* April 19, 2012, www.qsrweb.com; Karen Cho, "KFC China's Recipe for Success," *INSEAD Knowledge,* March 2009, http://knowledge .insead.edu.

12. "Green Mountain to introduce 'well-ness' drinks," *Bloomberg BusinessWeek,* September 6, 2012, www.businessweek. com; Leslie Patton, "Green Mountain CEO Working on Better K-Cup Sales Forecasting," *Bloomberg News,* May 3, 2012, www.bloomberg.com; Leslie Patton, "Dunkin' Brands to Test Pods for Green Mountain's Vue," *Bloomberg News,* April 26, 2012, www.bloomberg.com.

13. Mike Perrault, "Brand New: Marketing Plan to Be Unveiled," *Desert Sun (Palm Springs, California),* May 8, 2012, www.mydesert.com.

14. "How Green Is My Sneaker?" *Wall Street Journal,* July 21, 2010, www.wsj.com.

15. "Malaysia to Host Asia's First Legoland," *Phuket News (Thailand),* August 9, 2012, www.thephuketnews.com; "Legoland Malaysia to Open on Sept 15," *New Straits Times Press Business Times (Malaysia),* April 25, 2012, www.btimes.com.my; Deena Kamel Yousef, "Not Just Fun and Games: Amusements Industry to Top $31.8b by 2017," *Gulf News,* April 15, 2012, http://gulfnews.com/business; "Asia's First Legoland Hotel to Open in 2014," *Borneo Post,* April 25, 2012, www.theborneopost .com.

16. Rupert Neate, "Ad Men Use Brain Scanners to Probe Our Emotional Response," *Guardian (UK),* January 14, 2012, www.guardian .co.uk; John Tierney, "To Choose Is to Lose," *New York Times Magazine,* August 21, 2011, pp. 33+.

17. Jonnelle Marte, "McDonald's May Hike Prices in U.S., Not Europe," *Smart Money,* April 20, 2012, www.smartmoney.com; Lisa Baertlein, "McDonald's Profit Boosted by U.S., Europe," *Reuters,* April 20, 2012, www.reuters.com; Lucy Fancourt, Bredesen Lewis, and Nicholas Majka, "Born in the USA, Made in France," *Knowledge@ Wharton,* January 3, 2012, http://knowledge .wharton.upenn.ed.

18. Charles Duhigg, "How Companies Learn Your Secrets," *New York Times,* February 16, 2012, www.nytimes.com.

19. Patricia Odell, "Visa Attempts Olympic Gold in Social Media," *Chief Marketer,* May 9, 2012, http://chiefmarketer.com.

20. Verne Harnish, "Rules of Attraction," *Fortune,* April 30, 2012, p. 30.

21. Kyle Peterson, "Boeing Says New 737 Winglet Will Save Fuel," *Reuters,* May 2, 2012, www.reuters.com; Tim Katts, "Boeing to Ship Four South Carolina-Built 787s to Air India," *Bloomberg,* April 27, 2012, www .bloomberg.com.

22. Diane Martin and John Schouten, *Sustainable Marketing* (Upper Saddle River, NJ: Prentice Hall, 2012), p. 10.

23. Mark J. Miller, "Unilever CEO on Sustainability: 'Uncomfortable Targets' Necessary," *Brand Channel,* May 7, 2012, www.brandchannel.com.

24. Bruce Einhorn, "There's More to Oreo Than Black and White," *Bloomberg BusinessWeek,* May 3, 2012, www.businessweek.com; Victoria Lautman, "Kraft Foods's Brand New World," *Chicago Magazine,* June 2011, www.chicagomag .com; Robert Smith, "Rethinking the Oreo for Chinese Consumers," *National Public Radio,* January 27, 2012, www.npr.org.

25. Ashley Lutz, "Gamestop to J.C. Penney Shut Facebook Stores," *Bloomberg,* February 22, 2012, www.bloomberg.com.

26. See Paul W. Farris, Neil T. Bendle, Phillip E. Pfeifer, and David J. Reibstein, *Marketing Metrics,* 2nd edition (Upper Saddle River, NJ: FT Press, 2010), Chapter 1.

27. George Anders, "Inside Amazon's Idea Machine," *Forbes,* April 4, 2012, www .forbes.com; Richard L. Brandt, "Birth of a Salesman," *Wall Street Journal,* October 15, 2011, www.wsj.com.

28. Erin Dostal, "Report: B-to-B Marketers Don't Measure Campaigns," *Direct Marketing News,* March 20, 2012, www.dmnews.com.

29. Jim Roope, "Smartphones Let Retailers Target Shoppers," *CNN Radio,* April 4, 2012, www.wfmz.com.

30. Matt Heusser, "How Etsy.com Grows in a Unique Fashion," *PC World,* March 31, 2012, www.pcworld.com.

31. Hannah Karp, "Store Brands Step Up Their Game, and Prices," *Wall Street Journal,* January 31, 2012, www.wsj.com.

32. Ann Zimmerman, "Can Retailers Halt 'Showrooming,'" April 11, 2012, www.wsj .com.

33. Tanzina Vega, "Marketers Find a Friend in Pinterest," *New York Times,* April 17, 2012, www.nytimes.com; Bill Griffith, "Driving Shoe: L.L. Bean Bootmobile Stomps Kenmore Square," *Boston Globe,* April 13, 2012, www.boston.com.

34. Jennifer Waters, "Social Media Offers Sweet Revenge for Bad Service," *MarketWatch,* May 11, 2012, www.marketwatch.com.

35. Ann Carrns, "Big Banks Struggle to Help Customers on Twitter," *New York Times,* January 11, 2012, www.nytimes.com; "Better Living Through Twitter," *Wall Street Journal,* February 23, 2009, http://blogs.wsj .com/wallet.

36. David Burrows, "How to Bring Events Up to Gold Standard," *Marketing Week,* May 10, 2012, www.marketingweek.co.uk.

37. Josh Sanburn, "Fast-Casual Nation," *Time,* April 23, 2012, pp. 60-1; Keith O'Brien, "Supersize," *New York Times Magazine,* May 6, 2012, pp. 44+.

38. David Greenfield, "From Idea to Innovation," *Network Computing,* April 9, 2009, http://networkcomputing.in/; Erin Nelson, "Online: An Essential Path to Igniting Brand Passion," *Forbes,* March 26, 2009, www.forbes.com.

39. Santanu Choudhury, "Fiat, Tata to Rework Alliance in India," *Wall Street Journal,* May 2, 2012, www.wsj.com.

40. Michael Nutley, "There's a Lot More to Social Media than Fire-fighting a Wall of Gripes," *Marketing Week,* April 19, 2012, www.mar-ketingweek.co.uk; Nat Ives, "Ladies' Home Journal Lets Readers Write the Magazine," *Advertising Age,* January 9, 2012, p. 1.

41. Michael E. Porter and Mark R. Kramer, "Creating Shared Value," *Harvard Business Review,* January 2011, http://hbr .org/2011/01.

2

Analyzing the Current Situation

In this chapter:

PREVIEW

Marketers are constantly scanning the environment to identify, monitor, and interpret the forces and trends that affect markets and marketing decisions. This first step in the marketing planning process sets the stage for a marketing plan that will provide value, build relationships, and make a difference (see Exhibit 2.1). Over time, you'll gain the experience and knowledge to recognize early signs of changes in the marketing environment and be able to think through the consequences for your planned marketing activities.

In this chapter, you'll learn about scanning the internal environment, including the organization's mission, resources, product offerings, previous results, business relationships, keys to success, and warning signs. You'll also learn about scanning the external environment, including competitive factors and political-legal, economic, social-cultural, technological, and ecological trends. Finally, you'll see how to use your insights about the current situation to prepare and refine a SWOT (strength, weakness, opportunity, and threat) analysis.

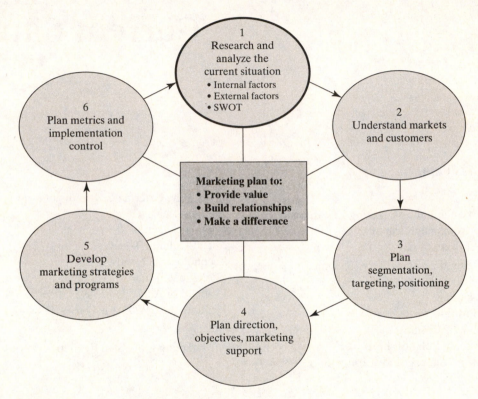

EXHIBIT 2.1 **Marketing Planning: Step 1**

APPLYING YOUR KNOWLEDGE

This is a good time to set up the structure of your marketing plan so that you can document the outcome of your environmental scanning and analysis efforts. Follow the outline shown in Exhibit 1.2, read the sample plan in the appendix, or check this book's companion website at www.pearsonhighered.com/wood/ to see what a typical marketing plan includes. Answering the questions in "Your Marketing Plan, Step by Step," at the end of this chapter will help you navigate the scanning and analysis process. Also review this chapter's checklist, which includes key questions to ask as you examine your current marketing situation.

CHAPTER 2 CHECKLIST   Your Current Marketing Situation

To analyze the marketing environment for planning purposes, examine these factors:

Internal Factors

✓ What is the organization's mission, and how will my marketing plan support it?

✓ What human, financial, informational, and supply resources can I count on for my marketing plan?

✓ What critical elements could make the difference between outstanding and poor marketing performance?

✓ What strengths and weaknesses do internal factors represent for my organization?

External Factors

✓ What are the most important external trends affecting my brands and my markets?

✓ How quickly are changes occurring in the external environment, and which developments require immediate attention?

✓ What opportunities and threats do external factors pose for my organization?

✓ What risks would my organization accept when dealing with these opportunities and threats?

Competitive Factors

✓ Who are our current competitors (by product, brand, or target market) and what companies or industries may develop into competitors?

✓ What are each competitor's market share, objectives, resources, strengths, and weaknesses? What are the implications for our ability to compete with them?

✓ How are competitors using marketing to build and reinforce customer relationships, and what can we learn from their successes and failures?

✓ How do key competitors usually respond to *their* competitors, and how can we use this information to plan for effective marketing?

UNDERSTANDING THE MARKETING ENVIRONMENT

To formulate a flexible and practical marketing plan, you need to monitor key factors in the **macroenvironment** that can affect the marketplace and marketing performance. These include broad political-legal, economic, social-cultural, technological, and ecological forces. In addition, you have to examine specific groups in the **microenvironment** that more directly influence marketing activities and performance, such as customers, competitors, channel members, partners, suppliers, and employees. An understanding of the marketing environment starts with environmental scanning.

Environmental Scanning

Because the business environment is more dynamic now than in the past, marketers are approaching *environmental scanning* with a new urgency. Some marketers monitor the environment in a passive way, taking note when they

PLANNING TIP

Watch for emerging trends that might disrupt your industry or markets.

identify a development that seems relevant to what the company is doing or that could signal a competitor's next move. However, the best marketers actively scan the environment at all times, not just when writing a marketing plan. This helps them envision many future possibilities and consider subtle changes for improving the plan and its implementation. It also helps them be more prepared to react if a "black swan" event (like a devastating storm of the century or a sudden and dramatic financial downturn) poses unusually severe challenges.[1]

Consider how the marketers of Procter & Gamble (P&G) examine the environment and react quickly to threats and opportunities. (To see P&G's home page, visit www.pg.com or scan this QR code.)

Procter & Gamble. With $82 billion in global sales and 24 brands that each ring up more than $1 billion in annual revenue, P&G is a powerhouse in household products (like Charmin and Downy) and personal care products (like Crest and Olay). Its marketers are always scanning the environment for key political-legal events such as new inflation controls in Venezuela, which required P&G to cut prices there by as much as 25%. Its marketers also watch the economic situation in countries where they buy and sell. In recent years, P&G has had to pay more for supplies of raw materials even as budget-minded consumers have been switching brands to save money. After P&G raised some prices to cover higher costs and improve profitability, it lost market share to competitors who held prices steady. P&G's marketers quickly decided to roll back prices on detergents and other items to remain competitive.

Although product innovation is a long-standing strength, the firm is also partnering with outside entrepreneurs and businesses to speed up new-product development. It recently moved the headquarters of its personal care unit to Singapore to get closer to fast-growing Asian markets, to research what local customers want, and to create new products for their needs. Taking a world view of social and cultural developments, P&G is heavily involved in marketing linked to the Olympic Games. The company was a corporate sponsor of the 2010 Vancouver Olympics and the 2012 London Olympics, and it plans to continue this high-profile Olympic sponsorship through the games in 2020.[2]

P&G's marketers recognize that environmental changes such as governmental price controls and economic downturns can have a major impact on profits. They must watch the external environment with an eye toward identifying the most significant events and trends, including opportunities to boost brand recognition through Olympics sponsorship. Are competitors raising prices as their costs go up, and by how much? How quickly will demand for beauty products grow in nations where incomes are relatively low but are increasing year after year? What social media sites are attracting the most consumer traffic, and what does that mean for P&G's marketing efforts? What technologies can P&G build on for more effective communication with customers? All of these issues will affect the firm's ability to achieve its goals through marketing.

SWOT Analysis

PLANNING TIP

Be aware that one firm's strength may be another firm's weakness.

Based on what you learn from scanning the environment, you'll prepare a **SWOT analysis** showing your organization's strengths, weaknesses, opportunities, and threats.

- *Strengths* are internal capabilities that can help the firm achieve its goals and objectives. For P&G, strengths might include production efficiency, well-known brands, and marketing know-how. Remember that a company need not actually possess the strengths—it must have clear *access* to the strengths, through alliances or other means.
- *Weaknesses* are internal factors that can prevent the firm from achieving its goals and objectives. For a catalog company, weaknesses might include an outdated order-fulfillment system, inadequate access to credit for buying products from wholesalers, and an inexperienced management team.
- *Opportunities* are external circumstances that the organization might be able to exploit for higher performance. As an example, increased media and regulatory attention to water-contamination issues might present an opportunity for a maker of water-filtering equipment. Under conditions of uncertainty, as when the economy is very unpredictable, marketers may evaluate opportunities in terms of acceptable risk, instead of looking only for the most attractive profit or market-share potential.[3]
- *Threats* are external circumstances, outside of the organization's direct control, that might hurt its performance now or in the future. For a family restaurant seeking to expand, threats could include increased competition, higher food costs, and high borrowing costs. Threats may be countered, but because they're not under the company's direct control, they can't be entirely eliminated.

The outcome of your internal and external analysis should be a grid like Exhibit 2.2, which will become an important part of the marketing plan. This exhibit shows a brief hypothetical SWOT for the Costco retail chain. Ideally, you should conduct a SWOT analysis of each major competitor (and key would-be competitors) to examine the current and potential influence on your marketing situation.

EXHIBIT 2.2   Hypothetical SWOT Analysis for Costco

Strengths	*Weaknesses*
(Internal capabilities that can help firm achieve marketing plan objectives)	(Internal factors that might prevent firm from achieving objectives)
1. Stringent cost controls	1. Limited selection of products in each category
2. Experienced, enthusiastic employees	2. Limited experience operating in fast-growing international markets

Opportunities	*Threats*
(External circumstances that can be exploited to achieve objectives)	(External circumstances that might prevent firm from achieving marketing plan objectives)
1. Economic conditions that make customers more price sensitive	1. Community opposition to new big-box stores
2. Development of more convenient customer-payment methods	2. Increased government regulation

ANALYZING THE INTERNAL ENVIRONMENT

PLANNING TIP

This analysis gives you the background to set objectives, target customers, and create strategies for providing value.

Look closely at your organization's mission, which provides overall direction for marketing planning efforts. Also review your organization's resources, offerings, previous results, business relationships, keys to success, and any warning signs that may point to significant changes ahead (see Exhibit 2.3). Your organization has definite strengths and weaknesses, which will show up in this analysis.

Mission

The **mission** states the fundamental purpose of a company, a nonprofit organization, or a governmental agency—its core ideology, in the terminology of Collins and Porras—defining the focus, indicating how it will provide value, and outlining its envisioned future. A statement of mission is important because it helps align strategy, resources, and activities as managers and employees work toward the organization's future.[4] The mission is also "a promise the company makes to its employees," says Jeffrey Abrahams, author of *The Mission Statement Book*. "That promise becomes an integral part of the branding of the company."[5]

Whether explained in a few words or a few sentences, a mission statement should be specific enough to give direction to those involved in marketing planning and implementation throughout the organization.[6] Furthermore, a good mission statement will suggest how the organization plans to make a difference. Exhibit 2.4 shows the mission statements of several different types of organizations. These succinct statements guide marketers in determining what customers their organizations will serve and what value they will provide through marketing. Unilever's statement, for example, defines the basic needs that the company will address and includes its broader, long-term goal of helping consumers "get more out of life." Coca-Cola's statement defines the focus as "the world" and mentions the drive to deliver emotional benefits and make a difference. Kiva's statement is the briefest of these examples and the most specific. In many ways, however, it is the most ambitious: Alleviating poverty is an enormous challenge, but it would make an enormous difference in the world. (See Kiva's home page by visiting www.kiva.org or by scanning the QR code.)

Resources

Next, look at the resources the organization has available or can obtain, including human, financial, informational, and supply resources. No company has access to unlimited resources; therefore,

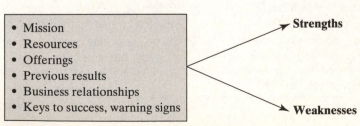

- Mission
- Resources
- Offerings
- Previous results
- Business relationships
- Keys to success, warning signs

Strengths

Weaknesses

EXHIBIT 2.3   **Analyzing the Internal Environment**

EXHIBIT 2.4 Mission Statements

Organization	Type of Business	Mission
Unilever	Manufacturer	To add vitality to life. We meet everyday needs for nutrition, hygiene, and personal care with brands that help people look good, feel good, and get more out of life.
Coca-Cola	Soft drinks	To refresh the world; to inspire moments of optimism and happiness; and to create value and make a difference.
MasterCard	Financial services	Every day, everywhere, we use our technology and expertise to make payments safe, simple, and smart.
Massachusetts General Hospital	Health care	Guided by the needs of our patients and their families, we aim to deliver the very best health care in a safe, compassionate environment; to advance that care through innovative research and education; and to improve the health and well-being of the diverse communities we serve.
Kiva	Nonprofit organization	To connect people through lending to alleviate poverty.

Sources: www.unilever.com; www.coca-cola.com; www.mastercard.com/us; www.massgeneral.org; www.kiva.org.

management must carefully balance resource allocation to ensure successful performance. Some questions to ask in examining internal resources include the following:

- *Human resources:* Does the workforce have the needed education, skills, and training? Do managers have the initiative and entrepreneurial drive to support the mission? Is the company using recruitment and training to prepare itself for the future? Are morale and turnover high or low? If applicable, what is the state of relations with unionized workers and their leaders?
- *Financial resources:* Does the company have the capital (or access to capital) to support marketing and achieve its objectives? What funding issues must be addressed over the period covered by the marketing plan, and what trade-offs might be needed? Will the company or nonprofit organization have the financial strength to implement all planned activities, or should activities be phased in as financing becomes available?
- *Informational resources:* Does the company have the data needed to understand its customers and the marketplace? What informational sources are available to support marketing planning, implementation, and control? Who in the organization is responsible for ensuring that informational resources are in place when needed?
- *Supply resources:* Does the company have (or can it obtain) steady and affordable supplies of parts, components, materials, and services needed for operations and production? Are its suppliers stable and committed to the organization? What new suppliers are emerging, and what new capabilities do they offer that will benefit the organization?

Resource availability is critical for performance in every industry and every market. Sometimes companies can arrange external sources or supplement existing resources through new strategic alliances, new supply-chain relationships, or short-term substitutions. The point is that marketers must look ahead to anticipate shortages and adjust their plans accordingly, which is what food and beverage manufacturers are doing as they look at global supplies of vanilla.

Vanilla shortage? Ice cream manufacturers, bakers, and other marketers have been closely monitoring vanilla supplies after extreme weather conditions and lower-than-expected harvests in some countries raised the possibility of a serious shortage. Most of the world's vanilla comes from Madagascar, and the spice is increasingly expensive because of the labor-intensive cultivation process and the long lead-time for establishing new sources. Should production levels plummet, vanilla prices could skyrocket and push up retail prices for ice cream, cookies, flavored coffees, and other foods and drinks made with the spice. With wholesale prices already on the rise, some manufacturers have started stockpiling extra vanilla, while others are exploring alternative sources such as buying vanilla from niche growers in Australia.[7]

Offerings

This part of the analysis examines what the organization is currently offering in the way of goods and services. If information is available, look at the product mix and the lines within that mix, asking questions such as the following: What products are being offered, at what price points, and for what customer segments? What value does each product provide by solving a customer's problem or fulfilling a need? What is the age of each product, and what are its sales, profit, and share trends over time? How does each product support sales of the line—are some products sold only as supplements or add-ons to others? How does each product contribute to the company's overall performance? Does one product account for a large portion of sales and profits?

Also analyze how the offerings contribute to relationships with distributors and customers. Not long ago, during an unusually warm summer, Unilever had difficulty meeting demand for two popular flavors of Good Humor bars sold through ice-cream trucks that roam neighborhoods in Northeastern states. The company was in the process of shutting down one production facility and shifting manufacturing to two other facilities. Without those two popular products, however, ice-cream truck entrepreneurs lost sales and customers were disappointed.[8]

Another question to ask: Are the company's products keeping up with movement in the industry and with technological advances? Think about all the changes you've seen in the electronic game industry, from video-game consoles like the Nintendo Wii and handheld devices like the Nintendo DS to smartphone game apps like Angry Birds and social games like Words with Friends. Any company that expects to remain competitive in this category must have (or plan) a product line that makes sense for today and tomorrow.[9]

Marketers should also determine how their organization's offerings relate to its mission and to its resources. Do the products use the firm's resources most effectively and efficiently while following the mission? Are other offerings needed to restore the focus or fulfill the long-term purpose described in the mission? Answering these questions helps you determine where you stand and how to prepare for future marketing activities.

Previous Results

The company's previous results also offer important clues to internal factors and trends that can affect results. By analyzing the previous year's sales, profits, and other financial results—and by comparing these results with trends over several years—you can get a big picture of overall performance. Analyze the results of the previous years' marketing programs to see what worked and what did not. If exact figures aren't readily available, look at percentage increases and decreases to understand the trends in the business.

PLANNING TIP

Put results into context by examining how environmental factors influenced performance.

Among the questions to ask are the following: Which products did well over the past year, and which did not? Which communications drew the best response? Which channels were responsible for the most sales? How did price changes affect results? What are the most recent trends in results? The point is to separate effective from ineffective activities and to understand how well marketing has performed in the past as a prelude to planning marketing programs for the future.

Business Relationships

A closer look at relationships with suppliers, distributors, and partners can help determine whether changes should be made in the coming year. Although cost is always a critical factor, companies must also ask whether their suppliers and distributors (1) have the capacity to increase volume if needed, (2) maintain a suitable quality level, and (3) can be true partners in providing value to satisfy customers. How has the roster of suppliers and dealers changed over time? Is the company overly dependent on one supplier, channel member, or partner? Does the company expect its partners to provide special expertise or services?

Determining which business relationships to pursue can be vital to a young organization's marketing plan. Consider how Instagram's relationships contributed to its success (visit its home page at http://instagram.com or scan this QR code).

Instagram. This company's iPhone app for enhancing and sharing cell-phone photos became an instant hit when it was introduced on Apple's App Store late in 2010. Within three months, Instagram had 1 million users; six weeks after that, it had gained another million users. The initial decision to build an iPhone app aligned Instagram with one of the world's most admired companies. As the app became increasingly popular, partnership offers poured in. However, the firm remained focused on building its user base, expanding to other smartphone systems, and improving the user experience rather than on diverting time and energy to formal relationships for future revenue. Once Instagram had more than 25 million users, it decided to engage a broader audience by forging ties with Hipstamatic and other photo app firms. It was acquired by Facebook just as it passed the 5 billion photo mark.[10]

Keys to Success and Warning Signs

Not everything in a marketing plan is equally important. Marketers should identify, in just a few sentences, the special factors that most influence the firm's movement toward fulfilling its mission and achieving superior performance. Pinpointing these keys to success can show you where to focus and can suggest how to balance priorities in planning the year's marketing strategies and programs. For example, Apple's keys to success are (1) design savvy, (2) technological innovation, and (3) brand image. The combination of these three elements has propelled the company to success in smartphones, computers, and digital entertainment devices.

Every organization should scan for the major warning signs that indicate potential problems with leveraging the keys to success and performing as planned. For Apple, one such issue might be a technological development that could make its iPhone or iPad obsolete. Other possible warning signs for Apple might be government regulations that affect technology standards and quality or privacy problems that could tarnish the brand image. Paying close attention to these issues will help Apple's marketers plan to reach their objectives.

ANALYZING THE EXTERNAL ENVIRONMENT

Within the external environment, marketers need to examine broad political-legal, economic, social-cultural, technological, and ecological trends (see Exhibit 2.5). They must also pay special attention to the resources, strategies, and activities of competitors. Whereas scans of the internal environment are designed to uncover strengths and weaknesses, scans of the external environment are designed to uncover opportunities and threats that can be effectively addressed in the marketing plan.

Exhibit 2.6 shows an example of how the external environment might affect the marketing plans of Texas-based Southwest Airlines. Notice that there are marketing implications—including possible changes in marketing—that result from a careful study of external forces. This external analysis represents one point in time, however, because the forces are constantly shifting and evolving. Only by regularly monitoring environmental trends can you identify any signs of change that you should investigate and plan to address through marketing.

Political-Legal Trends

A variety of political, legal, and regulatory guidelines apply to business and marketing practices, and violating these rules can be costly (in terms of fines, time, and reputation). Numerous U.S. state and federal laws cover competitive behavior, pricing, taxation, promotion, distribution, product liability, labeling, and product purity, among other elements. Moreover, U.S. government agencies such as the Federal Trade Commission and the Department of Justice watch for questionable business practices, as do their counterparts in other nations.

Businesses have to be aware of political and regulatory trends in every country where they operate, and must consider their business impact, including how governmental approvals might affect plans and implementation. As one example, Chinese regulators must approve any

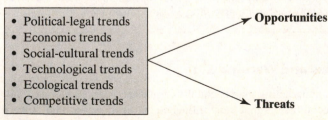

EXHIBIT 2.5   Analyzing the External Environment

EXHIBIT 2.6   The External Environment of Southwest Airlines

Element and Potential Impact	Possible Changes in Marketing
Political-legal trends: Restrictions that limit the timing and number of flights into or out of busy airports will affect Southwest's growth.	Identify the most promising new markets and lobby regulators to allow access to flight slots at airports in those areas; promote those new flights for competitive advantage.
Economic trends: Economic recovery can boost demand for business and leisure travel; tight credit conditions can restrict Southwest's ability to pay for new jets and facilities.	As demand rises, manage pricing to encourage buying and to maintain profitability; if credit is difficult to obtain, implement expansion plans more slowly.
Social-cultural trends: Population shifts and changes in centers of business activity affect demand for travel to and from certain areas.	Plan to add flights to areas experiencing population growth; research brand attitudes and buying behavior of businesspeople who travel to industrial centers; explore international flights to vacation destinations.
Technological trends: Higher consumer usage of smartphones and other mobile devices; availability of new technology for reservations, promotions, and customer service.	Offer multiple communication alternatives for travelers who want to find flights and fares, to be notified of flight delays, and more; engage customers on Twitter, YouTube, and other interactive sites.
Ecological trends: Concerns about environmental safety can affect attitudes toward air travel.	Publicize initiatives to improve fuel efficiency and increase use of eco-friendly materials; research customer attitudes toward issues directly affecting Southwest.
Competitive trends: Consolidation in the airline industry is creating larger, more powerful competitors; price wars can affect revenue and profits.	Differentiate Southwest on the basis of friendly service; maintain competitive pricing and fee-free extras to reinforce customer loyalty.

acquisition involving a firm with a significant business presence in China, a sometimes time-consuming process. In fact, Coca-Cola was unable to complete the acquisition of a Chinese company when local regulators eventually ruled against the deal. Google was allowed to acquire Motorola Mobility, but only after Chinese regulators delayed their decision for many months. This changed the timing of the search giant's global marketing plan for harnessing Motorola Mobility's valuable patents as part of its marketing strategy to build market share in smartphones.[11]

Another important legal and ethical issue for any company with a website or social media presence is the question of privacy. Businesses generally track the online behavior of consumers to learn more about online visitors to their sites. However, many consumers and privacy advocates are concerned about invasion of privacy and are unsure of how firms use tracking data. Companies tend to favor industry self-regulation of behavioral tracking, whereas privacy advocates are calling for government regulation to protect consumers. Meanwhile, many businesses and sites have begun participating in voluntary "do not track" programs to reassure consumers and defuse the situation.[12]

Economic Trends

In today's interconnected global economy, deepening recession (or rapid recovery) in one part of the world can affect consumer and business buying patterns thousands of miles away. To better understand the buying power of consumers (or business customers), marketers should analyze buyer income, debt, and credit usage. When personal income is rising, consumers have more buying power; lower debt and more available credit also fuel consumer buying. The reverse is also true: When consumers are losing their jobs, are facing wage cuts, or are worried about debt, they stop or slow spending. Similarly, businesses with higher debt may not buy as much or as often as businesses with lower debt and more available credit. For planning purposes, consider how specific local, regional, national, and international trends may affect the company's industry, its products, its competitors, and targeted geographic markets.

Foreign exchange trends can greatly influence cross-border marketing. For example, when the euro seems expensive to U.S. vacationers, the exchange rate actually makes U.S. destinations less expensive for visitors from Europe. Florida recently experienced a vacation boom when changes in the exchange rate brought European travelers to the state's newly affordable beaches and theme parks. The U.S. economy was recovering during the same period, and Florida's tourism industry also benefited from an influx of family vacationers who live within driving distance of Florida attractions.[13] (For more about Florida tourism, visit the official home page at www.visitflorida.com or scan the QR code here.)

Social-Cultural Trends

For marketers of consumer products, population trends and characteristics suggest the size of the potential market and hint at lifestyle changes that should be examined. For marketers of business products, indicators of market size and strength include trends in business formation and certain organizational characteristics that can affect current and future demand. However, these point-in-time examinations of demographic trends must be routinely updated to reflect any shifts, with more research to understand links with behavior and attitudes. Following is a brief overview of the role of consumer demographics, business demographics, and cross-cultural factors that can influence marketing; see Chapter 3 for more detail about markets and customers.

CONSUMER DEMOGRAPHICS Population growth is creating and expanding markets around the world, whether through higher birth rates, longer life spans, or immigration. Yet the population is actually shrinking in some areas as people move elsewhere, such as from urban to suburban or rural markets or from one state or country to another. For this reason, marketers need to follow the population trends in the markets where they currently do business or are considering doing business, using U.S. Census data and other research. They must also explore the composition of the consumer population. Because diversity is a key factor in planning for marketing strategy, it's important to study demographics such as age, gender, ethnic and religious background, education, occupation, and household size and income.

BUSINESS DEMOGRAPHICS Companies that operate in business markets need to scan the environment for information about the size and growth of the industries that they sell to, as measured by number of companies, number of locations or branches, number of employees, and sales revenues. They should also pay attention to trends in new business formation, which can signal emerging opportunities to market products such as office furniture, computers, accounting services, telecommunications services, and cleaning supplies.

CROSS-CULTURAL INFLUENCES   Thanks to globalization, social and cultural trends that blossom in one market can spread to many others. For instance, styles that emerge in the pop-fashion Tokyo district of Harajuku often catch on throughout the country and then pop up in other Asian markets. This opens opportunities for many marketers. American Eagle Outfitters recently opened its first store in Harajuku, and if local teens adopt its styles, that popularity will pave the way for expansion beyond Tokyo. At the same time, the Japanese retail chain Uniqlo is building on cross-cultural factors to bring its functional, affordable fashion to the world.

Uniqlo. When the first Uniqlo clothing store opened in 1984, the company's marketing aimed to educate brand-conscious Japanese consumers about the value of buying basic, reasonably-priced fashion items carrying only the Uniqlo label. Now the company is so well-established that 80% of all Japanese consumers own one or more Uniqlo items. It operates hundreds of stores in Asia, Russia, Europe, and the United States. Whereas competitors such as Zara and H&M move quickly to market the latest styles, Uniqlo concentrates on the universal appeal of wardrobe staples such as T-shirts designed by artists and designers in eye-catching colors.

No two Uniqlo markets are exactly alike. "Sometimes it takes us a while to understand our customer in a new market," says the CEO of Uniqlo U.K. For example, Uniqlo's marketers learned that even when springtime temperatures dip below zero, Russian consumers will visit stores in search of short-sleeved T-shirts. In Singapore, long-sleeved tops are popular despite the hot weather, because many of Uniqlo's shoppers travel to cooler climates. These insights are helping the company plan for marketing to achieve its ambitious long-term goal of becoming the world's largest apparel retailer by 2020.[14]

Technological Trends

Technology reaches into every aspect of the marketing mix, from digitally enhanced advertisements to new packaging materials and methods and beyond. A few of these trends include the ongoing global penetration of smartphones, advances in digital media, and the incorporation of electronic capabilities into a wider range of products. How will technology affect your product, customers, competitors, and marketing mix? To learn more about some key technology trends that can affect consumer behavior, check sources such as the Science and Technology section of USA.gov (see Exhibit 2.7).

The Internet has spawned countless marketing opportunities, from online retailing and social shopping to security solutions for viruses, stolen data, and other problems. Mobile technology is increasingly vital to marketers, as customers use brand- and retailer-specific apps to receive product and promotion information, check on inventory availability, compare prices, read customer reviews, and more. The list of retailers staying in touch with shoppers via app includes high-end stores such as Saks Fifth Avenue, department stores such as Macy's, and mass merchandisers such as Walmart. "We can greet each of our customers by name, guide them through our stores, and give them product recommendations and real-time savings, all from their mobile devices," says Walmart's head of mobile and digital marketing.[15]

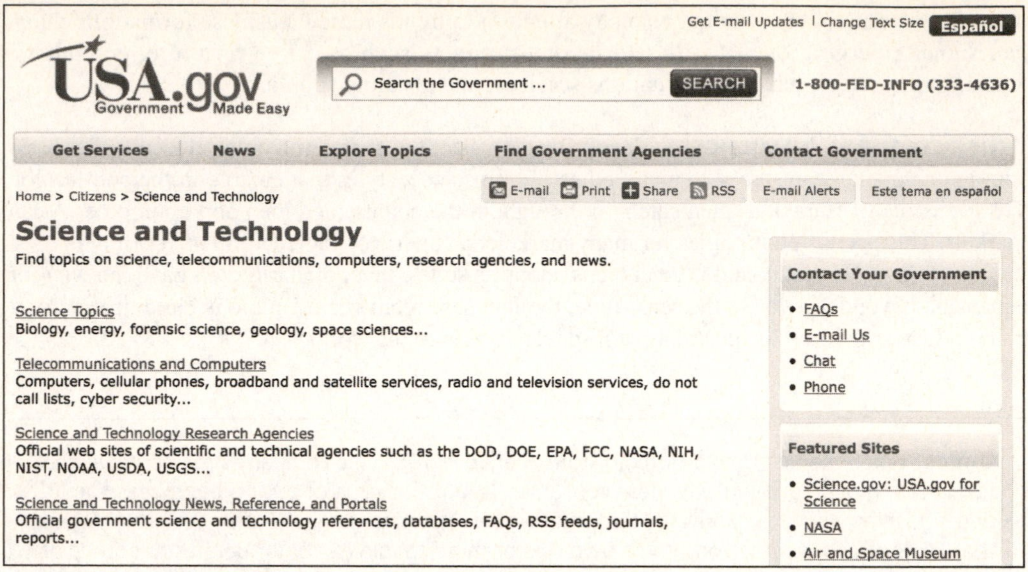

EXHIBIT 2.7   Science and Technology Updates on USA.gov

Broad questions about technological trends include the following: What cutting-edge innovations are being introduced, and how do they affect the organization's customers, suppliers, distributors, marketing, and processes? How are these technologies affected by, or generating, industry-wide standards and government regulations? What substitutes or innovations are becoming available because of new technology, and how are these changes likely to affect product categories, customer behavior, supplier strategies, and competitors' strategies? Understanding such trends can reveal threats (such as inventions or changes in standards that will make existing technology obsolete) and opportunities (such as quickly adopting a new technological standard).

Ecological Trends

The natural environment can influence companies in a variety of ways. Shortages of raw materials such as water, timber, oil, minerals, and other materials for production can cause major headaches for companies. Marketers also have to examine the various environmental issues that affect their organizations because of government regulation or social attitudes. Manufacturers of furniture, for instance, are increasingly concerned about using wood from sustainable sources, and many customers are insisting on products made from "green" raw materials. As a result, more marketers are applying for green certification labels to demonstrate that their goods and services are eco-friendly. However, the proliferation of labels and the wide range of standards for sustainability can be confusing to both consumers and businesses.[16]

More than 80% of U.S. consumers say they buy green products or are involved with green activities. Unfortunately, some marketers are taking advantage of this interest in sustainability to position their products as eco-friendly even when they're not, a case of **greenwashing**. Now, U.S. regulators are taking a very close look at green claims to prevent companies from misleading consumers. Clearly, marketers who want to earn the public's trust must be transparent about products' green benefits and must offer solid support for claims of environmental safety.[17]

Competitor Analysis

Analyzing competitors and the competitive climate can help marketers dig deeper into market dynamics, anticipate some moves that rivals might make, and create more practical and flexible marketing plans. Start by identifying current competitors, both successful and unsuccessful, and think about future sources of competition in order to avoid being blindsided by a new entrant. Examine each competitor's keys to success, strengths and weaknesses, and resources and strategies, with an eye toward what you can adapt and what you should avoid (see Exhibit 2.8). Also examine the timing of future competitive threats from emerging rivals, think about the opportunities they may exploit to enter the market, understand possible strengths and weaknesses, and consider what you can do to deflect competitive threats even before they've fully emerged.

Ultimately, customers determine the value of a firm's competitive advantage. This means any organization—large or small—has an opportunity to attract a loyal customer base by discovering what customers want and delivering it more effectively and efficiently (and perhaps more distinctively) than competitors. Consider Movie Tavern, a niche player that has become popular by offering a one-stop combination of food and film (see its home page at http://movietavern.com or scan the QR code).

Movie Tavern. Headquartered in Dallas, Movie Tavern is one of the pioneers of the food-and-film entertainment industry. Movie-goers can enjoy a full meal, nibble on snacks, or sip a drink while they view a first-run film, a 3-D movie, or a classic film in any of the company's 16 locations . Movie Tavern actually represents a double competitive threat: It not only competes with traditional movie theaters, it uses its reasonably-priced menu, complete with beer and wine, to compete with nearby restaurants.

Fewer than 1% of all U.S. movie theaters are currently equipped for food-and-film entertainment, but more competitors are entering the market alongside niche players like Movie Tavern and Studio Movie Grill. Alamo Drafthouse Cinema, for example, is a brew-pub theater that offers first-run movies and special movie festivals tied to seasonal or local themes. AMC, one of the largest U.S. theater chains, is testing Dine-In Theaters with upgraded seating and a diverse menu of drinks, appetizers, desserts, and entrees. Still, as an AMC executive observes, "Learning how to run a restaurant is a little different than running a theater." Knowing how to manage the food side of the business is one of Movie Tavern's key strengths in competing with any theater that enters the food-and-film business.[18]

According to Michael Porter, the five competitive forces affecting industry profitability and attractiveness are the rivalry among current competitors, the number of potential entrants into the industry, the bargaining power of suppliers, the bargaining power of buyers, and the potential threat presented by substitute products.[19] When it began, Movie Tavern was a new entrant that challenged AMC and other established theater chains. In turn, Movie Tavern's success is attracting new entrants, leading to increased rivalry within the industry. Buyers now have relatively few choices of food-and-film entertainment, but the situation will change as more suppliers enter the market. Buyers can currently choose from a wide array of substitute products, which also affects the competitive environment.

PLANNING TIP

Look for new ideas by probing customers' reactions to competitors' strengths and weaknesses.

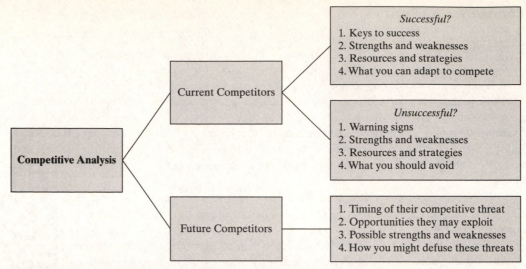

EXHIBIT 2.8   Analyzing Current and Future Competitors

Marketers need to determine which of Porter's generic competitive strategies is most appropriate for the company's unique situation.[20] With a **cost leadership strategy**, you seek to become the lowest-cost producer in the industry (Trader Joe's private-label grocery products are an example). With a **differentiation strategy**, you create a unique differentiation based on some factor valued by the target market (such as Movie Tavern's combination of food and film). With a **focus strategy**, you narrow the competitive scope to achieve a competitive advantage in your chosen segments. The strategy you choose for your marketing plan depends, in part, on refining your analysis of internal strengths and weaknesses and external opportunities and threats.

Refining the SWOT Analysis

During environmental scanning and analysis, you uncovered a number of strengths, weaknesses, opportunities, and threats. Now you're ready to refine the SWOT analysis for use in marketing planning. Specifically, how do you know what's a significant strength or weakness and which opportunities and threats are the most critical? First, examine your organization's previous performance to see how much of a strength or weakness each factor has been in the past. Also, compare the strengths and weaknesses you've identified with similar factors exhibited by your top competitors.

Next, see how each factor contributed to your ability to achieve a goal or prevented your organization from achieving a goal. Finally, consult strategic decision-makers inside the firm to learn their views on which are the most important opportunities to explore, threats to counteract, strengths to build on, and weaknesses to defend against.[21] Add this refined SWOT to your marketing plan, and refer to it as you continue the planning process.

Summary

The macroenvironment consists of broad political-legal, economic, social-cultural, technological, and ecological forces. The microenvironment consists of groups that more directly influence performance, such as customers, competitors, channel members, partners, suppliers, and employees. The outcome of environmental scanning is a SWOT analysis, which shows the organization's strengths, weaknesses, opportunities, and threats. A marketing plan can help you exploit strengths and opportunities while preventing threats and weaknesses from diminishing your marketing performance.

In scanning the internal environment, examine the organization's mission, resources, offerings, previous results, business relationships, keys to success, and warning signs. The mission shows the organization's fundamental purpose. Resources include people, money, information, and supplies. In scanning the external environment, examine political-legal, economic, social-cultural, technological, and ecological trends, as well as the competitive situation. Social-cultural influences include consumer demographics, business demographics, and cross-cultural factors. When considering the competitive environment, look at both current and potential competitors to learn from successes and to identify pitfalls to avoid in your marketing plan. Finally, based on the results of environmental scanning, refine the SWOT analysis.

Your Marketing Plan, Step by Step

Answer the following questions as you scan the environment and prepare a SWOT analysis for your marketing plan.

1. If your plan focuses on a real product or company, how will you research its internal and external environment and its competitors? In addition to examining the product or company's website and literature, look for online, printed, video, and audio content from the sources in the following list. If you're focusing on a hypothetical product or brand—or creating a marketing plan for an entirely new business or product—you can use publicly available information from the following sources to research close competitors and the industry as background for creating specific details for your plan.
   a. Industry groups, analysts, conferences, and research
   b. Business and news media
   c. Academic and professional groups
   d. Advocacy and community groups
   e. Government agencies and publications
   f. Professional and customer product reviews
   g. Social media sources such as company Facebook pages, YouTube videos, and blog posts
   h. Podcasts, webinars, executive interviews, and similar sources
2. Summarize what you learn about each internal and external factor named in Exhibits 2.3 and 2.5.
3. To get more information about competitors, start with their websites and social media activities. Also, check stores or distributors for written materials and details about products and other marketing particulars. Look at which distributors and retailers carry competing products and how those products are displayed, promoted, and priced. Do an Internet search for customer and distributor comments, both positive and negative, to identify competitors' weaknesses and strengths. Finally, check news sources and industry blogs for the latest developments about competitors' resources, results, and business relationships. Summarize the main points you learn about your current and emerging competitors.
4. What are your chosen product's or company's strengths and weaknesses? To find out, classify each bit of information you've collected about your product into one of four categories:
   a. "Positive internal" (potential strengths from factors in the internal environment)
   b. "Negative internal" (potential weaknesses from factors in the internal environment)
   c. "Positive external" (potential opportunities from factors in the external environment)
   d. "Negative external" (potential threats from factors in the external environment)
   Do the same with the information you've collected about competitors. Next, compare your product's positive and negative internal information with competitors' positive and negative

internal information. Using your judgment and these comparisons, determine which of your product's "positive internal" items represent significant strengths and which of your product's "negative internal" items represent significant weaknesses. Summarize your conclusions as part of the SWOT analysis in your marketing plan, using a grid similar to the one in Exhibit 2.2.

5. Review the information you've gathered about your product's external environment and classified as either "external positive" or "external negative." Thinking about your organization's mission and internal situation, as well as the competitive information you've gathered, which items on your list represent significant opportunities—and why? Which represent significant threats—and why? Refine the SWOT analysis and document it in your marketing plan.

Endnotes

1. Matthew Le Merle, "How to Prepare for a Black Swan," *Strategy +Business,* August 23, 2011, www.strategy-business.com.

2. Lisa Bernard-Kuhn, "P&G Exec Touts New Products," *Cincinnati.com,* September 6, 2012, www.cincinnati.com; Jessica Wohl, "Procter & Gamble to Move Beauty Unit to Singapore," *Reuters,* May 10, 2012, www.reuters.com; Ricardo Geromel, "Procter & Gamble Explains Why Israel Is the Startup Nation," *Forbes,* May 16, 2012, www.forbes.com; Mae Anderson, "P&G to Give Mothers of Olympians $1,000," *Bloomberg BusinessWeek,* May 8, 2012, www.businessweek.com; Lauren Coleman-Lochner, "P&G Drops After Cutting Forecast Amid Venezuela Price Controls," *Bloomberg,* April 29, 2012, www.bloomberg.com; Mae Anderson, "Procter & Gamble 3Q Net Income Slips," *Bloomberg BusinessWeek,* April 27, 2012, www.businessweek.com.

3. Stuart Read, Nicholas Dew, Saras D. Sarasvathy, Michael Song, and Robert Wiltbank, "Marketing Under Uncertainty," *Journal of Marketing,* vol. 73 (no. 3), May 2009, pp. 1–18.

4. James C. Collins and Jerry I. Porras, *Built to Last* (New York: HarperBusiness, 1994), pp. 220–221.

5. Quoted in Maureen Jenkins, "What's Our Business?" *Black Enterprise,* October 2005, p. 71.

6. Jim Nichols, "Your Mission: Create a Worthwhile Mission Statement," *Forbes,* May 3, 2012, www.forbes.com.

7. Lauren Torrisi, "Vanilla Shortage," *ABC News,* April 4, 2012, http://abcnews.go.com; Lauren Day, "Australian Vanilla Growers to Cash in on Global Shortage," *ABC News Australia,* May 2, 2012, www.abc.net.au; Murray Wardrop, "Vanilla Crisis Could Force Up Price of Ice Cream, *Telegraph (U.K.),* April 2, 2012, www.telegraph.co.uk.

8. Paul Sonne and Jennifer Levitz, "Not Cool: I Scream, You Scream, We All Scream 'Where the Heck's Our Ice Cream?'" *Wall Street Journal,* May 25, 2012, www.wsj.com.

9. "The Business of Gaming: Thinking Out of the Box," *Economist,* December 10, 2011, pp. 5-7.

10. Michael Lee, "Facebook Closes Instagram Deal at US$715 million," *ZDNet,* September 7, 2012, www.zd.net; Austin Carr, "An Insider's View on Instagram's True Value to Facebook," *Fast Company Design,* May 17, 2012, www.fastcodesign.com; Austin Carr, "Hipstamatic, Instagram to Unveil Photo-Sharing Partnership," *Fast Company,* March 21, 2012, www.fastcompany.com; Leslie Horn, "Instagram iPhone App Adds 1 Million Users in Six Weeks," *PC Magazine Online,* February 15, 2011, www.pcmag.com.

11. Brian Womack and Hugo Mille, "Google Wins Approval in China for Motorola Mobility Purchase," *Bloomberg,* May 19, 2012, www.bloomberg.com; Steven M. Davidoff, "China Flexes Its Regulatory Muscle, Catching Google in Its Grip," *New York Times,* May 15, 2012, www.nytimes.com.

12. Todd Sperry, "Twitter Joins 'Do Not Track,' Gives Users Privacy Option," *CNN,* May 17, 2012, www.cnn.com.

13. Kevin McQuaid, "Summer Travel Slump? Don't Tell Local Tourism Officials," *Sarasota Herald-Tribune,* May 15, 2012, www.heraldtribune.com; "Florida Tourism Numbers Show Slight Gain in 2012," *Bloomberg BusinessWeek,* May 17, 2012, www.businessweek.com.

14. Stephanie Clifford, "As U.S. Retailers Retreat, a Japanese Chain Sees an Opening," *New York Times,* May 22, 2012, www.nytimes.com; Samuel Thomas, "Harajuku's New Meeting Place for Fashionistas," *Japan Times,* May 1, 2012, www.japantimes.co.jp; Tina Gaudoin, "Uniqlo: Cheap and Very Cheerful," *Wall Street Journal,* April 19, 2012, www.wsj.com.

15. Adele Ferguson, "How the Humble App Is Changing the Face of Shopping, and Retailers," *Sydney Morning Herald (Australia),* May 19, 2012, www.smh.com.au.

16. Matt Evans, "Furniture Awash in Green-Claims Labels at High Point Market," *The Greater Triad Area Business Journal (Greensboro, North Carolina)*, April 20, 2012, www.bizjournals.com.

17. Anne Marie Mohan, "SPS 2012: Marketing 'Green' to the Mainstream," *Packaging World,* May 9, 2012, www.packworld.com; "FTC Increasing Scrutiny of Green Claims," *Environmental Leader,* March 20, 2012, www.environmentalleader.com.

18. "Movie Tavern Brings 200 Jobs to Gwinnett," *Gwinnett Business Journal (Georgia),* May 17, 2012, http://gbj.com; Andreas Fuchs, "Delectable and Delicious: In-Cinema Dining Continues to Grow in Popularity," *Film Journal International,* February 2012, p. 22; Karen Robinson-Jacobs and Robert Wilonsky, "Austin's Alamo Drafthouse Plans up to 7 Dallas-Area Theaters,"*Dallas Morning News,* May 16, 2012, www.dallasnews.com; Pamela McClintock, "The Evolving Upscale Movie Experience," *Hollywood Reporter,* April 1, 2011, p. 52.

19. Michael E. Porter, *Competitive Advantage* (New York: Free Press, 1985), p. 5.

20. Discussion draws on concepts in Porter, *Competitive Advantage*, pp. 11–26.

21. Mary K. Coulter, *Strategic Management in Action* (Upper Saddle River, NJ: Pearson Prentice Hall, 1998), p. 141.

Understanding Markets and Customers

In this chapter:

PREVIEW

No two markets are exactly the same, no two markets stay the same forever, and no company can afford to sell to or satisfy every customer in every market on earth. Even well-heeled giants like General Electric, General Motors, and Genentech must make informed decisions about which local, regional, national, and international markets to serve and about the specific customer groups they can develop marketing plans to satisfy most profitably.

This chapter discusses how to research and analyze markets and customers, Step 2 in the marketing planning process (see Exhibit 3.1). First, you'll learn how to define your market, examine overall characteristics, and calculate market share, a prelude to selecting markets and segments to target. Next, you'll learn more about understanding the needs and behavior of consumers and business customers in light of the constant change that affects marketing activities. Finally, you'll see how primary research and secondary research are used during the preparation of a marketing plan.

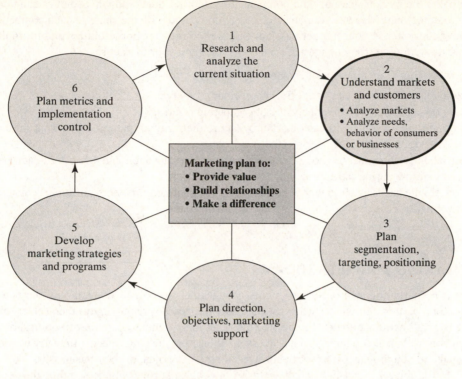

EXHIBIT 3.1   Marketing Planning: Step 2

APPLYING YOUR KNOWLEDGE

As you read this chapter and move ahead with marketing planning, continue to record your conclusions and decisions in a written marketing plan. Look at the sample plan in the appendix to see how companies document what they learn about markets and customers and the research they need to create an effective strategy. Also use this chapter's checklist when preparing to analyze your markets and customers. Finally, refer back to the research and notes you made after completing the "Your Marketing Plan, Step by Step" exercises in previous chapters.

CHAPTER 3 CHECKLIST   Analyzing Markets and Customers

Understanding the Market and Market Share

✓ How can the market be described in terms of product, customer need, and geography?

✓ What general demographics, characteristics, needs, behavior, and preferences pertain to this product and category in this market? How are these changing?

✓ What is the market share of your company, brand, or product, and what sources can you use to monitor share? How is your share changing compared with the share of each competitor?

✓ How can you use your marketing plan to make the most of opportunities and to minimize threats stemming from the market's characteristics and your market share?

Understanding Consumers and Business Customers

✓ What customer needs can your offering profitably satisfy?

✓ How do customers perceive the value of competing offerings relative to yours?

✓ Who are the customers in each market, what are their buying patterns, and what influences their needs and behavior?

✓ For business customers, who is involved in the buying decision and what does each person need to know during the buying process?

✓ How are the needs and behavior of business customers influenced by organizational connections and considerations?

ANALYZING MARKETS TODAY

Just as the marketing environment is highly changeable, so too is a **market**—all the potential buyers for a particular product. In a **consumer market**, people are buying for themselves or their families; in a **business market**, people are buying for their companies, nonprofit groups, or other organizations. When you think about a "market," think "people"—because ultimately it's people who make the buying decisions for themselves, their households, or their businesses.

As Exhibit 3.2 indicates, market analysis is a vital backdrop for understanding the dynamic needs and behavior of consumers and business customers you want to reach through your marketing plan. Nike has successfully dealt with different market situations by studying each market and understanding the needs and concerns of consumers, locally and globally.

Nike. Nike remains at the top of its game even after decades of fierce competition with global rivals such as Adidas and Puma. It rings up $20 billion in revenues year after year because it knows how to research, analyze, define, and target its markets. In meeting the sports needs of professional athletes and consumers who aspire to their personal best, Nike applies its knowledge of innovation, performance, and style to provide value. Even during difficult economic times, the company has been able to sprint ahead of competitors and increase market share because it knows its markets and customers so well.

In the past, Nike's high-profile TV and billboard ads set the tone for its marketing. It still uses fast-paced commercials, sometimes debuting them on Facebook or YouTube. In today's wired world, however, Nike aims to engage customers in digital dialogue and involve them in the brand's virtual sports community. During the recent Olympic Games, Nike was mentioned in thousands of tweets and attracted hundreds of thousands of new Facebook fans. Digital Sport, another part of this marketing strategy, began with the Nike+ program, a high-tech system that aims to help consumers work toward their fitness goals. A computer chip embedded in the wearer's Nike athletic shoes sends performance data to his or her mobile device (distance for runners, jump height for basketball players, and so on). Users can upload their statistics to the Nike+ site, chart their progress over time, and compare results with others.[2]

Consumer Analysis
- Needs
- Cultural considerations
- Social connections
- Personal factors

Market Analysis
- Market and needs definition
- Market changes
- Market share

Business Customer Analysis
- Needs
- Organizational connections
- Organizational considerations

EXHIBIT 3.2   Market and Customer Analysis

Also remember that people's preferences, behavior, and attitudes can shift at any time, creating new consumer or business markets and changing existing markets. Sometimes changes can be extreme, even to the point of markets disappearing, as happened to the Flip handheld camcorder. The popular and affordable Flip dominated the fast-growing market for handheld video recorders when its parent company was purchased by Cisco in 2009. Just two years later, Cisco shut down the Flip and exited the market, recognizing that consumers were turning to multi-function smartphones for video recording instead of buying individual devices like the Flip.[1]

As Nike knows, every market is different, which affects planning for the marketing mix of products, channel choices, and communications. The first step for Nike, as for other marketers, is to broadly define the market and its needs. (Learn more about Nike at its corporate home page http://nikeinc.com/ or by scanning this QR code.)

Broad Definition of Market and Needs

A market can be defined at five basic levels: (1) potential market, (2) available market, (3) qualified available market, (4) served or target market, and (5) penetrated market.[3] Exhibit 3.3 shows these definitions with a rental car example. The potential market contains the maximum number of customers that exists for a company's product (recognizing, of course, that no one product can appeal to every possible customer). Note that if the product already exists, the penetrated market consists of people who are already buying it. The remainder of the market consists

PLANNING TIP

When formulating your marketing plan, research and analyze the broad market for your product.

Type of Market	Definition	Rental Car Example
Potential market (*broadest definition*)	All customers who may be interested in a particular offering	Any driver who needs temporary transportation
Available market (*subset of the potential market*)	Customers who are interested, possess sufficient income, and have access to the offering	Any driver who can afford the rental fees and is in the area served by rental-car services
Qualified available market (*subset of the available market*)	Customers who are qualified to buy based on age (for products that cannot be sold to underage consumers) or other criteria	Drivers in the available market who have valid licenses and meet minimum or maximum age restrictions
Target market (*subset of the qualified available market to be served*)	Customers that the company intends to target for a particular offer	Drivers in the qualified available market who need to travel from airports to final destinations in the area
Penetrated market (*subset of the target market*)	Customers who are already buying the type of product sold by the company	Drivers in the target market who have previously rented cars

EXHIBIT 3.3   Defining the Market

of nonbuyers (potential customers) who are aware of the offering or value its benefits, have access to it, are of the proper age or have the skill to buy or use it, and can afford it. Marketers, therefore, want to narrow their focus by gaining a thorough understanding of customers in the potential, available, and qualified available markets.

For planning purposes, markets may be described in terms of geography as well as by product or customer definition. "The U.S. smartphone market" is a broad description of one target market that Apple seeks to serve with its iPhone. Because of international telecommunication standards, Apple must define each target market geographically: "The U.S. smartphone market" and "the London smartphone market" are two examples. Another way to define the market is in terms of customer need: "The Baltimore market for weed killer" is an overall description of the group of customers and prospects seeking a product to wipe out weeds. Within that market may be subsets of consumers and business customers who prefer eco-friendly products or who want to get rid of specific weeds such as poison ivy for aesthetic or health reasons.

Next, the company conducts research into the broad needs of the available market. Here, the emphasis is on identifying general needs prior to a more in-depth investigation of each segment's particular needs. This research also helps the company identify what customers value and how its image, products, services, and other attributes can be positioned for competitive differentiation. Consider the situation of Volkswagen, which is aiming to become the world's largest automotive manufacturer by 2018. (Get the latest corporate news about Volkswagen Group of America at www.volkswagengroupamerica.com or by following the QR code.)

Volkswagen. Volkswagen, based in Wolfsburg, Germany, designs cars and trucks for different markets and needs—design being one of its competitive strengths in all markets. As a result, each vehicle has styling, features, and benefits geared toward its specific target market. VW's sleek Lamborghini sports cars are valued as status symbols worldwide, while the VW Beetle is valued for its fuel efficiency as much as for its distinctive personality. The diesel-powered VW Amarok commercial pickup trucks offer the rugged handling and gas-sipping benefits valued by business buyers in Latin America.

   The mid-sized VW Golf, sporty and nimble for city streets and highways, has become Europe's best-selling car. VW is opening a new Audi plant in Mexico to supply cars to North America, where demand for this luxury brand has been strong. Looking ahead, VW's marketers plan to continue using their knowledge of customer needs in each market and their well-regarded design capabilities as competitive advantages in the high-stakes race for global market share. Reaching the goal of selling 10 million cars and trucks in one year will put VW in the industry-leading position it aims to achieve. [4]

Along with a broad understanding of needs, marketers look at general demographics to get a rough sense of what each market is like (in the aggregate). As an example, U.S. Census information shows the number of people and households in specific areas of the country. Marketers then look beyond sheer numbers, researching gender, age, education, marital status, income, home ownership, and other characteristics that relate to their products.

In the business market, marketers can use the **North American Industry Classification System (NAICS)** to classify industries and investigate industry size. Additional research about industries, products, and geographic markets is available from a wide variety of sources, including international trade organizations, global banks, foreign consulates, universities, and business publications. As with consumer markets, the next step is to obtain meaningful characteristics that relate to the product, such as the annual sales, number of employees, or industries served by the businesses in the market. Motorola Solutions, for instance, identifies markets by industry (such as the public safety sector, including fire and police departments), researches the communications needs of each industry market, and tailors complete solutions (such as two-way communications systems) to fit each industry's needs.[5]

Markets as Moving Targets

Markets are always in flux: Consumers move in or out, are born or die, start or stop buying a good or service; businesses change location, go in to or out of business, expand or divest units, start or stop buying a product. Thus, at this stage of the market analysis, marketers need to locate projec-

PLANNING TIP

Consider the markets of today and tomorrow when developing your plan.

tions of demographic changes in the markets and to forecast future demand for (or sales of) their type of product, as a way of sizing the overall market over time. (Forecasting is discussed in Chapter 10.)

   Is the population expected to grow or shrink, and by how much? How many new businesses are projected to enter or leave the market? What are the projections for total industry sales of the product over the coming years? Do these projections suggest a sizable market, a stagnant market, or a shrinking market? The answers to these questions influence what you put in your marketing plan regarding research, targeting, and objectives. Consider the market for mobile computing.

> **Mobile Computing.** Since its introduction, Apple's now-iconic iPad has dominated the market for tablet computers. Even though the first iPad lacked a camera and other features usually found on today's tablets, millions of customers were attracted to its portability, ease of use, and sleek design. The iPad was an instant hit. With an economic downturn dampening high-end PC sales, many consumers and businesses turned to the iPad as a fun and functional mobile alternative to the traditional laptop. Suddenly, companies throughout the computer industry had to adjust to new market realities and sizable shifts in demand.
>
> By 2012, sales of tablet computers were surging, with the iPad remaining well ahead of competitors such as Amazon's Kindle Fire and Samsung's Galaxy Tab. Meanwhile, Dell was scrambling to revise its marketing plan amid slower sales of desktop, notebook, and mini-notebook PCs. And chipmaker Intel began positioning itself for the future by designing smaller, speedier microprocessors to power the next generation of mobile devices.[6]

Much research is publicly available for major markets and for products, but marketers of groundbreaking products often must conduct their own research to project demand and sales. This part of the planning process also feeds into the SWOT analysis discussed in Chapter 2, because it can reveal new opportunities or threats that must be addressed.

Market Share as a Vital Sign

PLANNING TIP

Keep market share in mind to set realistic objectives and metrics.

Market share is the percentage of sales in a given market held by a particular company, brand, or product, calculated in dollars or units (ideally, both). Market share usually changes over time as companies and their competitors court customers, the market grows or shrinks, and competitors enter or exit. You can use market share information as a baseline for understanding historical market dynamics and a standard for setting and measuring marketing plan objectives.

In simple terms, market share is calculated according to this formula:

$$\frac{\text{One company's product sales in the market (units or dollars)}}{\text{Overall sales of such products in the market (units or dollars)}}$$

Thus, if Firm A sells 2 million units in the 50 states, and overall market sales for all competitors selling that kind of product are 10 million units, A's U.S. market share would be calculated as:

$$\frac{2,000,000}{10,000,000} = .20 = 20\%$$

Units are frequently used for market-share calculations because differences in company pricing policies can distort share comparisons. However, companies don't always report unit sales publicly. As a result, if a company wants to calculate its market share and those of its competitors, it may have to use dollar sales. Suppose Firm A sells $15 million worth of a product in the U.S. market, where overall industry sales of such products are $100 million. Its nearest competitor, Firm B, sells $12 million worth of products in the U.S. market. Then A's share would be 15% and B's share would be 12%.

As noted earlier, market share is a point-in-time snapshot showing the relative positions of competitors during a particular period—positions that can and do constantly change. For example, suppliers LG and Samsung together accounted for nearly 100% of the 2010 market for tablet-computer display panels, thanks to the incredible popularity of models like the iPad. In 2011, however, the estimated combined market share of these two Korean companies was down to about 81%: According to one report, LG held 46% of the market and Samsung held 35%. Why? Because competitors from Japan, China, and Taiwan were gaining ground with displays for up-and-coming tablets. New tablets introduced in 2012 changed market demand again, prompting changes in market share among display suppliers. As tablets get smaller and more complex, display manufacturers will have to meet even more stringent standards in the years ahead, which will affect share as well.[7]

Clearly, market share is one of a business's vital signs, to be monitored over time as a way of spotting potential problems as well as potential opportunities. Companies should develop share information for each product in each market, regularly update share numbers to track shifts, and examine shifts as possible triggers for control measures (discussed in detail in Chapter 10).

In addition, market share directly affects segmentation and targeting, because a company with marketing strategies to capture a larger and larger share of a shrinking market segment could end up with nearly 100% of a market too small to be profitable. Cisco stopped producing Flip video recorders—by far the dominant brand in compact, handheld camcorders—because it believed the market was on the brink of extinction, thanks to an ever-higher penetration of smartphones. After Kodak entered bankruptcy, it pulled out of the videocamera and digital camera markets to focus on image printing, in part because multifunction smartphones were replacing individual devices (as Cisco had realized).[8] On the other hand, most companies take special notice of markets in which demand is projected to skyrocket, using share over time to identify opportunities, to understand competitive dynamics, and to set and measure progress toward objectives.

ANALYZING CUSTOMER NEEDS AND BEHAVIOR

With the market analysis as backdrop, marketers use research to examine the needs, buying behavior, and attitudes of the customers in their markets. This research forms the foundation for decisions about which segments to target, the most effective way to position the product in each market, and what marketing strategies and tactics are most appropriate for profitably satisfying customers. The brief chapter-ending section on marketing research discusses how marketers can study and understand customers' behavior and buying decisions.

Forces in the external environment can play a key role in affecting the who, what, when, where, why, and how of consumer and business buying behavior. This is one of the reasons for studying the current situation, as discussed in Chapter 2. To illustrate, when the economy is in recession, many consumers and business customers change their buying patterns—sometimes purchasing less or less often, sometimes seeking out low-priced alternatives. For this reason, Nestlé and Unilever recently introduced smaller, lower-priced packages of their branded products for cash-strapped European consumers. "There are unemployed young people, students, single-parent families, and pensioners," explained Nestlé's top executive in Europe. "We can provide them with relevant options." Meanwhile, supermarkets, drug stores, and discount chains are also appealing to these same consumers with low-priced store-brand products.[9] In different economic circumstances, however, this buying behavior is likely to change again, forcing a new look at many marketing plans. (To see Nestlé's corporate site, visit www.nestle.com or follow this QR code.)

The attitudes and habits of consumers and business customers are clearly affected by the marketing-mix programs implemented by different companies competing for their attention, loyalty, and buying power. From the customer's perspective, no marketing tactic stands in isolation: It's only one tactic used by the company and one of many stimuli in the market (some of which are noticed and acted on, most of which are not). So marketers not only must understand their markets and the environmental forces shaping customer actions, but also must learn to see the totality of their marketing activities and the actions of competing firms through their customers' eyes.

Remember that stated needs are generally the tip of the iceberg; customers also have unstated needs (e.g., a good or service) and sometimes secret needs (e.g., relating to their self-concept or other internal needs). Thus, it is vital to understand the problem each customer seeks to solve and what that customer really wants from the solution. Remember that the needs, wants, attitudes, behavior, and decision-making processes of consumers differ, in general, from those of business customers. The next sections highlight important influences to understand when preparing plans for consumer and business markets (see Exhibit 3.4).

Consumer Markets

Who is buying or using the product? When, where, how, and why? What is the consumer's decision-making process for buying that product, and how are the process and the decisions changing over time? Look at both internal and external sources of data for this analysis of consumer needs, decision making, and behavior.

PLANNING TIP

Determine needs by behavior as well as what consumers say.

When making decisions about more complex purchases, such as a car, consumers generally take more time, gather more information about alternatives, weigh the decision more carefully, and have strong feelings in the aftermath of the purchase. Inexpensive items bought on impulse, such as candy, are not usually subjected to as much scrutiny before or after the purchase. By

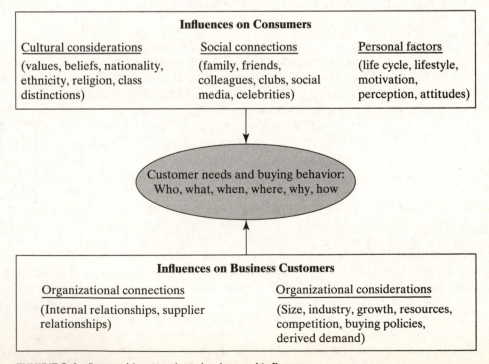

EXHIBIT 3.4   Researching Needs, Behavior, and Influences

investigating the entire process consumers follow to buy, use, and evaluate their products, marketers can determine how, when, and where to initiate suitable marketing activities.

Early in the buying process, for example, marketers may need to emphasize benefits that solve consumer problems. Later in the process, marketers may need to communicate where the product can be purchased; still later, marketers may want to reassure consumers that they made the right buying decision. The exact nature and timing of the marketing activities will depend on what the marketer learns about consumer decision making (as well as on the marketer's strategy and resources, of course).

Although the level of influence varies from individual to individual, consumer needs, wants, and behaviors are affected by cultural considerations, social connections, and personal factors.

CULTURAL CONSIDERATIONS As buyers, consumers feel the influence of the national or regional culture in which they were raised as well as the one in which they currently live. This means that consumers in different countries often approach buying situations from different perspectives because of differing values, beliefs, and preferences. Without research, marketers can't know exactly what those differences are or how to address them.

Subcultures are distinct groups within a larger culture that exhibit and preserve distinct cultural identities through a common religion, nationality, ethnic background, or lifestyle. A variety of subcultures drive U.S. consumers' decisions and behavior. For example, Cuban Americans frequently have different food preferences than, say, Chinese Americans. Teenagers—an age subculture—tend to prefer different clothing styles, music, and travel choices than seniors.

Class distinctions, even when subtle, also influence consumer behavior. The members of each class generally buy and use products in a similar way; in addition, people who aspire to a different class may emulate the buying or usage patterns of that class. Savvy marketers learn how such distinctions operate and then apply this knowledge to decisions about products, marketing communications, distribution arrangements, price levels, and service strategies.

SOCIAL CONNECTIONS Consumers have a web of social connections that influence how they buy—connections such as family ties, friendships, work groups, and civic organizations. Family members, for example, directly or indirectly control household spending for many goods and services. Children ask parents to buy products advertised on television; parents buy things to keep children healthy or safe; families make group decisions about vacations. Social connections include friends and fans on Facebook, Twitter, and other social media networks.

PLANNING TIP

Monitor social media to see what consumers say about your brand.

Understanding how social connections affect the buying process is critical for marketers creating plans for products intended for specific family members, usage, or occasions. *Social gifting* has recently emerged as a trend in which consumers' social connections play a key role.

Social gifting. Want to be reminded about friends' birthdays or anniversaries? Need ideas for appropriate gifts? Social-gifting apps address these two needs by enabling consumers to buy and send a gift card or to arrange for delivery of a product for any occasion. Wrapp, based in Sweden, lets users send friends digital gift cards for H&M, Sephora, or other retailers through their connections on Facebook (or by text message or e-mail). Karma, owned by Facebook, allows users to monitor their Facebook friends' posts in certain categories (including birthdays and relationships) and suggests appropriate gifts for each situation. The buyer uses Karma's app to choose a gift and a greeting, then Karma notifies the recipient about the gift. Starbucks is also building on these types of social connections by promoting digital gift cards sent via Facebook.[10]

As with class distinctions, aspirations to different social connections can be a powerful influence on buying behavior. In apparel, for example, preteens want to look as grown up as possible, so they emulate teen fashions; teenagers dress like the celebrities they admire; and managers seeking to move up follow the clothing cues of higher-level managers. Within each social group, consumers look to certain opinion leaders for advice or guidance about buying decisions.

PERSONAL FACTORS   Personal factors are another major category of influences on consumer buying, covering life cycle, lifestyle, and psychological makeup, among other factors. *Life cycle* refers to the individual's changing family situation over time—single, cohabiting, engaged, married, married with children, divorced, remarried, and so on. Each of these life-cycle phases entails different buying needs, attitudes, and preferences that, in turn, can be identified through research and addressed through marketing. Engaged couples, for instance, are targeted by marketers selling formal wear, wedding invitations, catering services, and other wedding goods and services; new parents are targeted by marketers selling entirely different products.

Lifestyle is the pattern of living that a person exhibits through activities and interests—how the individual spends his or her time. To understand the complexities of lifestyle and its influence on consumer buying, marketers use sophisticated techniques to examine variables known as **psychographic characteristics**, which together form a picture of the consumer's lifestyle. Some markets are better approached through psychographics. For example, when the online travel site Expedia entered the Indian market, it emphasized its strength in arranging for hotels, transportation, and vacation activities for nearly every lifestyle or interest. Whether customers want a last-minute getaway to an island resort or a packaged tour of European cities, Expedia markets itself as a convenient, all-in-one travel site that saves time and money.[11]

Internal elements such as motivation, perception, and attitudes—all part of the consumer's psychological makeup—can strongly influence consumer behavior. **Motivation** stems from the consumer's drive to satisfy needs and wants. **Perception** is how the individual organizes environmental inputs (such as ads, conversation, and media) and derives meaning from them. When marketers talk about "cutting through clutter," they mean how to make their message stand out among many messages bombarding consumers throughout the day—not just to capture attention but to motivate consumers to respond. **Attitudes** are the individual's lasting evaluations of and feelings toward something, such as a product or a person. Especially after an event that puts an entire product category in a negative light, such as a safety recall or publicity about contamination, marketers need to plan for encouraging positive attitudes and perceptions.

Business Markets

PLANNING TIP

Dig deeper to understand underlying needs and concerns.

Like consumer markets, business markets are made up of people—individuals who buy on behalf of their company, government agency, institution, or not-for-profit organization. In the context of business buying, however, these people are generally influenced by a different set of factors than when buying as consumers. Marketers therefore need to examine organizational considerations and connections when analyzing business-buying decisions and behavior.

ORGANIZATIONAL CONNECTIONS   Although exactly who does the buying differs from company to company, officially designated purchasing agents are not the only people involved with the buying decision. Buyers are usually connected with other internal players. For instance, another employee or manager may initiate the buying process by suggesting a purchase; those who actually use the product may play a role by providing specifications, testing alternatives, or evaluating purchases; and buyers may need connections to the managers who are authorized to approve a purchase.

Depending on the organization and its structure, other internal players may wield some type of influence, such as insisting on compatibility with existing goods or services or controlling access to buyers. Not every player will participate in every purchase, so marketers must understand the decision process that takes place inside key customer organizations and plan appropriate marketing activities to reach the right players at the right time with the right message.

Finally, learn about the organization's current relations with competing suppliers, including long-term contracts, evaluations, requirements, and other elements. Many firms have long-term buying relationships with suppliers who meet preset quality and performance standards. Companies that outsource functions, the way U.K. mortgage firm International Personal Finance outsources its cloud computing file storage to Fujitsu U.K., generally sign multiyear agreements with the chosen supplier. This means other suppliers have a long wait before they can even try to bid for the business.[12] Researching a business customer's supplier connections and requirements is a good first step toward getting on the short list of approved suppliers and making the sale.

ORGANIZATIONAL CONSIDERATIONS   Organizational considerations include the company's size and industry, share and growth, competitive situation, buying policies and procedures, financial constraints, and the timing of purchases. In researching these factors, marketers need to find out, for example, whether a corporation buys centrally or allows each unit to buy on its own, whether companies participate in online marketplaces, and what funding and scheduling issues affect the purchase. Internal priorities are another organizational consideration.

Business buying is also affected by **derived demand**, the principle that demand for business products in an industry is based on demand for related consumer products. As an example, a surge in demand for motorcycles, cars, and small trucks in Asia has prompted BASF, a chemical company based in Germany, to expand the production and distribution of its automotive paint coating materials for that market. The company is also looking ahead to new automotive coating materials suitable for all-electric and hybrid cars, which are increasingly popular.[13]

Derived demand requires that business-to-business (B2B) marketers be aware of emerging trends and needs in consumer markets and be ready to help customers serve *their* customers. If suppliers are unprepared to deliver on time and within budget, marketers that serve consumers will have difficulty providing the value that their customers demand when and where needed. On the other hand, derived demand can also mean slower orders and sales for B2B marketers. During the recent economic downturn, low demand for air travel prompted many airlines to reduce flight schedules and find ways to slash expenses, which affected suppliers such as Boeing. Southwest Airlines delayed delivery of 20 new multimillion-dollar Boeing 737 jets until at least 2017, for instance. On the other hand, All Nippon Airways, which had hoped for speedy delivery of the new, fuel-efficient 787 Dreamliner, was forced to wait for more than two years while Boeing ironed out production problems. This delay caused a change in marketing plans for new routes and new schedules.[14] (Follow this QR code to visit the Boeing home page or click on www.boeing.com.)

PLANNING MARKETING RESEARCH

This chapter has covered a wide range of issues that should be researched in order to give organizations a better understanding of markets and customers during the marketing planning process. Often the best way to start is with **secondary research**—information already collected for another purpose. Secondary research is more readily available and less expensive than **primary research**, research conducted to address a specific marketing question or situation. Exhibit 3.5 shows a few of the many ways in which research can be used to support your marketing plan.

Secondary Research

Secondary research is often the starting point for a situation analysis, and it can be quite valuable—if you understand its limitations. Check the dates and the sources. Some sources offer new or updated statistics and profiles on a regular basis; others provide a snapshot covering a specific period, which can be useful but may become quickly outdated. Also consider the source's credibility to be sure the information is from an unbiased and reputable source. Industry information from the U.S. Department of Commerce's Bureau of Economic Analysis, for example, is based on government studies and statistics (see Exhibit 3.6). If a source reports data but did not actually conduct the research, find out where the information came from and whether it was changed from the original. If you don't know anything about the source, try to verify the information's accuracy before you rely on it for marketing purposes.

Plan to use multiple sources of secondary research so you can get the benefit of different viewpoints; also check each source's details against the others. Look for the details you need

EXHIBIT 3.5 How Research Supports a Marketing Plan

Type of research	Definition	Examples of support for a marketing plan
Secondary	Research using data already collected for another purpose	• As part of situational analysis, to gain a broad overview of demographic trends in a certain market by examining U.S. Census data • As part of metrics, to compare actual response to company communications with typical response rate within the industry
Primary	Research conducted to address a specific marketing question or situation	• As part of product strategy, to investigate the benefits and attributes that customers want when buying this type of product • As part of channel strategy, to determine what kind of in-store display will capture shopper's attention and result in the highest sales • As part of pricing strategy, to understand how customers value the offering and competing offerings • As part of communication strategy, to see whether customers receive, understand, and respond to a particular message or campaign

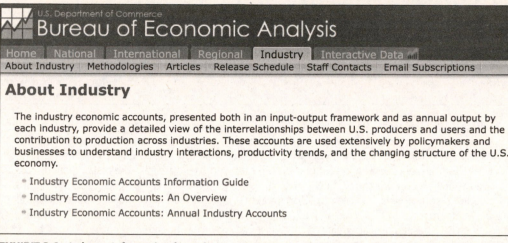

EXHIBIT 3.6   **Industry Information from the U.S. Department of Commerce Bureau of Economic Analysis**

in each source, taking note of how current the information is and extracting the specifics to be included in various sections of your marketing plan. Be prepared to explain and interpret the information in the context of your brand's situation.

Often, secondary research is too general to answer detailed questions about particular markets and types of customers. That's where primary marketing research comes in. Marketers who are qualified to do so can conduct primary research to support the planning process. Some companies have specialists on staff to conduct primary research or prefer to hire outside specialists to do so.

Primary Research

Primary research starts with a definition of what you need to know about a specific market and how that knowledge will help you create a more effective marketing plan. For example, a carpet manufacturer might want to know more about the buying process families use to determine when to buy new carpeting for an existing home. This knowledge can help its marketers better plan the timing and content of communications to trigger interest in the brand and in specific carpet products. The manufacturer can also gain insight into stated and unstated needs that carpeting can satisfy, such as making a room more comfortable (stated) and communicating social status (unstated).

The next step is to plan for collecting data through observation, surveys (online, by phone, or by mail), experiments, and other research methods. Marketers are increasingly interested in ethnographic research, online research, and neuromarketing.

ETHNOGRAPHIC RESEARCH   When marketers use *ethnographic research*, they observe how customers behave in actual product-purchase or usage situations and ask questions to clarify the reasons for their behavior. The Walt Disney Company uses ethnographic research to better understand the attitudes and behavior of an important target market for cable TV programming, tween boys (ages 6–14). Trained researchers observe tween boys as they shop, visit them at home to learn what they choose and use and why, and watch what they do in their free time. Based on this research, Disney now has tween actors in its TV shows carry skateboards with the bottoms facing outward (to show off the personalization, which tweens like to do) and creates characters who work hard to improve their skills (which tweens admire).[15]

LEGO used ethnographic research to study preteen girls' play patterns before introducing a new product line aimed at girls.

LEGO. LEGO has traditionally been much more successful in marketing block sets to boys (and adults) than in marketing block sets designed for girls. When the company planned a new line of block sets for girls, it began by sending marketers on lengthy research trips to observe U.S., U.K., German, and Korean girls at play and to talk with their families. The researchers discovered that girls weren't fond of the mini-figures packaged with current LEGO sets. "The girls needed a figure they could identify with, [one] that looks like them," notes a product designer on the team.

LEGO researchers also learned that girls enjoy role-playing and storytelling as they build. Based on these findings, the company created LEGO Friends, themed sets with plastic "character" mini-dolls and blocks in bright pink, lavender, and blue colors. To jump-start storytelling, LEGO came up with a fictional setting (Heartlake City) and included accessories like a veterinary clinic and a beauty salon. "We had nine nationalities on the team to make certain the underlying experience would work in many cultures," explains the senior creative director. Although some critics have complained about what they see as gender stereotypes, the company says its aim is to "engage even more girls in the skill-developing experience of LEGO play." Actual first-year sales were double the company's projection, indicating an enthusiastic market response.[16]

ONLINE RESEARCH   Many marketers employ *online research*—research conducted via the Internet—because the cost is relatively low, it can be implemented and fine-tuned on fairly short notice, and the results are available in short order. On the other hand, the results will not be entirely representative of a product's market because not all consumers and business customers use online media or participate in online surveys. Nonetheless, many companies use formal online surveys or informally study consumer comments in online communities such as Facebook for clues to attitudes and purchase intentions.

Companies that use *behavioral tracking* want to research what customers do when they visit certain websites or click on certain ads. Google, for instance, tracks users' online activities so it can examine behavior patterns and serve up ads based on interests revealed by those patterns. This does, however, raise ethical concerns, as will be discussed later, and marketers must also comply with all applicable laws and regulations, which often vary from country to country.

NEUROMARKETING   One of the newest areas of marketing research is *neuromarketing*, investigating consumers' physiological and neurological reactions to marketing activities. Neuromarketing may help firms dig deeper into what happens inside consumers when they see products in stores, view or hear advertising messages, buy and use goods and services, and evaluate their buying decisions. Amazon, for instance, uses eye-tracking technology to analyze the way consumers look at its retail pages and has redesigned some screens based on this research.[17]

Using Marketing Research

If marketing research is not available or must be carried out, you should indicate this in your marketing plan and include the research as part of your plan's budgets and schedules. Also plan to conduct ongoing marketing research to help measure results during implementation. For instance, you might use advertising research to test messages and media as well as to study customer response; you might use test marketing to gauge reaction to new products. Research studies of customer satisfaction, market share changes, and customer attitudes and buying patterns are also valuable for spotting and analyzing clues to the company's effect on the market and customers (as well as seeing how competitors are doing).

PLANNING TIP

Summarize research findings, identify key needs and influences, and plan for new research.

At times, you may be forced to make decisions based on incomplete data; given the fast pace of the global marketplace, you'll rarely have enough time or money to conduct exhaustive research covering every contingency. Therefore, you'll have to assess the risk of waiting for more research compared with the risk of seizing an opportunity before it slips away or before competitors gain an edge.

Finally, as noted earlier, privacy is a major issue in marketing research. Although marketers can do a better job of targeting segments and planning marketing activities by gathering and analyzing vast amounts of data, research also raises some questions about privacy. Most people are aware that supermarket purchases, web-surfing habits, and other behavior can be easily tracked. But what specific information is collected and how is it used? Can individuals be personally identified? How are individuals protected by privacy laws, industry self-regulation, and companies' privacy policies? The U.S. Federal Trade Commission (FTC) is taking a closer look at companies' use of behavioral tracking research. (For more information, visit the FTC site at www.ftc.gov/ or scan the QR code here.) So keep privacy in mind as you plan.

Summary

When analyzing markets, start by broadly defining the general market and the needs of those customers. Markets are always changing, as consumers or business customers enter or leave and start or stop buying a product. For this reason, firms should project market changes and analyze demand in detail before selecting a specific segment to target. Many companies track their market share over time, compared with that of competitors, to understand market dynamics and establish a marketing metric.

Research is important for analyzing consumers and business customers. In consumer markets, cultural considerations, social connections, and personal factors help shape needs, wants, and behavior patterns. Marketers also research how consumers think and act in each stage of the buying decision process. Business buyers are influenced by both organizational considerations and organizational connections. Companies can use secondary research and primary research to gain a better understanding of their markets and customers. However, marketers may be forced to plan marketing activities based on incomplete data in order to keep up with fast-moving market opportunities or to counter competitors.

Your Marketing Plan, Step by Step

Continuing your analysis of the current marketing situation, use the following questions as starting points for learning more about both markets and customers. Document your answers in your marketing plan.

1. Where will you find secondary research about consumer markets? Try to locate at least three solid sources. In addition to searching specific key words, consider the following:
   a. Population data from the U.S. Census (www.census.gov)
   b. International demographic data from the United Nations (http://unstats.un.org/unsd/demographic/products/vitstats)
   c. The American Customer Satisfaction Index (www.theacsi.org)
   d. Google Trends (www.google.com/trends)
   e. College and university library sources (such as www.bber.umt.edu/default.asp)
   f. Research groups (such as http://pewresearch.org)
2. Where will you find secondary research about business markets? In addition to searching specific key words, locate three or more good sources, such as the following:
   a. U.S. government resources (http://business.usa.gov)
   b. NAICS industry data (www.census.gov/eos/www/naics/)
   c. *Industry Week* magazine (www.industryweek.com/)
   d. *Businessweek* magazine (www.businessweek.com)
   e. *E-Commerce Times* (www.ecommercetimes.com/)
   f. College and university library sources (check your school's resources)
3. From the information you've collected, extract details to define the market for your product, including the potential available, qualified available, and target markets. Summarize your findings in a grid similar to that in Exhibit 3.3. Be as specific as possible in your definitions, recognizing that you may have to adjust these definitions later (after you complete your research and plan your targeting strategy). If your marketing plan is for a product already in existence, also define the penetrated market. For a marketing plan that focuses on business customers, include NAICS codes in your definitions.
4. If your marketing plan focuses on a real product, research and estimate its current market share (in unit or financial terms). Whether your plan focuses on a new, real, or made-up product, estimate the market shares of the major competitors in the industry, based on your research. How have share trends in this product category changed over time? What environmental factors seem to have affected these share changes? What are the implications for your marketing plan?
5. For marketing plans that focus on consumer markets, use secondary research to find data about how culture, social connections, and personal factors are likely to affect the people in your defined markets. Explain your findings in your marketing plan and include two specific ideas for how your marketing plan will make use of these insights.
6. If your plan focuses on business customers, research how organizational connections and considerations (including derived demand) are likely to affect the businesses, nonprofits, or institutions in your defined market. Read respected industry blogs for clues to influences on business buying. Explain your findings in your marketing plan, including at least two specific points about how your marketing plan will tap into these influences.

Endnotes

1. David Pogue, "The Tragic Death of the Flip," *New York Times,* April 14, 2011, www.nytimes.com.

2. "Nike Wins Brand Battle on Social Media, According to Socialbakers," *Hispanic Business,* August 14, 2012,

www.hispanicbusiness.com; Allan Brettman, "Nike Brand President Charlie Denson Delivers Speech at SportAccord Convention," *Oregonian,* May 23, 2012, www.oregonlive.com; Scott Cendrowski, "Nike's New Marketing Mojo," *Fortune,* February 13, 2012, www.fortune.com; Jeff Brooks, "The Rise of 'Advertility,'" *Adweek,* November 9, 2009, www.adweek.com; Eleftheria Parpis, "Nike Plays New Game," *Adweek,* February 23, 2009, p. AM12.

3. See Gary L. Lilien and Arvind Rangaswamy, *Marketing Engineering,* 2nd ed. (Upper Saddle River, NJ: Prentice Hall, 2003), p. 159.

4. Andreas Cremer, "Volkswagen Hopes Revamped Golf Will Help It Catch Toyota," *Reuters,* September 3, 2012, ww.reuters.com Joseph A. Mann Jr., "Volkswagen Takes on Toyota for Share of the Latin American Light-truck Market," *Miami Herald,* May 20, 2012, www.miamiherald.com; John Reed, "Design Through Discipline," *Financial Times,* May 24, 2012, www.ft.com; Chris Reiter, "Volkswagen Profit Beats Expectations on Higher Audi Sales," *Bloomberg,* April 26, 2012, www.bloomberg.com.

5. Kate Maddox, "Solutions Marketing a Complete Mix for B2B," *B2B Online,* May 14, 2012, www.btobonline.com.

6. Brian Caulfield, "Intel to Build Chips Apple 'Can't Ignore,' For iPad, iPhone, CEO Says," *Forbes,* May 10, 2012, www.forbes.com; Chandra Steele, "History of the iPad," *PC Magazine,* March 12, 2012, www.pcmag.com; Salvador Rodriguez, "iPad Domination," *Los Angeles Times,* May 23, 2012, www.latimes.com.

7. Donna Tam, "LG and Samsung Loosen Their Iron Grip on Tablet Displays—Slightly," *CNet,* May 30, 2012, http://news.cnet.com.

8. "Eastman Kodak 1Q Loss Widens," *Wall Street Journal,* April 27, 2012, www.wsj.com.

9. John Revill, "Food Makers Rethink Europe," *Wall Street Journal,* May 28, 2012, www.wsj.com.

10. Douglas MacMillan, "What Facebook Will Get out of Gift-Giving App Karma," *Bloomberg BusinessWeek,* May 23, 2012, www.businessweek.com; Samantha Pearson, "Social Gifting Comes to Brazil," *Financial Times,* May 15, 2012, www.ft.com; Nivedita Bhattacharjee, "Social Gifting," *Reuters,* April 30, 2012, www.reuters.com.

11. Saumya Prakash, "India Is Expected to Be the Fastest Growing Online Travel Market in the Asia-Pacific Region in 2012," *Business Standard (India),* May 28, 2012, www.business-standard.com.

12. Karl Flinder, "Fujitsu UK Head on the Way Forward," *ComputerWeekly,* March 29, 2012, www.computerweekly.com.

13. Tim Wright, "Auto OEM Coatings," *Coatings World,* March 19, 2012, www.coatingsworld.com; "BASF Expands Coatings Business in ASEAN," *Coatings World,* January 2009, p. 18.

14. "Southwest Airlines Delays Boeing 737 Deliveries," *Crain's Chicago Business,* May 16, 2012, www.chicagobusiness.com; Susanna Ray, "Boeing Misses 2011 Delivery Target on 787 Delays as Airbus Beats Its Goal," *Bloomberg,* January 5, 2012, www.bloomberg.com.

15. Brooks Barnes, "Disney Expert Uses Science to Draw Boy Viewers," *New York Times,* April 14, 2009, www.nytimes.com.

16. Tiffany Hsu, "Lego Goes to the Girls: New Products Feminist or Sexist?" *Los Angeles Times,* August 31, 2012, www.latimes.com; Mark J. Miller, "Lego Hits Brick Wall with Lego Friends for Girls," *BrandChannel,* February 22, 2012, www.brandchannel.com; Brad Wieners, "Lego Is for Girls," *Bloomberg Businessweek,* December 14, 2011, www.businessweek.com; M. Nipper, "LEGO Group Commentary on Attracting More Girls to Construction Play," *LEGO,* January 12, 2012, www.lego.com.

17. Kris Van Cleave, "Eye-Tracking Technology Helps Marketers and Medical Professionals Alike," *WJLA ABC (Washington, D.C.),* May 7, 2012, www.wjla.com; Rupert Neate, "Ad Men Use Brain Scanners to Probe Our Emotional Response," *Guardian (UK),* January 14, 2012, www.guardian.co.uk.

4

Segmenting, Targeting, and Positioning

In this chapter:

PREVIEW

Who is your market? Instead of trying to market to a single neighborhood, city, state, nation, region, or planet—on the assumption that everyone has the same needs, behaviors, and attitudes—most marketers focus on specific customer groups within a given market. This chapter explores the process of segmentation, targeting, and positioning, which constitutes Step 3 in marketing planning (see Exhibit 4.1).

    You'll first review the overall process and then learn about the variables used to identify customer segments within consumer and business markets, which are important for your marketing

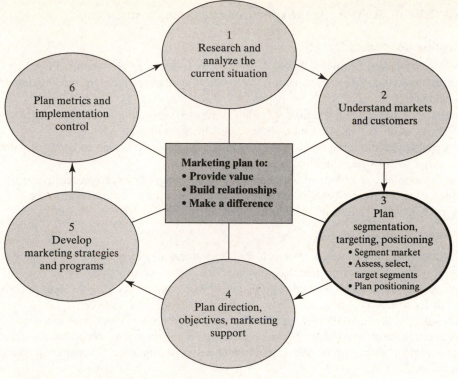

EXHIBIT 4.1   Marketing Planning: Step 3

plan. Next, you'll see how marketers evaluate segments and choose coverage strategies for those to be targeted. Finally, you'll learn about positioning strategies for competitive advantage. Once you determine which groups you will market to, you can set goals and objectives for your marketing plan, as discussed in Chapter 5.

APPLYING YOUR KNOWLEDGE

After reading this chapter, continue working on your marketing plan by summarizing your decisions and priorities in a written marketing plan document. Also, look at sample marketing plans for ideas about discussing segmentation, targeting, and positioning decisions. Take a moment to read this chapter's checklist questions about segmenting consumer and business markets, and then review what you've learned from the "Your Marketing Plan, Step by Step" exercises in earlier chapters.

> **CHAPTER 4 CHECKLIST   Identifying and Evaluating Segments**
>
> ### Segmenting Consumer Markets
>
> ✓ Can demographics be used to group consumers by needs or responses that differ by gender, household size, family status, income, occupation, education, religion, race, nationality, or social class?
> ✓ Can geographic variables be used to group consumers according to needs or responses that differ by nation, region, state, city, postal code, climate, or distance?
> ✓ Can psychographic variables be used to group consumers according to needs or responses that differ by lifestyle, activities, or interests?
> ✓ Can behavioral and attitudinal variables be used to group consumers according to needs or responses that differ by benefits expected, usage occasion, user status, loyalty status, technological orientation, attitudes, or price sensitivity?
>
> ### Segmenting Business Markets
>
> ✓ Can demographics be used to group business customers according to needs or responses that differ by industry, business size, business age, and ownership structure?
> ✓ Can geographic variables be used to group business customers according to needs or responses that differ by nation, region, state, city, climate, postal code, and distance?
> ✓ Can behavioral and attitudinal variables be used to group business customers according to needs or responses that differ by benefits expected, usage occasion, user status, loyalty status, technological orientation or usage, purchasing patterns, attitudes, or supplier standards and evaluation?
>
> ### Evaluating Segments
>
> ✓ Which segments should be eliminated due to legal or ethical issues, potentially negative reaction, or poor fit with resources and competencies?
> ✓ Which segments fit well with company resources, mission, goals, priorities, and offerings?
> ✓ How attractive is each segment in terms of market factors, competitive factors, economic and technological factors, and the business environment?

SEGMENTING CONSUMER AND BUSINESS MARKETS

As markets shift and the marketing environment evolves, what was once considered a mass market has now become fragmented and diverse. For example, marketers of widely used products such as breakfast cereal used to count on network TV advertising to reach millions of people during prime time. Today, network TV audiences are dwindling as a growing number of U.S. consumers time shift and media shift. Some order movies and sporting events on demand at any hour; some download episodes from iTunes to watch immediately or later on a TV, laptop, digital media player, or smartphone; some stream movies live from the Internet; some click through hundreds of cable TV channels for a spontaneous viewing experience; and some click to search and view videos on YouTube. Viewers who were unhappy about some shows being cancelled by TV networks can watch all-new episodes through Netflix and DirecTV, another major change in the TV industry.[1]

Just as no two people's media habits are alike, no two people have exactly the same backgrounds, needs, attitudes, behaviors, tastes, and interests. As a result, marketers are moving away from *mass marketing*—using one marketing mix to reach what was once seen as a single mass market—and toward *segment marketing*. *Segments* were defined in Chapter 1 as sizable groupings of consumers or business customers with similarities (such as similar needs, buying preferences, or attitudes) that respond to marketing efforts.

Segments and Niches

Market segmentation is the process of grouping customers within a market according to similar needs, habits, or attitudes that can be addressed through marketing. If all the people in all the segments (either consumers or business customers) reacted in the same way to the same marketing mix, there would be no need for segmentation. But because no two people are exactly alike, companies can address those differences through marketing.

In the milk market, for instance, one segment consists of people who want to limit their fat intake and therefore are interested in buying low-fat milk products. Another segment consists of people who prefer flavored varieties and therefore will pay attention to ads featuring chocolate-milk drinks. A third segment consists of people who want to limit milk intake for health reasons and therefore seek out soy milk and other substitutes. The customers within each segment have similar needs or are seeking the same benefits, so they tend to react in the same way to the marketing activities geared for that segment (whether it's a product, an ad, a discount, or a store display). Yet people outside the segment are less likely to notice, let alone respond to those marketing efforts.

Within a segment, marketers can often identify **niches**—smaller segments with distinct needs or benefit requirements, such as people who buy low-fat milk in individual serving sizes at meal time. Over time, tiny niches can expand into small yet profitable segments, and possibly into much larger segments. That's what happened when gluten-free foods burst into the mainstream. (To see Gluten Freely, a site started by General Mills, follow this QR code or visit www.glutenfreely.com.)

Gluten-free foods. At one time, the segment of consumers with celiac disease or a sensitivity to gluten was a niche targeted by only a few specialty food manufacturers and health-food stores. California-based Pamela's Products was one of these firms, offering gluten-free flour and baking mixes. Within the past few years, however, the number of people seeking out gluten-free foods for health or lifestyle reasons has grown dramatically. In 2001, yearly U.S. sales of gluten-free foods were estimated at about $200 million; today, yearly U.S. sales are estimated at $2 billion, with strong growth expected.

General Mills was one of the first major marketers to recognize the segment's growth potential and to modify hundreds of products specifically for these customers' needs. Targeting this segment, the company operates a website called Gluten Freely and a related Facebook page, which serve as one-stop resources for information about gluten-free living. Frito-Lay now labels its gluten-free snacks to attract customers in this ever-larger segment. Also, supermarkets are beginning to target this formerly small segment in a big way: Wegmans, for example, has introduced a line of gluten-free store-branded foods, shelved in the natural foods section.[2]

Reasons to Segment

Segmentation allows marketers to focus their resources on the most promising opportunities. This improves marketing efficiency and effectiveness as the organization gets to know each segment's customers and what they want and need. Such customer intimacy also enables marketers

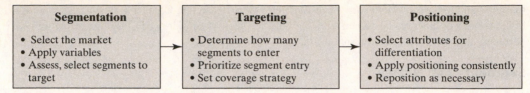

EXHIBIT 4.2 Segmentation, Targeting, and Positioning

to notice changes in the segment and to respond quickly. Finally, segmentation gives marketers the choice of entering segments in which only a few competitors are active or in which their most powerful or well-funded rivals are *not* competing.

As shown in Exhibit 4.2, segmentation lays the foundation for decisions about targeting and coverage strategy. The **target market** is the segment of the overall market that you choose to pursue. With these decisions, you're ready for positioning—giving the brand or product a distinctive and meaningful place (position) in the minds of targeted customers, a topic discussed later in this chapter.

Select the Market

The first step in segmentation is to select the general market(s) in which the company will target customers, based on the market definition, situational analysis, and SWOT (strength, weakness, opportunity, and threat) analysis. Eliminate markets or segments that have no need for the offering or are inappropriate for other reasons, such as geographic distance, lack of purchasing power, ethical questions, or troubling environmental threats. Also eliminate segments that are illegal or out of bounds for other reasons beyond the company's control. For instance, more than a dozen states no longer allow sugary soft drinks to be sold in school vending machines, which puts that segment (defined by age and place of purchase) out of bounds for soda marketers.[3]

Now marketers are ready to identify distinct segments within the markets they have defined. People and businesses differ in many ways, but not every difference is meaningful from a marketing perspective. The purpose of segmentation is to form groups of customers that are internally similar yet sufficiently different that each group will not react in exactly the same way to the same marketing activities. If all segments were similar or responded in the same way to marketing, segmentation would not be needed—the company could simply use one marketing mix for the entire market. Therefore, marketers create segments by applying one or more variables to the chosen consumer or business market.

APPLYING SEGMENTATION VARIABLES TO CONSUMER MARKETS

Marketers can isolate groupings within consumer markets using behavioral and attitudinal, demographic, geographic, and psychographic variables (see Exhibit 4.3). Consumer markets can be segmented with just about every one of these variables; the choice depends on the company's detailed marketing research profiling customers and analyzing their buying behavior. Sophisticated marketers often apply a combination of variables to create extremely well-defined segments or niches for marketing attention.

Common sense also plays a role: Some variables simply don't lend themselves to certain markets. For example, the consumer market for paper towels might be segmented in terms of

EXHIBIT 4.3   Segmentation Variables for Consumer Markets

Type of Variable	Examples
Behavioral and attitudinal	Benefits perceived/expected, occasion/rate of usage, user status, loyalty status, attitude toward product, usage, technological orientation, price sensitivity
Demographic	Age, gender, family status, household size, income, occupation, education, race, nationality, religion, social class
Geographic	Location (by country, region, state, city, neighborhood, postal code), distance, climate
Psychographic	Lifestyle, activities, interests

education, but it's unlikely that the resulting groupings will reveal differing needs or responses to marketing efforts. On the other hand, income and household size are likely to be better variables for segmenting this market, since either (or both) may result in groupings that have different needs or that respond differently to marketing activities. The following sections take a closer look at the main consumer segmentation variables.

Behavioral and Attitudinal Variables

Behavioral and attitudinal variables are, in many cases, the best way to identify a consumer group for marketing purposes. This is because such variables help marketers analyze the specific value that a group of consumers expects from a particular offering. Note that benefits required or expected, usage occasion and status, loyalty status, technological orientation, and attitudes

PLANNING TIP

Behavioral and attitudinal variables create segments that cross demographic and geographic lines.

toward products or usage generally cross demographic and geographic lines, yielding segments based on how consumers act or feel rather than on where they live or how old they are. For example, air travelers look for different benefits: Business travelers may put more value on convenient schedules, whereas vacation travelers may put more value on affordability. Therefore, marketers will use different messages for each of these segments to highlight what those customers need or the benefits they seek.

These variables are especially important for L'Oreal, the French company that looks beyond gender and age to increase its share of the $97 billion worldwide skin-care market.

L'Oreal. L'Oreal segments the market for men's skin care products by looking at both behavior and attitudes and tailoring its marketing for each geographic region. Its research found that in China, for instance, men want to look and feel good for professional as well as personal reasons. L'Oreal's Men Expert line appeals to this segment—and its sales in China are higher than in Western European markets. L'Oreal also sells its Garnier men's products in Chinese supermarkets where men can buy them without having to visit a women's beauty counter. In addition, L'Oreal is building on men's positive attitudes toward toned skin to increase its sales in India. Finally, the company arranged for Hugh Laurie to appear in advertising as its global face of men's skin-care. Laurie, who starred in the long-running TV hit *House,* says his role is to reinforce the attitude that "using cosmetics can be a very masculine decision after all."[4]

Segmenting by usage occasion helps marketers group consumers based on the occasion(s) when they buy or use a product. User status—whether a consumer has ever used the product, is a first-time user, or is a regular user—is particularly important when a company wants to increase sales by selling to nonusers, first-time users, or light users. Do consumers in the market tend to be brand loyal or do they constantly switch—and why? Companies often mount one marketing program to reinforce loyalty and another to court switchers from other brands.

Legendary motorcycle marketer Harley-Davidson, for example, enjoys such remarkable loyalty that some customers proudly wear its brand as a tattoo. Its vision is to "fulfill dreams through the experience of motorcycling," indicating that segmentation is based on customers' aspirations, a variable not dependent on geographic boundaries. With this in mind, the company has made a major marketing push in India, where the top executive observes, "Harley-Davidson is an iconic, lifestyle brand and Indian consumers understand that."[5] (To see Harley-Davidson's home page, go to www.harley-davidson.com or follow the QR code here.)

Demographic Variables

Many organizations apply demographic variables because these are common and easily identified consumer characteristics. In addition, they often point to meaningful differences in consumer needs, wants, and product consumption, as well as media usage. L'Oreal and other skin-care marketers segment customers on the basis of gender, knowing that men and women have different needs, attitudes, and behavior patterns. Banks often segment according to income (different levels have different needs for investments and other services), family status (different needs for mortgages and other types of credit), and work or retirement status (different needs for banking services, investment advice, and so on).

Segmenting on the basis of income can help marketers of upscale goods and services, such as luxury Silversea Cruises, identify consumer segments with the means to buy their products. It can also help marketers of lower-priced products focus on customers who need to stretch their dollars. An example is the retail chain Dollar General, which segments by income and geography and now rings up $15 billion in annual sales. Its 10,000 U.S. stores are smaller than those of Walmart and other discount giants and carry far fewer items, in order to make shopping quick and easy for time-pressured customers.[6] Marketers must avoid stereotyping customers when using demographic variables such as race, nationality, and income. Dollar General understands that low-income customers value national brands like Fisher-Price, for instance, even if they can afford to buy only limited quantities or for specific occasions—and it knows its high-income customers are attracted by Dollar General's low prices.[7]

Combining demographic variables can focus marketing even further. For example, Charles Schwab looks at household income, investment assets, and several other variables when segmenting the market for brokerage services. Adding other variables, especially behavioral and attitudinal variables linked to customers' underlying wants and needs, will reveal needs and benefits that can be addressed, segment by segment, through marketing. This is what USAA does.

USAA. Military families (defined by occupation) are the primary demographic segment served by USAA, which offers banking, investment, insurance, and other financial services. Within this larger segment, USAA has identified behavioral variables that help it better serve targeted customers. For example, USAA's marketers know that military families tend to move frequently, and they need flexible arrangements to be able to deposit checks, look at bank balances, discuss investment options, and request information about insurance. Targeting those with a positive attitude toward technology, USAA was among the first firms to allow customers to scan and deposit checks electronically, from a home computer or a smartphone, instead of in person or at an ATM. Customers can use its apps to check their accounts and to handle many transactions privately and securely via smartphone, iPad, or other mobile devices. Research shows that USAA customers are heavier-than-average users of smartphones; during a typical week, more than 6 million customers log in to their USAA accounts by phone. By 2018, USAA expects to be handling 1 billion smartphone contacts every year.

Applying another variable—attitude toward personal service—created a subsegment of customers who prefer dealing with people. "We still hear a number of members say that's how they prefer to do deposits with us," explains a USAA manager. So USAA arranged to have thousands of UPS stores equipped to accept checking deposits, scan them, and transmit them electronically. It also offers videoconferencing so customers can consult "face to face" with banking and investment experts.[8]

Geographic Variables

Companies routinely use geography to segment consumer markets. The decision to use geographic variables may be based on a company's ability to sell and service products in certain areas or climates, its interest in entering promising new markets, or its reluctance to sell in certain areas because of environmental threats or unfavorable climate. For instance, Apple uses geography to segment the consumer market for iPhones because different regions around the world require phones geared to different telecommunications systems. Pizza Hut has used LivingSocial, a daily deal site, to promote a special discount offer for its Pizza Mia small-size pizza, aiming to attract customers to its 270 stores in Australia.[9]

PLANNING TIP

Geographic segmentation may cover a single neighborhood or an entire continent.

Still, companies that segment by geography must carefully note meaningful differences within each area and similarities that cross geographic boundaries. For example, Macy's has returned to its merchant roots by segmenting shoppers geographically to supplement its national merchandise assortments. Macy's carries a larger stock of swimsuits in stores located near water parks and coastal resorts. It stocks krumkake bakers in Minneapolis-area stores and Elvis-themed Christmas ornaments in Memphis-area stores. This type of segmentation is helping Macy's add local touches to compete with other national department stores and with local specialty stores.[10] (Scan the QR code or click to www.macys.com to see the retailer's home page.)

Psychographic Variables

Segmenting on the basis of psychographic variables such as lifestyle, activities, and interests can help companies gain a deeper understanding of what and why consumers buy. Sometimes psychographic segmentation is the only way to identify a consumer group for special marketing attention, because activities and interests tend to cross demographic and geographic lines. People who share an interest in sports, for instance, may live anywhere and be of almost any age or gender.

Marketers who apply psychographic variables in combination with other variables may be able to create one or more segments that will respond to different marketing initiatives. The key is to identify the specific psychographic variables (and any other variables) that correspond to meaningful differences. Fiat, for example, combines demographic, geographic, and psychographic variables to identify segments for marketing attention. Its Fiat Ride & Drive program brings test-drive vehicles to auto shows around the United States and to other events, including big-city jazz festivals, encouraging customers to get behind the wheel and then comment about the experience via social media.[11]

APPLYING SEGMENTATION VARIABLES TO BUSINESS MARKETS

As Exhibit 4.4 shows, business marketers can segment their markets using three major categories of variables: (1) behavioral and attitudinal, (2) demographic, and (3) geographic. In many cases, marketers use a combination of variables, including industry (a demographic variable), size of business (another demographic variable), location (a geographic variable), and purchasing patterns (a behavioral variable). Again, the purpose is to create segments that are internally similar but that don't have the same needs or don't respond exactly the same as other segments when exposed to the company's marketing activities.

Behavioral and Attitudinal Variables

Segmenting by behavior or attitude (such as purchasing patterns, user status, attitude toward technology, loyalty status, price sensitivity, order size/frequency, attitudes, or benefits expected) is especially effective because it helps marketers understand what specific business segments want and value, as well as how and why they buy. Staples, for example, has analyzed its database of small business customer purchasing information to uncover buying patterns and identify relevant demographic details about those customers. This allows the office-supply retailer to more accurately segment its market, communicate specific offers for each segment, and achieve higher response to its marketing efforts.[12]

Purchasing patterns can vary widely; for example, companies have differing buying policies and practices and buy at different times or intervals. Understanding buying cycles and policies can help marketers design and deliver the right offer at the right time. Similarly, companies that are frequent users may require a different offer or message than first-time buyers.

EXHIBIT 4.4   Segmentation Variables for Business Markets

Type of Variable	*Examples*
Behavioral and attitudinal	Purchasing patterns and process, user status, benefits expected, supplier requirements and evaluation, attitude toward product and usage, technological orientation, loyalty status, order size/frequency, buyer/influencer/user attitudes
Demographic	Industry, business size, business age, ownership structure
Geographic	Location (by country, region, state, city, neighborhood, postal code), distance, climate

Demographic Variables

The main demographic variables in business markets are industry, business size, business age, and ownership structure. Industry segmentation is a good starting point, but it doesn't necessarily result in groupings that are sufficiently different to warrant different marketing approaches. Therefore, marketers typically segment further on the basis of size (as measured by annual revenues or unit sales, number of employees, or number of branches) or even rate of growth, reasoning that businesses of different sizes or growth rates have different needs. And combining demographics with behavioral and attitudinal variables allows B2B marketers to fine-tune marketing for specific segments.

Marketers that segment according to business age are looking for differing needs or purchasing patterns that relate to how long the business has been in existence. Businesses in the formation stage often have a higher need for office or factory space, computers and equipment, accounting and legal services, and other offerings needed for starting a new business. In contrast, older businesses may need repair services, upgraded computers and equipment, and other goods and services related to maintaining an existing business. Segmenting by ownership structure also can reveal meaningful differences. For instance, the insurance and accounting needs of sole proprietorships are not the same as those of corporations. Only by segmenting the market can marketers identify these differences for appropriate marketing attention, as Praxair is doing.

Praxair. Headquartered in Danbury, Connecticut, Praxair supplies industrial gases and coatings to businesses worldwide. The $11 billion company segments by industry (identifying 25 industry segments such as chemicals, textiles, and automotive) and by type of business (manufacturer or distributor). A manufacturer opening a new plant creates an opportunity for Praxair to supply it with the gases or coatings needed for start-up and then for ongoing operations. Environmental issues play a role in Praxair's segmentation, as well: The firm is now targeting industrial customers that want to reduce emissions in their manufacturing operations. Finally, because Praxair must consider how industrial customers will take delivery of gases (via pipeline, for instance, or by tanker truck), geography is also an important variable.[13]

Geographic Variables

Business marketers, like their consumer counterparts, can use geographic variables such as nation, region, state, city, and climate to segment their markets, as Praxair does. This allows the grouping of business customers according to concentration of outlets, location of headquarters, and geography-related needs or responses. It also enables business marketers to consider how geographic differences affect each segment.

By applying geographic as well as demographics and behavioral/attitudinal variables, marketers can get a better picture of each segment and have more information on which to evaluate the attractiveness of individual segments. Here's how Caterpillar uses geographic variables in its business markets. (To visit Caterpillar's home page, scan the QR code or go to www.cat.com.)

Caterpillar. Applying multiple segmentation variables helps Caterpillar market construction and mining equipment, plus turbines and other engines, worldwide—with annual sales topping $60 billion. Construction firms, government buyers, and mining companies in different areas have different needs, demographics, behavioral characteristics, and attitudes toward the equipment they use. With geographic segmentation, Caterpillar looks at how earth-moving equipment will be used in each region. It's targeting China and India, in particular, where large-scale construction and factory projects are being undertaken by government and industry. Infrastructure improvement is not growing as quickly in North America as in Asia, but expansion of the mining industry is boosting demand for Caterpillar's specialized mining machinery.

Another way to segment Caterpillar's market is by preference for purchase or rental. It created the Cat Rental Store brand so its dealers in Europe could offer equipment rentals to construction firms that need machinery for short periods or particular jobs. Rentals are more popular among U.K. construction firms than among French and German construction firms, but with easier access to convenient rentals, Caterpillar expects to expand its business throughout Europe.[14]

ASSESSING AND TARGETING SEGMENTS

PLANNING TIP

Determine criteria for assessing the attractiveness of segments under consideration.

Once you have applied segmentation variables to a market, you need to assess each segment so that you can select the most promising ones for targeting and also determine your coverage strategy for these segments.

Segment Evaluation

In preparation for evaluation, screen out segments that are extremely unsuitable or unattractive, based on poor fit with the firm's resources, goals, mission, and priorities (identified during the analysis of the current situation). Also eliminate segments that require specialized skills or extraordinary resources that are beyond your organization's reach or mission.

Exhibit 4.5 shows factors used to evaluate segments and identify the most promising ones for marketing attention. As this exhibit indicates, market factors are one key measure of attractiveness, including current and future opportunity for sales and profits. Large, more profitable, or faster-growing segments are generally more attractive than smaller, less profitable, or slower-growing segments. In assessing opportunity, marketers also look at how each segment would affect the company's ability to reach its overall goals, such as growth or profitability.

A second factor is the potential for competitive superiority. Can the company effectively compete or lead in the segment? How intense is the competitive pressure in each segment? How well differentiated are competing products and companies that are already targeting each segment? A third factor is the extent of environmental threats. Based on the environmental scanning and analysis, what macroenvironmental threats, such as more restrictive regulatory guidelines, exist now or could emerge to hamper the company's performance in the segment? Would entering a particular segment stir up controversy and hurt the company's image among stakeholders? Economic and technological factors are the fourth category; these include investment required for entry, expected profit margins, and barriers to entry/exit in the segment. Check government sites such as Export.gov for background information to help assess macroenvironmental factors in other countries (see Exhibit 4.6).

Fit with company resources and competencies

Market factors Size; growth rate; life-cycle stage; predictability; price elasticity; bargaining power of buyers; cyclicality of demand	**Economic & technological factors** Barriers to entry and exit; bargaining power of suppliers; technology utilization; investment required; margins
Competitive factors Intensity; quality; threat of substitution; degree of differentiation	**Business environment factors** Economic fluctuations; political and legal; regulation; social; physical environment

Identify most promising segments and order of entry

EXHIBIT 4.5   Assessing Segment Attractiveness
Source: Graham Hooley, Nigel F. Piercy, and Brigitte Nicoulaud, *Marketing Strategy and Competitive Positioning*, 5th ed. (Harlow, England: FT Prentice Hall, 2012), Fig. 10.3, p. 245.

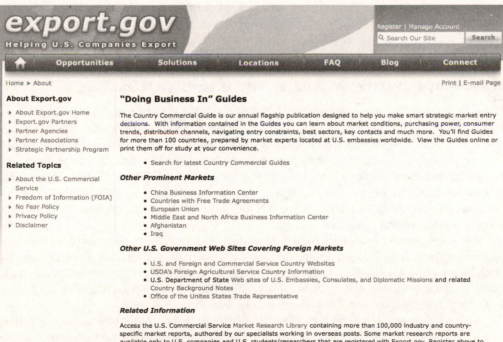

EXHIBIT 4.6   Researching International Markets at Export.gov

EXHIBIT 4.7   Sample Segment Ranking

Segment	Score for market factors	Score for competitive factors	Score for fit with resources, competencies	Score for economic, technological factors	Score for potential environmental threats	Overall score
A	3	5	2	4	3	17
B	5	4	4	3	4	20
C	2	2	3	2	5	14

Scoring key: 5 = highly attractive, 4 = moderately attractive, 3 = average, 2 = moderately unattractive,
          1 = highly unattractive

Now that you've screened out segments you will *not* enter, determine how many segments you *will* enter and rank the remaining segments in order of priority for entry. Some marketers do this by weighing the evaluation criteria to come up with a composite score for each segment. This shows which segments are more attractive and allows comparisons based on higher profit potential, faster projected growth, lower competitive pressure, or other criteria.

Different marketers plan for different ranking systems and weighing criteria, based on their mission and objectives, resources, core competencies, and other considerations. As shown in the simplified ranking in Exhibit 4.7, some segments may score higher for competitive superiority but lower for fit with organizational resources, for instance. The overall score generally determines which segments are entered first; here, segment B has the highest overall score and will be the top priority for marketing attention. Other marketers prefer to rank segments according to similar needs or product usage. And some examine how much risk they would be willing to accept in each segment, ranking segments from most acceptable to least acceptable risk.[15]

Concentrated, Undifferentiated, and Differentiated Marketing

PLANNING TIP

Summarize your ranking and targeting decisions in the marketing plan.

What coverage strategy will you use for the segments you want to enter? One strategy is to target all segments with the same marketing strategy, which is **undifferentiated marketing**. This mass-market approach ignores any segment differences and is based on the assumption that one marketing strategy for the entire market will yield results in all segments. Exhibit 4.8 shows this coverage strategy at far left. Although undifferentiated marketing requires less investment in product development, advertising, and other tactics, it is rarely used today because it doesn't adequately address the needs of fragmented, diverse markets.

Many companies use **concentrated marketing**, identifying the most attractive segment and concentrating marketing attention on only that one (such as Segment A, Segment C, or Segment C_2 in Exhibit 4.8). The advantage is that the company can focus all its marketing activities on a single customer grouping. However, if the segment stops growing, attracts more competition, or changes in other ways, it might become unattractive almost overnight.

Instead, companies that target multiple segments generally use **differentiated marketing** to create a separate marketing strategy for each segment. Colgate, which once used mass marketing to target everyone who needed toothpaste—one product for all, one benefit for all, one campaign for all—has become expert at differentiated marketing. It targets an immensely diverse

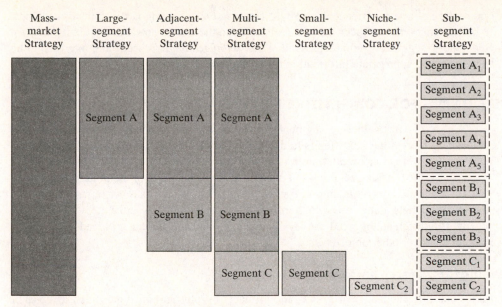

EXHIBIT 4.8   Market Coverage Strategies
Source: Roger J. Best, *Market-Based Management*, 6th ed. (Saddle River, NJ: Pearson Prentice Hall, 2013), Fig. 5-15, p. 174.

group of segments with individual marketing mixes: people who want whiter teeth, people who want less tooth tartar, people who have sensitive teeth, and so on.

Differentiated marketing entails considerable research to understand each segment's needs and results in higher costs for different products, different advertising campaigns, and so on. These costs must be taken into account when preparing the marketing plan and related budgets. If your resources won't stretch to cover all the targeted segments, you may need a rollout strategy for entering one segment at a time, in order of priority.

Segment Personas

Some companies apply the customer insights they gain from segmentation by developing **segment personas**, detailed but fictitious profiles representing how individual customers in targeted segments behave, live, and buy. Instead of marketing to a faceless, anonymous group based on research data, the company uses personas to get a well-rounded, more human picture of a typical person in each segment. Segment personas give marketers a deeper understanding of what shapes the needs, preferences, buying behavior, and consumption patterns in each group. "A persona is a design tool that helps [marketers] make informed decisions, and it's an archetype we use to target our client audiences," says an ad agency executive. "We cut across traditional demographic and psychographic information and bring it to life through photos, names, and a bio."[16]

One firm specializing in sales management software interviewed dozens of customers in its targeted segments and then developed a series of detailed personas to portray what motivates people in each segment. One segment persona, nicknamed Anya, describes a confident and competitive sales professional who spends extra time preparing for meetings with customers. A second segment persona, nicknamed Luke, describes an enthusiastic new salesperson, an expert networker who has less experience than Anya. The firm created cardboard cutouts of each persona to help its marketers connect with the real people in these segments. Another software firm created a generic segment persona representing the "average" buyer's needs and interests, to be sure its website had appropriate information for all audiences.[17]

POSITIONING FOR COMPETITIVE ADVANTAGE

After selecting segments for entry and determining the coverage strategy, the next step is to decide on a positioning strategy to differentiate the brand or product on the basis of attributes that customers find meaningful. Marketing research can uncover customers' views of the brand and its competitors, revealing key attributes that influence customer buying decisions.

Then the marketer must determine which attribute (or combination of attributes) supports the most meaningful differentiation and conveys a competitive advantage that will lead to achieving sales, market share, or other objectives.

Meaningful Differentiation

Companies can differentiate their brands and products by physical attributes such as product features, service attributes such as convenient installation, channel attributes such as wide availability, and pricing attributes such as bargain pricing. The choice depends on what customers value and how competitors are perceived. If customers value wide availability of a product, that point of differentiation is a potentially meaningful basis for positioning. However, it won't be a powerful point of differentiation if a competitor has already used that attribute to differentiate its product or brand. Also, a positioning will not work if it conflicts with the company's mission, goals, or resources.

Here are some examples of positioning based on meaningful differentiation:

- Toyota Prius: eco-friendly, fuel-efficient car
- FedEx: fast, reliable, on-time delivery
- EasyJet: affordable, no-frills air travel in Europe
- Shutterfly: convenient, high-quality online photo management

In each case, the positioning conveys the value that the brand provides and sets the brand apart from competitors in a sustainable way. FedEx's positioning on the attribute of on-time delivery—backed up by day-in, day-out performance—has given the company a distinct image and competitive edge because of the value this attribute represents to customers. Similarly, when Toyota introduced the Prius during the 1990s, hybrid cars were a distinct niche, but the green positioning helped establish Toyota's sustainability credentials. Today, eco-friendly positioning is increasingly common in the auto industry, which means Toyota must continue to innovate and add to its competitive differentiation.[18] (Take a look at Toyota's U.S. home page by clicking to www.toyota.com or following this QR code.)

Positioning and Marketing Leverage

Positioning alone won't build competitive advantage, although it can act as the driving force for marketing strategies and programs, setting the tone for the rest of the marketing plan. Thus, to leverage the company's investment in marketing, all marketing programs should support and reinforce the differentiation expressed in the positioning. This is especially important for a start-up, which must establish what its brand stands for and why customers should choose it rather than a competing brand. Nuovo Trasporto Viaggiatori shows high-stakes marketing in action in Italy.

Nuovo Trasporto Viaggiatori (NTV). In 2012, Nuovo Trasporto Viaggiatori—which translates to "New Passenger Transport"—inaugurated its high-speed Italo rail service in Italy. Start-ups are rare in an industry that requires a heavy investment ($1.3 billion, in this case) in equipment and infrastructure. However, top management expects that Italo's positioning as speedy, modern, and stylishly comfortable transportation will appeal to a lot of people who travel between major Italian cities like Rome and Milan for business or pleasure. The firm's long-term goal is to capture at least 20% of the market and to break even by carrying about 8 million passengers per year. To achieve its goals, Italo must attract passengers from Trenitalia, the state-run railway system, and from airlines that fly the same domestic routes. Yet there is plenty of room for market growth because fewer people use high-speed trains in Italy than in countries such as France.

Italo's positioning is carried through in all aspects of the marketing mix. The logo, for instance, features a stylized rabbit sprinting on a vivid red background. The trains—all new—are outfitted with roomy leather passenger seats, a cinema car showing free movies, and a club car featuring more spacious seating and personalized service. Passengers enjoy free Wi-Fi and free satellite TV service, and they can order snacks or meals at their seats. Inside each train station, Italo's sleek service areas are architect-designed for eye appeal, comfort, and efficiency, with information desks, Wi-Fi, weather updates, and other amenities. The total effect is more like the luxury of first-class air travel than an ordinary train trip—by design. Finally, Italo's pricing is tiered, depending on the route, level of service, time of day, and day of week. Can this high-speed start-up achieve its ambitious goals?[19]

Positioning is not a one-time thing, because the environment is always changing, just as customer perceptions often change over time. You must be ready to reevaluate the basis of your product's or brand's differentiation and plan for repositioning, if necessary. Tropicana, owned by PepsiCo, recently switched to 100% Florida-grown oranges for its orange juices. It then repositioned the brand to emphasize the U.S. origin of all its oranges, a differentiation that research shows is important to U.S. consumers and that also sets Tropicana apart from rival Coca-Cola's Simply Orange juice.[20]

Summary

Market segmentation is the process of grouping customers within a market according to similar needs, habits, or attitudes that can be addressed through marketing. The purpose is to form groupings that are internally similar yet sufficiently different so that each grouping will not react in exactly the same way to the same marketing activities. Segmentation is the basis for targeting decisions about which market segments to enter and the coverage strategy to use.

Once segments have been chosen, the company creates a positioning strategy for effective differentiation on the basis of attributes that are meaningful to the targeted segments.

The market segmentation process is: (1) select the market, (2) apply segmentation variables, and (3) assess and select segments for targeting. Consumer markets can be segmented using behavioral/attitudinal, demographic, geographic, and psychographic variables. Business markets can be segmented using behavioral/attitudinal, demographic, and geographic variables. Next, evaluate each segment and rank selected segments in order of entry, then determine how to target them through concentrated, undifferentiated, or differentiated marketing. Some marketers put a human face on segments by using segment personas, detailed but fictitious profiles representing how targeted customers behave, buy, and live.

Your Marketing Plan, Step by Step

Use the following questions as starting points for the segmentation, targeting, and positioning decisions you will document in the marketing plan you're developing.

1. Review your previous market and customer research. Which overall market will you select for your brand, product, or service?

2. If your offering is for consumers, look at Exhibit 4.3. Which of these variables might help you group consumers according to similar needs or attributes that will respond to marketing attention? You're trying to identify segments that are internally similar yet are different from other segments (for marketing purposes). For example, within the overall market for a household product, can you form segments of consumers who expect different benefits? Would consumers who expect Benefit A respond in a different way to your marketing compared with those who expect Benefit B? Can you segment the overall market for your product using age, location, or lifestyle to create groups of consumers that share some similarity but that are different from other segments? Remember, the test is whether segments would respond differently to a particular marketing activity. If all segments would respond in the same way, you don't need separate segments.

3. If your offering is for businesses, look at Exhibit 4.4. Which of these three types of variables might help you group businesses according to similar needs or attributes that will respond to marketing? You want to identify segments that are internally similar yet are different from other segments (for marketing purposes). For example, within the overall market for a high-tech offering, can you form segments of business customers with similar technological orientation? Can you group customers and prospects according to industry or business size or both? Will these segments respond differently to marketing efforts?

4. Now evaluate the segments you have created, as in Exhibit 4.5, bearing in mind what you learned when you scanned the internal and external environment earlier in the planning process. Can you screen out segments that don't make sense for the product or brand, or that are a poor fit with your company's mission, capabilities, resources, or priorities? Do some segments represent risks that your company will not take?

5. Of the remaining segments, which would you rank highest and lowest on market factors, competitive factors, economic/technological factors, and business environment factors? For instance, are some segments particularly attractive because they're growing quickly (market factor) or there is little threat of substitution (competitive factor)? Are some segments unattractive because of unusually restrictive regulations (business environment factor) or very low profit margins (economic factor)? Create a segment ranking similar to that of Exhibit 4.7 to support your decision process.

6. Based on your assessment of the segments, select the most promising one for targeting. Next, determine whether your marketing plan should provide for concentrated marketing (one marketing mix for one segment), undifferentiated marketing (one marketing mix for all segments), or differentiated marketing (different marketing mixes for different segments). Explain your reasoning for the targeting and coverage strategy you select when you document your marketing plan.

7. Considering what you know about each targeted segment and your customers' needs, preferences, and behavior, what handful of attributes should you emphasize for meaningful

differentiation of your offering? Describe why customers in your targeted segments would find these attributes meaningful (do customers value speedy delivery, for instance?). Use this information to draft a one-sentence positioning statement for your offering for each targeted segment.

Endnotes

1. Cory Barker, "Why Hulu, Netflix, and Others Don't Need to Revive Canceled TV Shows," *TV.com,* August 7, 2012, www.tv.com; Alex Sherman and Andy Fixmer, "Canceled TV Shows Get a Digital Afterlife," *Bloomberg Businessweek*, May 24, 2012, www.businessweek.com; Bill Carter, "Prime-Time Ratings Bring Speculation of a Shift in Habits," *New York Times,* April 22, 2012, www.nytimes.com.

2. Gary Quackenbush, "Pamela's Products Completes $1M Gluten-Free Bakery Expansion," *North Bay Business Journal (Calif.),* May 28, 2012, www.northbaybusinessjournal.com; David Hatch, "General Mills Tries Gluten-Free Sales in the Cloud," *U.S. News and World Report,* May 15, 2012, http://money.usnews.com; Susan Donaldson James, "Frito-Lay Jumps into Gluten-Free Craze with New Labels," *ABC News,* May 24, 2012, http://abcnews.go.com; "Wegmans Launches Gluten-Free Line," *Supermarket News,* May 31, 2012, http://supermarketnews.com.

3. Nicole Ostrow, "Banning Sugary Soda from Schools Fails to Cut Teen Consumption," *Bloomberg Businessweek,* November 15, 2011, www.businessweek.com.

4. Nina Sovich, "Because the Guys Are Worth It, Too," *Chicago Tribune,* May 10, 2012, www.chicagotribune.com; Amy Kazmin, "India's Men See Skin Care as Fair Game," *Financial Times,* June 26, 2011, www.ft.com; MacKenzie Wilson, "Hugh Laurie: L'Oreal's New Leading Man," *BBC America,* July 6, 2011, www.bbcamerica.com.

5. Karen Freeman, Patrick Spenner, and Anna Bird, "Three Myths About What Customers Want," *Harvard Business Review Blog,* May 23, 2012, http://blogs.hbr.org; Anita Sharan, "The Harley Temptation," *Hindustan Times,* May 6, 2012, www.hindustantimes.com.

6. Spencer Jakab, "A Discount Retailer Even Walmart Envies," *Wall Street Journal,* June 3, 2012, www.wsj.com; Mark Fisher, "Dollar Stores Get Wider Range of Customers," *Dayton Daily News,* May 26, 2012, www.daytondailynews.com.

7. Randy Hofbauer, "Dollar General in Command," *Private Label Buyer,* July 8, 2010, www.privatelabelbuyer.com.

8. "How USAA Innovates Online Banking," *Bank Technology News,* August 31, 2012, www.americanbanker.com; John Adams, "As Mobile Matures, USAA Plots Its Next Steps," *Payments Source,* February 15, 2012, www.paymentssource.com; Wayne Heilman, "Great Service Across Platforms," *The Gazette (Colorado Springs),* May 22, 2011, p. B1; Jeremy Quittner, "Security or Convenience? USAA Lets Mobile Users Choose," *American Banker,* November 16, 2011, www.americanbanker.com; Sara Lepro, "USAA Gives Remote Deposit a Face," *American Banker,* November 12, 2010, p. 1.

9. Campbell Phillips, "LivingSocial Jumps on the Fast Food Bandwagon with Pizza Hut," *Power Retail,* May 14, 2012, www.powerretail.com.au.

10. Walter Loeb, "Macy's New Focus," *Forbes,* May 31, 2012, www.forbes.com; Matthew Boyle, "A Leaner Macy's Tries to Cater to Local Tastes," *Businessweek,* September 3, 2009, www.businessweek.com; Cotten Timberlake, "With Stores Nationwide, Macy's Goes Local," *Bloomberg Businessweek,* September 30, 2010, www.businessweek.com.

11. Rich Thomaselli, "Chrysler Takes the Test Drive Out of the Dealership," *Advertising Age,* June 4, 2012, www.adage.com.

12. Jonathan Hornby, "The Case for Data-Driven Test and Learn Processes," *Chief Marketer,* June 4, 2012, http://chiefmarketer.com.

13. Vincent Valk and Ian Young, "Industrial Gases: Emerging Markets, New Applications Lift Growth," *Chemical Week,* February 27, 2012, p. 19; "Praxair Increasing Prices On Nitrogen, Other Gases Starting June 1," *Wall Street Journal,* May 16, 2012, www.wsj.com.

14. "Caterpillar Takes Less Prescriptive Approach," *International Rental News,* May–June 2012, p. 8; Corinna Petry, "Caterpillar's N. America Outlook Robust," *American Metal Market,* April 27, 2012, p. 8; "Caterpillar Expands Operations in India," *Hospitality, Tourism, and Leisure,* December 5, 2011, n.p.

15. See Stuart Read, Nicholas Dew, Saras D. Sarasvathy, Michael Song, and Robert Wiltbank, "Marketing Under Uncertainty," *Journal of Marketing,* May 2009, pp. 1–18.

16. Daniel B. Honigman, "Persona-Fication," *Marketing News,* April 1, 2008, p. 8.

17. David Meerman Scott, "How Well Do You Know Your Buyer Personas?" *Web Ink Now,* July 22, 2008, www.webinknow.com; David Meerman Scott, "Switch from Features to Buyer Personas," *Web Ink Now,* April 15, 2011, www.webinknow.com.

18. Alan Ohnsman and Yuki Hagiwara, "Toyota Prius Escapes Niche to Surge into Global Top Three," *Bloomberg News,* May 29, 2012, www.bloomberg.com/news.

19. Gaia Pianigiani, "On High-Speed Rails, a New Challenger in Italy," *New York Times,* April 29, 2012, p. 16; Phil Patton, "Ferrari of Railyard Has an Auto Pedigree," *New York Times,* May 6, 2012, www.nytimes.com; Murray Hughes, "Italo Will Be 'Fast, Agile, and Fun,'" *Railway Gazette International,* January 2012, p. 35; Keith Fender, "Could Italy Set the Model for America?" *Trains Magazine,* April 2012, p. 12.

20. Natalie Zmuda, "Tropicana Goes Back to Nature in New Global Pitch," *Advertising Age,* February 20, 2012, p. 3.

Planning Direction, Objectives, and Marketing Support

In this chapter:

PREVIEW

Where do you want your marketing plan to take you? You know which groups of consumers or businesses you want to market to, but what do you want to achieve? The ultimate purpose of a marketing plan is to help your organization achieve *objectives*—short-term performance targets—that will, in turn, bring you closer to achieving *goals,* long-term performance targets tied to the mission. Without goals and objectives, you won't know whether your marketing is successful. You set objectives in Step 4 of the marketing planning process (see Exhibit 5.1) as a foundation for developing marketing strategies and programs.

    As discussed in this chapter, you start by determining the overall direction for the marketing plan, consistent with your organization's current situation and priorities and with the customer segments you've selected. Next, you'll learn how to set effective marketing, financial, and

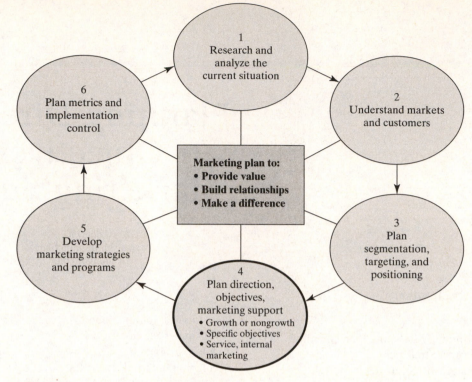

EXHIBIT 5.1   Marketing Planning: Step 4

societal objectives for the period covered by your plan. Societal objectives are, increasingly, an important way to show stakeholders what the company stands for and how it will make a difference. Finally, you'll see how customer service and internal marketing provide support for marketing-mix decisions based on the strategic direction in your plan.

APPLYING YOUR KNOWLEDGE

After reading this chapter, document your chosen direction, objectives, and marketing support decisions in a written plan. These decisions indicate what your plan seeks to accomplish in marketing to your targeted customer segments—how you will judge the success or failure of your marketing efforts. Refer to this book's appendix for examples of goals and objectives. Also consult this chapter's checklist for questions to ask when developing objectives for your marketing plan. Don't forget that you will be planning for metrics to use in tracking progress toward these objectives, as discussed in Chapter 10.

> **CHAPTER 5 CHECKLIST   Do Your Objectives Measure Up?**
>
> ✓ Is the objective specific and time defined?
> ✓ Can progress toward the objective be measured periodically via metrics?
> ✓ Is the objective realistic yet challenging?
> ✓ Is the objective consistent with the organization's mission, goals, priorities, and strategic direction?
> ✓ Is the objective consistent with the organization's resources, strengths, and capabilities?
> ✓ Is the objective appropriate, given environmental opportunities and threats?
> ✓ Does the objective conflict with other objectives?

DETERMINING MARKETING PLAN DIRECTION

Where does the company want to be in the future, and how will it get there? Now that you have decided on the segments you'll target, these are the next big questions your marketing plan should ask and answer. As examples, Redbox seeks to enlarge its U.S. customer base by adding to its network of DVD rental kiosks, and Coca-Cola seeks higher market share in soft drinks through global expansion. These firms, like many businesses and nonprofit organizations, have marketing plans for growth. Growth isn't always an appropriate direction, however; in dealing with difficult challenges, some companies may strive to maintain current sales or profit levels, whereas others may choose retrenchment (see Exhibit 5.2).

PLANNING TIP

Be guided by the mission, goals, and situational analysis when planning your direction.

   Although economic downturns can be difficult for businesses in the short term, they sometimes (but not always) present opportunities for long-term survival and, ultimately, for growth. Look at the newspaper industry, where major upheavals are forcing drastic changes in marketing and operations. Many papers are formulating plans to minimize losses and to prepare for the unpredictable yet inevitable impact of digital demand.

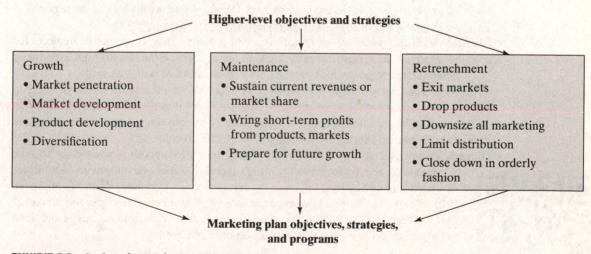

EXHIBIT 5.2   Options for Marketing Plan Direction

Source: Marian Burk Wood, *Essential Guide to Marketing Planning*, 2d ed. (Harlow, Essex, England: Pearson Education, 2010), Fig. 5.1, p. 95.

Newspaper marketing. Newspapers everywhere are reeling from the aftermath of recession, lower circulation, and the movement of display and classified advertising from print to electronic media. More than 20% of all U.S. newspapers have already implemented marketing plans to charge for online access, and other changes are in the works at many papers worldwide. The marketing plan of the *Times-Picayune* of New Orleans, for instance, is geared toward repositioning the paper as a multimedia brand, in order to set the stage for a stronger financial future. The newspaper has cut its print schedule to three days per week but will continue posting news and ads on its website every day. "For us, this isn't about print versus digital, this is about creating a very successful multi-platform media company that addresses the ever-changing needs of our readers, our online users, and our advertisers," explains an executive with the parent company.

In Canada, the company that owns the *Ottawa Citizen, Calgary Herald,* and *Edmonton Journal* has eliminated the Sunday editions of those newspapers in order to save money. Its marketing plan aims to counter losses and to restore revenue in two ways. First, the company's going after a higher volume of online advertising to replace some of the revenue that previously came from print advertising. Second, it's now charging readers for access to news features posted on some of the papers' websites. The company is monitoring the results day by day and is prepared to make additional changes if needed.[1]

What are your choices for growth strategies and nongrowth strategies? The next two sections explain what each entails and their implications for marketing planning.

Growth Strategies

In pursuit of growth, marketers can develop plans for one (or a combination) of these four broad strategies[2]:

- **Market penetration** is a growth strategy in which the company sells more of its existing products to customers in existing markets or segments. It's especially viable for companies that can build on established customer relationships and positive value perceptions to improve market share or stimulate higher demand.
- **Market development** involves identifying and reaching new segments or markets for existing products, an investment in future sales and profits. Brands with high awareness, good reputations, and positive word of mouth can be effective with this strategy.
- **Product development** is a growth strategy in which the company sells new products to customers in existing markets or segments, requiring an investment in product innovation and related activities. Starbucks follows this strategy by introducing new noncoffee menu items (like Evolution Fresh juices) to appeal to its café customers.[3]
- **Diversification** is a growth strategy of offering new products in new markets to take advantage of new opportunities, through internal product-development capabilities or by starting or buying a business for diversification purposes. Diversification can help an organization avoid overreliance on a small number of products and markets.[4] On the other hand, too much diversification can dilute available resources and open the organization to competitive attacks on multiple fronts.

Rovio, the Finnish company behind the hugely popular Angry Birds brand, has aggressively pursued growth through product development and market penetration. (Follow the QR code to see Rovio's home page or visit www.rovio.com.)

Rovio and Angry Birds. More than 1 billion people worldwide have downloaded Angry Birds games and launched red birds from slingshots to tear down the defenses of green pigs. Just two years after introducing the first Angry Birds game, parent company Rovio was ringing up annual revenues of $100 million, with a whopping 64% profit margin. Loyal customers have eagerly awaited each new version of the game. When Angry Birds Space became available, 50 million people downloaded the game in the first 35 days.

Now Rovio's marketing plan for global growth calls for new versions and variations of the Angry Birds game (such as Bad Piggies), new branded products, and brand licensing, all to increase sales and profits in both new and existing markets. Licensing deals are putting Angry Birds characters on snacks, toys, jewelry, playground equipment, and dozens of other types of merchandise. The company is also expanding by opening branded theme parks in China, customized with attractions and merchandise for this fast-growing market. It has a deal for a branded debit card in Russia, another market where Rovio sees growth potential. "We want to make Angry Birds a permanent part of pop culture," says the head of marketing, comparing the brand to Hello Kitty and other brands that have remained successful over time.[5]

Nongrowth Strategies

Growth isn't always desirable or even possible. In tough economic times, for instance, organizations often marshal their resources and strive simply to maintain current sales or market share, using marketing for defensive reasons. Another maintenance strategy is to seek the highest possible profits from current products and current customers without trying for growth. Sometimes companies are forced into a period of retrenchment because of rising costs, slower sales, lower profits, or a combination of these three factors.

With sufficient time, management attention, and financial realignment, the most drastic change of direction—bankruptcy—sometimes leads to a turnaround. General Motors (GM), for example, struggled through several money-losing years before declaring bankruptcy in 2009, at the height of the global financial crisis. It emerged from bankruptcy just weeks later, with government help and dramatically lower expenses. At that point, GM's new marketing plan called for a streamlined product line that included new eco-friendly, fuel-efficient models like the Volt, while doing away with brands like Hummer, Pontiac, and Saturn. Based on months of financial and marketing changes, and on an improving economic situation, GM returned to profitability in a better competitive position than it had been for some time.[6]

Less drastic decisions include withdrawing from certain markets, deleting particular products, cutting back on marketing, limiting distribution, or closing a division. Sometimes companies limit or halt growth during a certain period, in a particular division, or in selected markets. This can help a marketer become more efficient, positioning itself for future growth. Clearly, strategies for slow or no growth call for different marketing plans than those used for more aggressive growth.

SETTING MARKETING PLAN OBJECTIVES

After choosing a direction for the marketing plan, you'll set objectives as short-term destinations along the path toward longer-term organizational goals. The exact objectives set will depend on your current situation, the

PLANNING TIP

Check that achieving one objective doesn't prevent you from achieving another objective.

environmental issues and keys to success you have identified, the customers you'll target, your organization's mission and goals, and your chosen positioning. By comparing your actual results to your objectives and goals (through the use of metrics), you will be able to see whether your plan is succeeding or whether it must be changed in some way.

As summarized in this chapter's checklist, objectives will be effective for guiding marketing progress only if they are:

- **Specific, time defined, and measurable.** Objectives must be specific and must include both deadlines and quantitative measures so that marketers can plan the timing of activities and evaluate interim results. Marketers also should be able to measure progress by looking at sales figures, customer counts, satisfaction surveys, or other indicators that the plan is moving the company toward its destination. USAA, a Texas-based insurance and financial services firm, makes customer relationships its highest priority and monitors results by counting how many customers defect during each period. Not surprisingly, USAA has one of the best records for customer loyalty of any firm in its industry, with a retention rate of 98%.[7]

- **Realistic but challenging.** Marketing plan objectives should be rooted in reality yet be sufficiently challenging to inspire high performance. You need to consider the current situation to decide whether an objective is achievable or out of reach. As an example, if a sudden or severe economic downturn is dampening demand, you may need to adjust your objectives. Or you may need to change your objectives because of increased demand or other factors, which is what happened to Ford recently. As the economy improved, the company was able to boost production by adding new suppliers and improving supply-chain efficiency. With higher demand, Ford increased sales objectives for the Focus and other popular vehicles. In turn, one of its plants set goals to boost engine production well beyond previous output to support Ford's higher sales goals.[8]

- **Consistent with the mission and overall goals.** Objectives set for the marketing plan should support the organization in fulfilling its mission and advancing toward its long-range goals. During the years when Ford was losing money and struggling to survive, it set short-term sales and market-share objectives to support its long-term goal of returning to profitability. Once it regained profitability, Ford set and achieved higher market-share goals for three consecutive years as it pursued growth throughout all the markets it serves.[9]

- **Consistent with internal environmental analysis.** Challenging objectives are empty words unless the organization has the appropriate resources and strengths to follow through. For instance, Amazon.com is pursuing aggressive growth goals in new products and markets, backed by its technological and logistical capabilities, its in-depth knowledge of customer buying patterns, and its strength in e-book publishing and distribution.[10]

- **Appropriate in light of opportunities and threats.** Objectives must make sense in the face of marketplace realities, opportunities, and threats. For example, tablet computers and multifunction smartphones are increasingly replacing standalone digital music devices. Should Apple set ever-higher sales objectives for iPods if it anticipates that its iPhones and iPads will attract much more consumer interest?[11] Similarly, Netflix—which rents DVDs by mail and streams video entertainment to subscribers—is known for its ambitious objectives. But with ever-increasing competition from YouTube, Amazon, and others, is it realistic for Netflix to aspire to 60 million or more streaming subscribers in the United States alone?[12]

At 23andMe, a genetic testing service, every manager and employee sets individual six-month objectives to support the company's overall objectives. Week by week, employees submit a summary of their accomplishments so that management can see at a glance whether they're making progress toward overall objectives. This attention to detail helps the fast-growing firm determine quickly whether its marketing is having the desired effect and how each marketing project contributes to overall performance.[13]

Types of Objectives

Marketers usually set three types of objectives in their marketing plans (see Exhibit 5.3). **Marketing objectives** are targets for managing specific marketing relationships and activities with customers and with channel partners. **Financial objectives** are targets for managing financial results, including sales, revenue, and profits. **Societal objectives** are targets for achieving particular results in social responsibility, such as increasing recyclable product content or building a community center. These objectives help you build relationships, provide value, and make a difference through your marketing plan. The following sections explain and show examples of each type of objective.

Marketing Objectives

Marketing objectives should include targets for managing customer relationships because these are so critical to company success. E-marketing expert Judy Strauss advises, "Objectives to raise profit, increase market share, or change stakeholder attitudes and behaviors are meaningless unless companies make effective plans to manage their most valuable asset: customer relationships."[14] Depending on the industry, direction, mission, and available resources, marketers may set targets for acquiring new customers, retaining customers, increasing customer loyalty, and increasing customer satisfaction. Customer acquisition and retention are especially vital in mature markets such as wireless telecommunications, which is why Verizon Wireless and its competitors use marketing for such objectives.

EXHIBIT 5.3 Marketing Plan Objectives

Type of Objective	Purpose	Samples
Marketing	To use marketing to manage key relationships and activities	• Customer relationships • Channel relationships • Product development • Market share • Order fulfillment • Brand awareness
Financial	To use marketing to attain certain financial results	• Sales revenue by product • Sales revenue by channel • Breakeven by product • Return on investment • Profitability
Societal	To use marketing to achieve results in social responsibility	• Greener/cleaner operations • Community involvement • Sustainable sourcing • Charitable activities

Some firms set additional objectives for managing relationships with other stakeholders, such as channel partners. Not-for-profit organizations usually set objectives for managing relations with members and contributors, as well as for attracting donations, grants, and corporate sponsorships. Other objectives in this category might cover marketing activities related to market share, new product development, and other vital areas.

Some sample marketing objectives might include the following:

- *Customer acquisition.* Expand the customer base by adding 200 new customers each month for the next year.
- *Customer retention.* Reduce the annual customer defection rate to 10% by the end of the year.
- *Customer satisfaction.* Score 96% or higher on the next yearly customer satisfaction survey.
- *Channel relationships.* Expand distribution by placing products in four additional supermarket chains within six months.
- *Unit sales.* Sell 500 units in each targeted segment during every month next year.
- *Market share.* Capture 2% of the U.S. market by March 31 and 3% by June 30.
- *Product development.* Develop and introduce five new products by December 31.
- *Order fulfillment.* Cut the time for fulfillment of orders from 48 to 24 hours by May 15.

All marketing objectives set for a particular year's plan must lead the company toward its long-term goals. In recent years, fast-food giant McDonald's has increased revenues through marketing objectives that focus on customer relationships. (Scan the QR code to see McDonald's U.S. home page or go to www.mcdonalds.com/us/en/home.html.)

McDonald's. After decades of sales increases driven, in part, by opening thousands of new restaurants, McDonald's changed its marketing strategy to focus on the basics of bringing loyal customers back to existing restaurants again and again. The multiyear "Plan to Win" strategy aims to retain customers, increase the number of visits, and bring customers in to restaurants during different times of the day. Financial objectives linked to marketing objectives translate these relationship targets into revenue and profitability targets for each region and for the company overall.

To give current customers new reasons to eat at its restaurants, McDonald's has introduced new menu items, such as beverages and snacks, including its enormously successful McCafé coffees and limited-time products like the McRib and Chicken McBites. It has refreshed perennial favorites by offering new sauces or sides, appealing to variety-seeking customers, and has added breakfast items to increase visit frequency. Moreover, the updated restaurant ambiance and free Wi-Fi in many areas encourage customers to bring family or friends and linger over a second cup of coffee or a shake. One thing McDonald's isn't changing, however, is its commitment to serving people quickly—in effect, its order fulfillment. "We talk about hospitality, we talk about friendly relationships, but we live in a world of speed today," the CEO says.[15]

Financial Objectives

Although the exact financial objectives will vary from organization to organization, businesses generally quantify sales volume and product targets, profitability targets such as margin or pretax profit, return on investment (ROI) targets for marketing, and breakeven targets (see the discussion of pricing in Chapter 7). Not-for-profit organizations might set targets for fundraising, among other financial objectives.

PLANNING TIP

Be sure objectives are achievable, given your resources and marketing tools.

To be effective in guiding marketing activities, financial and marketing objectives should be consistent. However, sometimes a marketing objective has to be modified or set aside to achieve an overriding financial objective, or a financial objective may have to be postponed or changed if a particularly important marketing objective (such as launching a major new product) is to be achieved.

The following are some sample financial objectives:

- *Sales revenue.* Achieve $150,000 yearly sales revenue by December 31.
- *Product sales revenue.* Sell $3,000 worth of Product A every month.
- *Channel sales revenue.* Increase monthly Internet sales to $50,000 by end of year.
- *Profitability.* Increase the gross profit margin to 25% by end of year.
- *Return on investment.* Achieve 12% ROI on funds invested in direct marketing activities.
- *Breakeven.* Reach the breakeven point on the new service offering by July 15.

IBM, which rings up $107 billion in annual global sales, builds multiyear objectives for sales revenue and other financial measures into its marketing plans. (Visit IBM's U.S. home page by following the QR code or by going to www.ibm.com.)

IBM. Nicknamed "Big Blue," IBM is never at a loss for marketing data to support its plans for growth and to measure its results in high-tech products and services such as supercomputers (like Watson), cloud-computing services, processing of retail and bank transactions, and other offerings. Its pretax profit margin in 2003 was 10.6%, yet IBM is aiming to achieve a pretax profit margin of 20% in the near future. One way to reach this goal is to do more business in software and services, which carry higher profit margins than computer hardware. As a result, IBM has set specific five-year goals for increasing its presence in these sectors.

To get to those goals, its marketing plan includes short-term financial objectives for overall revenue growth and for sales growth by type of product and geographic region. IBM is also marketing its capabilities to corporations and governments in emerging markets, with an eye toward longer-term growth and profitability as economic development builds demand for technology infrastructure and data management know-how. IBM, now more than a century old, continues to reinvent its marketing through objectives that move it forward toward a higher-profit future.[16]

Societal Objectives

These days, customers, suppliers, employees, civic leaders, and other stakeholders are looking more closely at what companies do for society—part of the push for more transparency and to be involved with organizations that make a difference. Recent surveys indicate that consumers expect businesses to get involved in good causes and to put as much weight on social responsibility issues as on financial performance.[17] At the same time, companies realize that they can do more for society in the course of their daily activities and give their marketing or financial objectives a boost at the same time.[18] Moreover, having a strong track record in social responsibility can help a company regain stakeholder confidence and protect its reputation if it encounters problems. And social responsibility is a way to differentiate brands in today's intensely competitive marketplace.

PLANNING TIP

Choose a cause that makes sense for your organization, customers, and employees.

Now, a growing number of organizations are including societal objectives in their marketing plans. As shown in Exhibit 5.3, some societal objectives may call for cleaner operations or "greener" (more ecologically friendly) products, charitable donations, volunteerism or other involvement with community projects, energy conservation, and other socially responsible actions. For example, IKEA has a long-term goal for building 50% of its wooden products from certified sustainable lumber by 2017, which will make the company the world's largest buyer of sustainable wood. Sustainability is literally built into the company's products and operations. "Our products are about form, functionality, style, and sustainability," explains IKEA's chief sustainability officer. "Our business model is to make sustainable products affordable for as many people as possible."[19]

Fulfilling societal objectives polishes company or brand image and shows that the organization is doing something constructive about issues that are important to stakeholders. Setting objectives is not enough; stakeholders want to know what the company actually accomplishes. (If companies do little more than talk about protecting the environment, they risk being accused of greenwashing.) A growing number of small and large businesses, including IKEA, post social responsibility reports on their websites to publicly showcase their social performance. Find out more on the Business for Social Responsibility site (www.bsr.org) and the Corporate Social Responsibility Newswire site (www.csrwire.com).

Cause-related marketing (also known as *purpose marketing*) falls under the umbrella of social responsibility because it links the marketing of a brand, good, or service to a particular charitable cause or to some larger societal purpose. Although the charity benefits, this isn't outright philanthropy because of the explicit marketing connection. Cause-related marketing can be very effective in motivating consumer buying: In one study, 75% of the respondents said they were more likely to buy a good or service when a percentage of the price is donated to a designated cause.[20]

Some sample societal objectives include the following:

- *Reduce waste.* Increase the proportion of recyclable product parts to 50% by the end of next year.
- *Obtain materials from sustainable sources.* By year-end, buy 50% of cotton fabric from certified sustainable sources.
- *Issue awareness.* Build awareness about preventing skin cancer by attracting 15,000 visitors to a special page on the company's website.
- *Community involvement.* Encourage employees to volunteer for local projects on company time, receiving pay for up to 40 hours of volunteerism per year.

Social business enterprises, founded for the purpose of benefiting society in some way, place a higher priority on social objectives than on financial or marketing objectives. Some seek legal status or voluntary certification as a *benefit corporation,* intended primarily for societal benefit (follow the QR code or visit www.bcorporation.net for more about such corporations). These organizations must set and meet appropriate financial and marketing objectives to have the resources and strength to achieve their social objectives.

PLANNING MARKETING SUPPORT

Before you plunge into the details of planning your marketing mix, you need to set objectives for two aspects of marketing support: customer service and internal marketing (see Exhibit 5.4). Customer service is important in any business because it offers opportunities to reinforce competitive differentiation and to start or strengthen customer relationships. **Internal marketing**—marketing to managers and employees inside the organization, across functional lines—is equally important for building internal relationships as a foundation for implementing the marketing plan and satisfying customers. A few firms, including the Florida-based software firm Voxeo, have appointed a Chief Customer Officer (CCO) to coordinate service and internal marketing initiatives at the top-management level. "We're doing whatever we need to do to make sure customers are exceptionally happy," says Voxeo's CCO—with metrics tied to specific objectives and measures.[21]

Setting objectives for these two areas of marketing support are discussed in the following sections; these objectives set the stage for marketing-mix decisions and programs (as discussed later in this chapter).

Customer Service

From the customer's perspective, service is part of the product or brand experience, and thus it has a major influence on customers' perceptions and responses. When setting customer service objectives, then, you must understand what your customers need and expect, what they consider satisfactory, and how service reflects on the brand or product. Although good customer service cannot make up for a bad product or spotty distribution, it can enhance the brand's image and may even allow a company to raise prices despite competitive pressure or other challenges.

In general, customers have different customer service needs and expectations at different points in the buying process:

- *Customer service before the sale.* Before they buy, customers often need assistance obtaining information about the product and its usage, features, benefits, and warranty; matching the right product to the right situation or need; researching add-ons like availability and

Internal Marketing Objectives		Customer Service Objectives
• Keep employees focused on customers • Keep employees involved in marketing • Keep employees informed about marketing • Improve employee performance and satisfaction	Support marketing objectives and the marketing mix	• Meet targeted segment's needs, expectations • Attract, retain, satisfy customers • Reinforce the product or brand positioning • Allocate service resources appropriately

EXHIBIT 5.4   Objectives for Customer Service and Internal Marketing

pricing of replacement parts; and understanding how installation, training, or other post-sale services operate. In some cases, mobile marketing and social media marketing can help fill the need for pre-sale service.

• *Customer service at the moment or point of sale.* When they are about to buy, customers may need help choosing a specific model; scheduling delivery, pickup, or use; choosing among payment options or preparing purchase orders; arranging trade-ins or taking advantage of promotional offers; completing paperwork for warranty registration; or handling other sale-related issues.

• *Customer service after the sale.* After the purchase has been completed, customers sometimes need assistance installing a product, ordering refills or spare parts, scheduling maintenance or repair services, training users, or dealing with other post-sale needs.

The marketing plan should set objectives for allocating service resources to deliver the appropriate level of customer service for each segment. It should also provide for improving self-service options when appropriate. Knowing that customer service is rarely perfect every time, marketers should include objectives for **service recovery**, how the organization will recover from a service lapse and satisfy its customers.

In setting service-recovery objectives, companies should think about the process (such as what customers must do to register a complaint and what employees are supposed to do in response) and the results (such as measuring satisfaction with customer service). For service on the fly, some companies are planning for a Twitter presence. They designate employees to watch for tweets about customer problems and to post timely responses. Two employees at the U.K. firm Autoglass, for instance, monitor comments on Facebook and Twitter. If they identify a service problem, they post an apology right away and ask the customer to provide more details via direct message, e-mail, or phone call so that Autoglass can put things right—right away.[22]

Internal Marketing

Internal marketing objectives are used to focus the entire organization on the customer and to generate support for the marketing plan. At the very least, internal marketing should ensure that there are proper staffing levels across functions and within the organization structure to carry out the marketing plan. It should also help marketers secure cooperation and involvement from other departments engaged in implementation, such as research and development, and keep employees informed about marketing activities so that they can communicate knowledgeably with customers and with each other. Another objective is to increase employee performance and satisfaction in a job well done. Upward communication is also vital, because it gives senior managers a feel for what the market wants and how marketing is meeting customers' needs. Without such support, external marketing programs have less chance of succeeding.

Depending on the company's resources and priorities, internal marketing communication can take place through internal newsletters, videos, and web pages; training and marketing or sales meetings; and other techniques. In fact, some big companies have created an internal marketing agency to coordinate the many communications needed to keep managers and employees informed about marketing strategies and programs.[23]

Here's how Germany's Adidas uses internal marketing worldwide. (For a peek at the Adidas U.S. home page, follow the QR code or go to www.adidas.com/us.)

Adidas. Since Adidas bought Reebok in 2005, the combined athletic apparel and equipment company has worked hard to ensure that its global workforce of 46,000 managers and employees understands the brand distinctions and strategies. Through meetings and internal blogs, wikis, electronic newsletters, and other social media vehicles, the company provides an overview of its overall long-term marketing direction and addresses what local employees need to know to be effective day to day. Internal marketing was especially important in the period leading up to its role as one of the official sponsors of the 2012 London Olympic Games and as designer of outfits for British athletes and Olympic volunteers. At the end of its high-profile Olympic marketing activities, Adidas used internal marketing to sum up the impact and thank the internal audience for their enthusiasm and support.[24]

Shaping the Marketing Mix

The organization's mission (which you reviewed as part of the situation analysis) plus the marketing direction, goals, and objectives all combine to guide decisions about the marketing mix, marketing support, and specific marketing programs. By properly implementing the programs in the marketing plan and using metrics to gauge the results, marketers should be able to move in the chosen direction and progress toward accomplishing financial, marketing, and societal objectives.

Imagine the complexities that the U.K.–based Vodafone faces in planning, tracking, and evaluating hundreds of marketing programs targeting more than 200 million wireless phone customers in multiple countries. Each program plays a part in achieving Vodafone's global marketing, financial, and societal objectives on the local and international levels.[25] Understanding the essential link between strategy, goals, objectives, and marketing-mix programs is the only way its managers can make appropriate, effective, and productive decisions.

Summary

A marketing plan may point the way toward growth (including market penetration, market development, product development, and diversification), maintenance of current sales levels, or retrenchment. Once the direction is set, marketers establish objectives for the marketing plan that are specific, time defined, and measurable; realistic but challenging; consistent with the organization's mission and goals; consistent with resources and core competencies; and appropriate for the external environment. Marketing objectives are short-term targets for managing marketing relationships and activities; financial objectives are short-term targets

for managing financial results; and societal objectives are short-term targets for managing social responsibility results.

For marketing support, marketers need to set objectives for customer service and for internal marketing. Customer service can be provided before, during, and after the sale, with service geared toward customer segments and marketing plan objectives and with appropriate objectives for service recovery. Internal marketing involves marketing to people inside the organization, and is necessary for building external relationships and implementing the marketing plan.

Your Marketing Plan, Step by Step

These questions will get you started on deciding your direction and objectives for the marketing plan you're developing. To see how objectives, customer service, and internal marketing are addressed in a marketing plan, review the sample in this book's appendix.

1. Based on your product or organization's current situation, SWOT analysis, and long-term goals, will you use your marketing plan to pursue a growth or nongrowth strategy? Of the specific options shown in Exhibit 5.2, which will you choose for your plan—and why?

2. Now that you know the direction you will follow, create a table with three columns. The first column will contain marketing objectives; the second, financial objectives; and the third, societal objectives. Think about the marketing objectives you need to achieve in order to move in the direction you've chosen. Will you need to set objectives for market share, unit sales volume, number of distributors, or brand awareness? For a new business, is customer acquisition a priority? For an existing business, is customer retention a priority? List at least three marketing objectives for your plan.

3. Next, consider the financial objectives you need to set. Will you be seeking to achieve a particular level of sales revenue or profit by product or channel or market? For a new product, what breakeven objective will you set? What other financial objectives are important to achieve? List at least three financial objectives for your

plan, bearing in mind the interrelationship with your marketing objectives.

4. Think about the societal objectives to be specified in your plan. Which environmental issues might your plan address? What about philanthropic activities and community involvement? Is there a particular issue that you want to associate with your brand or product? How can societal objectives help you reach your other objectives or compete more effectively? List at least three societal objectives you will include in your plan.

5. Check your objectives against this chapter's checklist. Are the objectives relevant, consistent, realistic, measurable, and time defined? Are your targets specific enough to guide your marketing activities in the short term?

6. What types of internal marketing and customer service support are necessary to move the organization in the direction you've chosen? Review Exhibit 5.4 as you define objectives for internal marketing, such as communicating with employees. What, when, and how will you do this? Who will be responsible, and how will results be measured? Also define customer service objectives, including targets for service recovery, if appropriate.

Endnotes

1. Lauren Indvik, "20% of Newspapers Now Have Online Paywalls," *Mashable,* August 28, 2012, www.mashable.com; Christine Haughney, "Newspapers Cut Days from Publishing Week," *New York Times,* June 3, 2012, www.nytimes .com; Steve Ladurantaye, "Postmedia Cuts More Jobs," *The Globe and Mail (Canada),* May 28, 2012, www.theglobeandmail.com; Cain Burdeau, "Times-Picayune to Cut Paper to 3 Days a Week," *Bloomberg Businessweek,* May 24, 2012, www.businessweek.com.

2. H. Igor Ansoff, "Strategies for Diversification," *Harvard Business Review,* September–October 1957, pp. 113–124; Philip Kotler, *Kotler on*

Marketing (New York: The Free Press, 1999), pp. 46–48.

3. Howard Penney and Rory Green, "Did Starbucks Make One Move Too Many?" *Fortune,* June 6, 2012, http://finance.fortune .cnn.com.

4. Roger J. Best, *Market-Based Management* (Upper Saddle River, NJ: Pearson Prentice Hall, 2013), p. 420.

5. Deborah Netburn, "'Angry Birds' Maker Rovio Thinks Pig, Unwraps Game 'Bad Piggies,'" *Los Angeles Times,* September 4, 2012, www.latimes.com; David MacDougall, "Angry Birds Flying Beyond Games, Around the World," *Associated Press,* June 3, 2012,

www.sacbee.com; "Angry Birds Creator to Float on Stock Market," *Daily Mail (UK),* May 8, 2012, www.dailymail.co.uk; Michael Kan, "Angry Birds Maker Rovio Plans for Amusement Parks in China," *PC World,* May 9, 2012, www.pcworld.com; Mark Hachman, "Rovio's Golden Egg: Its 2011 Profits," *PC Magazine,* May 7, 2012, www.pcmag.com.

6. Fred Meier, "GM Posts $1 Billion Q1 Profit, Dragged Down by Europe," *USA Today,* May 3, 2012, www.usatoday.com; Nick Bunkley, "Resurgent G.M. Posts 2010 Profit of $4.7 Billion," *New York Times,* February 24, 2011, www.nytimes.com.

7. Mark Miller, "The Truth Behind Brand Loyalty," *Mediapost,* June 7, 2012, www.mediapost.com; Jeremy Quittner, "USAA Tech Overhaul Makes Remote Banking Less Remote," *American Banker,* July 12, 2011, p. 1.

8. Alex Mishimoto, "Ford Adding More Production Shifts to Keep Up with Demand," *Motor Trend,* May 31, 2012, www.motortrend.com; Bart Mills, "Ford Sets Lofty Goals for Lima Plant," *Lima News (OH),* February 20, 2012, n.p.

9. David Shephardson, "Ford Can't Keep Up with Auto Demand," *Detroit News,* May 31, 2012, www.detroitnews.com; Alex Taylor III, "Fixing Up Ford," *Fortune,* May 11, 2009, http://money.cnn.com.

10. Kunur Patel, "Amazon Preps to Take On Apple, Others in Mobile Ads," *Advertising Age,* May 28, 2012, p. 1; Eric Savitz, "Amazon Q1 Blows Past Estimates," *Forbes,* April 26, 2012, www.forbes.com.

11. Matt Burns, "Apple Q2 2012: 35.1M iPhones, 11.8M iPads, 4M Macs, and 7.7M iPods," *TechCrunch,* April 24, 2012, www.techcrunch.com.

12. Tim Carmody, "Add It Up: Crunching Numbers for Apple, Amazon, Netflix, and Jeremy Lin," *Wired,* February 15, 2012, www.wired.com.

13. Liz Welch, "The Way I Work: Anne Wojcicki, 23andMe," *Inc.,* May 29, 2012, www.inc.com.

14. Personal communication with Judy Strauss.

15. Tiffany Hsu, "McDonald's: Big Changes Afoot," *Los Angeles Times,* May 24, 2012, www.latimes.com; Eli Greenblat, "McDonald's Growth Falters," *Sydney Morning Herald (Australia),* April 24, 2012, www.smh.com.au; "McDonald's Records

5.6% Global Sales Increase for 2011," *Advertising Age,* January 24, 2012, www.adage.com; Beth Kowitt, "Why McDonald's Wins in Any Economy," *Fortune,* August 23, 2011, http://management.fortune.conn.com; Emily Bryson York, "McDonald's Tying Summer Olympics to New Effort to Promote Children's Well-Being," *Chicago Tribune,* April 27, 2012, www.chicagotribune.com.

16. Ashlee Vance, "How Marketing Sparks IBM Stock," *MSN Money,* March 8, 2012, http://money.msn.com; Spencer E. Ante, "IBM Turns to Software," *Wall Street Journal,* May 13, 2010, www.wsj.com; Jessi Hempel, "IBM's Sam Palmisano: A Second Act," *Fortune,* March 4, 2011, http://tech.fortune.cnn.com; Beth Jinks, "IBM Tapping 'Gusher of Data' to Reach 2015 Targets, CEO Says," *Bloomberg,* March 12, 2012, www.bloomberg.com.

17. Matt Carmichael and Dante Chinni, "Trying to Decide on a Cause-Marketing Category?" *Advertising Age,* January 16, 2012, www.adage.com; Mark Dolliver, "The Positive Effects of Cause-Related Marketing," *CMO,* April 5, 2011, www.cmo.com.

18. "Good Business, Nice Beaches," *Economist,* May 19, 2012, www.economist.com.

19. Heather King, "Ikea's Steve Howard on Bringing Sustainability to the Masses," *Green Biz,* February 23, 2012, www.greenbiz.com.

20. Elaine Wong, "When the Going Gets Tough, P&G Gets Philanthropic," *Brandweek,* March 7, 2009, www.brandweek.com.

21. April Joyner, "Make Room for the Chief Customer Officer," *Inc.,* April 3, 2012, www.inc.com.

22. Steve Evans, "Social Media Is Now Part of Our Core Business," *Computer Business Review,* May 23, 2012, www.cbronline.com.

23. Jake Langwith, "The Rise of the Internal Marketing Agency," *ClickZ,* April 12, 2012, www.clickz.com.

24. Andrew Davidson, "Adidas Boss Plays to Win," *Sunday Times (London),* January 8, 2012, p. 6; Jan Runau, "A Snapshot of the Adidas Group's Internal Communication Efforts," *Adidas Group Blog,* September 20, 2011, http://blog.adidas-group.com; James Hall, "Adidas Aims to Be True Winner of 2012 Games," *Daily Telegraph (London),* May 30, 2011, p. 3.

25. Tony Case, "Going Global," *DM News,* December 2011, p. 26.

Developing Product and Brand Strategy

In this chapter:

PREVIEW

Successful products are a major building block in marketing success. To compete in today's global economy while moving toward your firm's marketing goals and objectives, you'll need to plan for new and improved products that meet your customers' needs and expectations. Formulating product and brand strategy is part of Step 5 of the marketing planning process (see Exhibit 6.1). In this chapter, you'll learn about the various elements to be considered in product strategy, including the value you provide to customers and the management of a product throughout its life cycle. You'll also explore key branding decisions to be made as you write your marketing plan.

APPLYING YOUR KNOWLEDGE

After studying this chapter, review the sample plan in this book's appendix for ideas about product and brand strategy. Then continue your project by answering the questions in "Your Marketing Plan, Step by Step," at the end of this chapter. Finally, document your decisions in your written plan, using this chapter's checklist as a guide to analyzing offerings and developing product strategy.

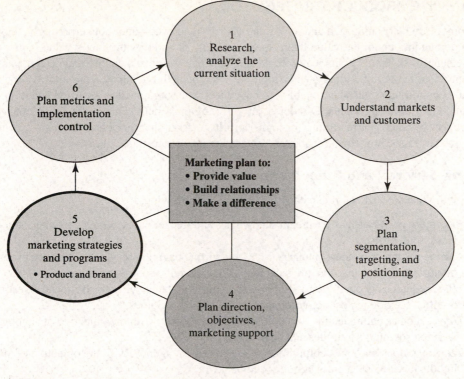

EXHIBIT 6.1   Marketing Planning: Step 5

CHAPTER 6 CHECKLIST   Planning Product Strategy

Current Offerings

✓ What products are being offered, at what price points, and for what customer segments and channels?

✓ What are the unit sales, revenues, shares, and profit trends of each product over the years?

✓ How are newer products faring in relation to older products?

✓ How does each product contribute to the company's performance and goals?

Product Plans

✓ How does each product support the organization's objectives and strategic direction?

✓ What opportunities for adding value through product modifications or introductions exist?

✓ How do each product's features and benefits, quality, packaging, services, and branding provide value for customers? What enhancements would add value and improve competitive position?

✓ Where is each product in the life cycle? How can each be aligned with plan objectives?

✓ What changes to product lines and product mixes will help the company pursue its goals?

PLANNING PRODUCT STRATEGY TODAY

Customers are better informed and have more choices than ever—and, not surprisingly, they are more demanding about the value they expect from any product. A product's value is provided by the benefits delivered by its features and supplementary services, quality and design, packaging and labeling, and branding (see Exhibit 6.2). As this exhibit shows, your strategy must be based on a thorough understanding of your customers, your organization's current situation, and external environmental forces. Of course, any offering must help achieve your marketing-plan objectives, whether you're aiming for higher profits, market share, or other targets—especially since resources are limited and marketers are accountable for results.

Goods, Services, and Other Products

What will your product be? It can consist of any of the following:

- *Tangible goods* such as ice cream sandwiches and freezer cases, which customers can buy, lease, rent, or use
- *Services* such as wireless phone services and virtual payment services, which are primarily intangible but may involve physical items (such as cell phones/smartphones)
- *Places* such as geographic regions courting tourists, states vying for business investment, or cities seeking to host activities such as the Olympic Games
- *Ideas* such as eating healthy or supporting human rights, with the objective of shaping the targeted segment's attitudes and behavior
- *Organizations* such as a corporation or a government agency, with the objective of affecting the targeted segment's attitudes and behavior
- *People* such as movie star Johnny Depp and pop star Lady Gaga, with the objective of affecting the targeted segment's attitudes and behavior

When preparing a marketing plan for a service, think about what customers prefer and how customers and employees will deal with the characteristics of intangibility, variability, inseparability, and perishability. You can use marketing to emphasize the positive aspects of

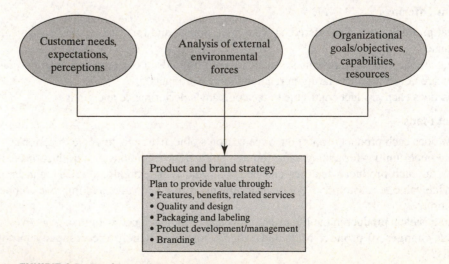

EXHIBIT 6.2   Product and Brand Strategy

EXHIBIT 6.3   Planning for Services

Intangibility	Variability
• Services have no physical existence, can't be experienced before being produced	• Service quality can vary from one experience to the next, depending on provider, facility, time of day, etc.
• Plan to market tangible aspects of a service, such as expert personnel or new equipment	• Plan to market staff's training and experience, standardized processes for quality management

Inseparability	Perishability
• Service production and delivery can't be separated from consumption	• Services can't be held in storage for future sale or consumption.
• Plan to market efficiency, effectiveness, emotional benefits of customers interacting with service employees	• Plan marketing to increase usage during slow periods, shift usage from peak periods to slower periods

these characteristics and to minimize the potential downsides of these characteristics, as Exhibit 6.3 suggests. For instance, Fandango and Moviefone recently teamed up to allow moviegoers to see which movies are playing in local theaters and to buy tickets in advance using a PC, tablet computer, or smartphone. This partnership turns perishability—the fact that services can't be stored for the future—into a positive by enabling customers to secure tickets for the time they choose. Both services are also active in social media so customers can get the latest news about movies wherever and whenever they want.[1] (Visit Fandango's home page by following this QR code or by going to www.fandango.com.)

Features, Benefits, and Services

Features are specific attributes that enable a product to perform its function. In physical goods such as backpacks, features include padded shoulder straps and strong zippers; in intangible services such as online banking, features include integrated display of all account information and one-click funds transfer. Features deliver **benefits**, the need-satisfaction outcomes that

PLANNING TIP

Seek to add value while achieving marketing, financial, *and* societal objectives.

customers want from a product. For example, customers who buy cordless drills are seeking the benefit of creating holes for nails and screws, although some may seek additional benefits such as convenience or status. Thus, consumers and business customers buy products not for the features alone, but for the value in providing benefits that fulfill needs or solve problems (which you can uncover through your market and customer analysis). What needs and problems do your customers have, and how will your product satisfy or solve them?

Exhibit 6.4 shows sample needs, features, and benefits for a product and a service. Each product targets a different consumer or business segment that's described according to behavior (do-it-yourselfers) or demographics (families with young children). In each case, note how the benefit interprets the feature in relation to each segment's specific need. If you analyze each feature of your product in this way, you'll get a better understanding of the value delivered to satisfy customer needs. As you plan, keep an eye on how needs, environmental influences, and

EXHIBIT 6.4   Sample Needs, Features, and Benefits

Product	Targeted Segment	Need	Feature	Benefit
Cordless drill (tangible)	Do-it-yourselfers (behavioral description)	Drill holes without electricity	Extra battery pack included	Drill can be used for long periods
Theme park (intangible)	Families with young children (demographic description)	Entertain children	Supervised wading pool	Toddlers can play safely

competitive offerings are evolving, because these can change at any point, possibly forcing you to change your marketing plan.

Beware of "feature bloat," adding so many features that customers become confused, frustrated, or dissatisfied. Before you plan for extra features, be sure they will help you achieve specific marketing plan objectives—and not at the expense of the bottom line, if financial goals are particularly critical. Understanding your targeted segment is the key. The many features of an iPhone are designed to appeal to heavy users of apps, for instance, but not to value-conscious or tech-wary consumers who use their cell phones only to make or receive calls.

More companies are building customer loyalty and profits through a product strategy calling for **mass customization**, creating products, on a large scale, with features or attributes tailored to the needs of individual customers. This approach to product marketing requires special planning and company capabilities, however.

Mass customization. From trench coats to swing sets to chocolates, a wide variety of products are now being customized to fit individual customers' needs and tastes. The British fashion brand Burberry invites customers to design their own deluxe trench coats, choosing fabric, collar, lining, colors, accents, and other details to make each a one-of-a-kind product. Families can customize the design of the wooden indoor or outdoor play sets they buy from CedarWorks in Maine to meet their individual needs. Mass customization is an option offered by some food marketers, as well. Customers can put photos and messages on M&M's, choose one or more colors, and even personalize the packaging for birthdays, weddings, and other special occasions. Heinz allows customers to design custom ketchup-bottle labels with personal photos and messages.

The key, explains expert B. Joseph Pine II, is to create products that can be modularized so that customers can build their own, module by module (fabric/collar/lining/etc. for Burberry coats, color/photos/etc. for M&M's). Marketers that use mass customization put some limits on customers' choices to make the products affordable while allowing for hundreds if not thousands of variations through mix-and-match choices. Mass customization isn't for every firm: Procter & Gamble tested Reflect, a site where customers could buy custom-blended beauty products. After deciding that its blockbuster brands (Olay, among others) had more profit potential, P&G shuttered Reflect, even though the site had attracted hundreds of thousands of visitors.[2]

In your marketing plan, also consider how the supplementary services can deliver valued benefits to satisfy customer needs, now and in the future. Some supplementary services may supply information for better use of the product, as in training; some services may offer consultation for problem solving or customization of the product; some services may involve safety or security, as in storage of products or data. Services can differentiate your offering, help you defend against competitors, and support your marketing efforts to acquire new customers.

Quality and Design

Often defined in terms of performance capabilities, the most important definition of **quality** is how well the product satisfies customers. By this definition, a high-quality product (good or service) is one that does a competitively superior job of fulfilling customer needs. Savvy marketers know that the basic functionality of acceptable quality is the price of entry in the contemporary global marketplace. Word of mouth (or online, word of mouse) can quickly sink a product with inferior quality—and just as quickly generate interest in a product with excellent quality. Good quality is no guarantee of success, but it can help attract new customers, retain current customers, capture market share, charge higher prices, earn higher profits, or meet other objectives.

PLANNING TIP

Determine how customers perceive your product's quality compared with competing products.

Your marketing plan should take into account customers' tendency to switch to a competing product if they believe its quality is superior (meeting their needs more consistently or more quickly). Quality is a major concern among cell phone users, for example, which is part of the reason for the higher **customer churn** (turnover in customers) at telecom carriers. Although price plays a role, quality often trumps price when customers consider switching among services.

Another focus of product strategy is design, inextricably linked to quality. A good design means more than style; it means that the product can perform as it should, can be repaired easily, is aesthetically pleasing, and meets other needs. Services are affected by design as well. The newly opened Lurie Children's Hospital of Chicago features gardens, scientific exhibits, and artwork to engage children, plus home-like family rooms where young patients and their relatives can relax together.[3] If your marketing plan is for a web-based service, remember that your site should be designed as attractive, functional, and "sticky"—engaging enough to keep customers there for more than a few seconds.

Design is at the forefront of many product categories, from computers and entertainment electronics to home appliances and workshop tools. When good quality is the minimum that customers will accept, the "emotional quality" of design is the marketing battleground that more companies are choosing for differentiation. Look at the category of sports helmets—such as for skiing and bicycling—where appearance adds an emotional element beyond the functional benefit of safety. Sweden's POC, recently acquired by Utah-based Black Diamond, makes aesthetically appealing helmets for skiers, high priced and high style. Also in Sweden, two designers came up with a bicycle helmet that is not a helmet at all, but a fashionable collar containing a helmet-like inflatable protection device. The device doesn't interfere with the enjoyment of bicycling, because it only inflates in a crash (similar to the way an airbag works) to protect the cyclist's head.[4]

Sustainability is driving many design decisions these days, as well. As one example, Terracycle designs useful products (such as tote bags, pencil cases, and shipping pallets) from discarded product packaging, cigarette butts, and other waste that otherwise wouldn't be recycled.[5] (Terracycle's home page is at www.terracycle.com—scan this QR code to visit.)

Packaging and Labeling

From the customer's perspective, packaging adds value by keeping tangible products safe and in convenient containers until they are used; labeling adds value by communicating product contents, uses, and warnings. Thus, Kellogg breakfast cereals stay fresh and uncrushed in the plastic-lined cardboard packaging, and Motrin pain reliever tablets are kept out of tiny hands by child-resistant containers; both packages bear labels with information about product ingredients

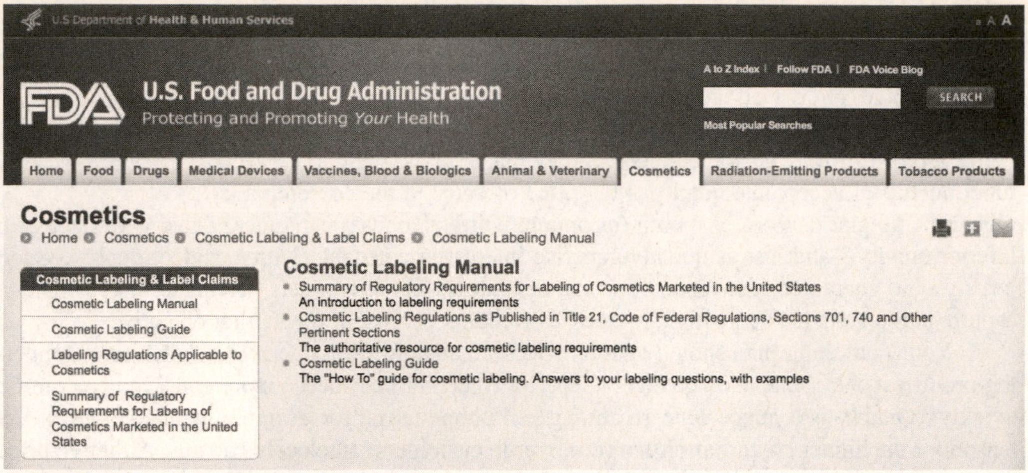

EXHIBIT 6.5 U.S. Food and Drug Administration Cosmetic Labeling

and consumption. When planning for labels, check on compliance with laws mandating warnings (such as about the health hazards of cigarettes or alcohol), the allowable use of certain phrases (such as "low fat"), and even the required size or type of words (for warnings or other details). Exhibit 6.5 shows a link to the U.S. Food and Drug Administration's summary of labeling requirements for cosmetic products.

Packaging and labeling play an important marketing role by highlighting points of differentiation, explaining the product's features and benefits, reinforcing what the brand stands for, and attracting attention among customers and channel partners. In addition, marketers should plan packaging and labeling to "sell" from the shelf, because the majority of shoppers make their buying decisions while in the store. Consider, too, how packaging can help polish brand image by communicating and delivering benefits that stakeholders value, such as a commitment to sustainability. For instance, both Coca-Cola and PepsiCo have marketing plans to promote soft-drink bottles made, in part, from plant materials.[6]

Another angle involves adding value to the packaging or labeling that customers use. UPS doesn't make packaging for products, but it does want to make a green name for itself.

UPS. UPS is a big part of many companies' marketing plans, especially during the busy holiday shopping season, when it delivers as many as 120 million packages per week. One challenge, as described by a senior executive, is, "How do you make the box no bigger than required, protect the product, maximize transport costs, and minimize carbon footprint?" To help business customers address this issue, UPS recently introduced an Eco Responsible Packaging Program, including a calculator for measuring the environmental effect of various packaging and shipping options. Among other customers, the rock band Pearl Jam has sought UPS's help in devising green shipping plans for its national tours.

UPS operates a variety of alternative-fuel vehicles and has set a goal of reducing fuel usage by 20% before 2020. Its annual sustainability report discloses how the firm is progressing toward that goal. Guided by a chief sustainability officer, Big Brown has other programs in the works to incorporate sustainable practices throughout its global operations and to reinforce its green reputation.[7]

PRODUCT DEVELOPMENT AND MANAGEMENT

The fourth major element of product strategy is managing the product's movement through the **product life cycle** of introduction, growth, maturity, and decline (see Exhibit 6.6). Even experts have difficulty predicting the exact length and shape of a product's life cycle, which limits the practi-

PLANNING TIP

Aim to have different products in different stages of the life cycle at any one time.

cal application of this theory. However, you can look at sales trends for clues to a particular product's life-cycle stage and use the existence of life-cycle stages as an idea-starter for your planning. New products with low but growing sales are in the introduction stage; young products with rapidly increasing sales are in the growth stage; existing products with relatively level sales are in maturity (profits are generally highest here); and older products with decreasing sales are in decline. Knowing this, how can you use your marketing plan to maximize profits during maturity, for example, or to postpone decline by changing product features or benefits?

During the development of your marketing plan, build in environmental screening and analysis to understand your product's movement through the life cycle and the marketing challenges you will face at each stage (see Exhibit 6.7). Product life-cycle stages can be influenced by many factors, including technology, competition, consumer lifestyles, and societal attitudes.

For tech products in particular, the period between introduction and decline is shorter than ever. Consider the brief life of the personal digital assistant (PDA).

Personal digital assistants. The personal digital assistant (PDA), with its calendar, contact, and organizing features, was first introduced in the 1990s and popularized by Palm. As technology advanced, rivals leapfrogged each other with new models every few months, moving from monochrome to color screens and adding new capabilities year after year. By 2005, however, PDA sales had almost reached their peak. From then on, the PDA was headed for decline as customers became enamored of more-advanced multifunction mobile devices such as the iPhone and tablet computers. Palm struggled financially, switching its focus from PDAs to smartphones before being acquired by Hewlett-Packard in 2010. A year later, after Palm had tried to diversify by marketing a tablet computer to compete with Apple's iPad, Hewlett-Packard discontinued the Palm brand and all Palm products.[8]

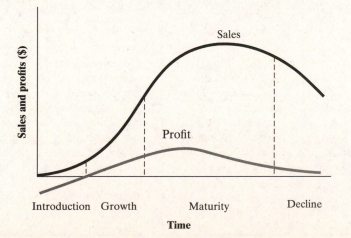

EXHIBIT 6.6   Product Life Cycle: Sales and Profits

Idea Generation and Screening	Initial Concept Testing	Business Analysis	Design Prototype	Market Testing	Commercialization
• Based on customer needs and wants, identify new product ideas	• Research customer value of product concepts	• Estimate development, production, and marketing-mix costs	• Design and produce working prototypes	• Test customer reaction through limited market trials or simulated testing	• Plan targeting and timing of launch
• Screen out unprofitable or unsuitable ideas	• Refine concept based on research	• Compare costs with potential share, sales, profitability to identify good candidates	• Test prototype functionality, customer appeal	• Test different marketing-mix combinations for support	• Plan production and marketing-mix support for launch

Introduction	Growth	Maturity	Decline
• Launch the new product	• Enhance product (new features, improved quality, added services, new packaging)	• Add brand or line extensions	• Reposition, reformulate, or cut struggling products
• Support launch with marketing-mix programs to build customer awareness, make product available, and encourage trial	• Support rising sales with expanded channel coverage, pricing for market penetration, and communications to start and reinforce customer relationships	• Defend market share through competitive pricing, channel expansion, communicating differentiation, and promotion to reinforce customer loyalty	• Manage profitability through careful pricing, pruning channel outlets, and minimal or highly targeted communications

EXHIBIT 6.7 **Product Strategy Through the Life Cycle**

New Product Development

When you plan for a new product, look closely at potential opportunities for providing value to targeted customers. Also build on internal strengths (identified through the situational analysis you conducted earlier) to create competitively superior products. Your marketing plan for new product development must cover these basic steps:

- *Idea generation.* Collect ideas from customers, managers and employees, suppliers, distributors, and other sources. **Crowdsourcing**—inviting customers and others outside the organization to participate by submitting concepts, designs, content, or advice—is an increasingly popular way to generate ideas. As mentioned in Chapter 1, *cocreation* goes even further, involving customers more deeply in collaborating on product ideas and innovation.
- *Idea screening.* Eliminate inappropriate or impractical ideas early in the process to avoid wasting time and resources later.
- *Initial concept testing.* Test to discover whether customers in the targeted segment understand and like the most promising new product ideas; refine or drop concepts that test poorly. Remember that a concept may test well in one segment or market but not in any others, which will affect the business analysis and marketing plan.
- *Business analysis.* Assess the business prospects of the remaining ideas and eliminate any that could be too expensive or that won't contribute to the marketing plan's objectives.
- *Prototype design.* Design and produce a prototype to determine the practicality and cost. If different technology or skills are needed, making a prototype will bring such issues into focus before full production.
- *Market testing.* Test the new product and various introductory marketing activities to gauge demand and competitive strength. Google thoroughly tests every change to its search services before making a final decision; because everything is online, the company can try different versions and gather feedback to make a decision very quickly.[9]
- *Commercialization.* Introduce the new product in some areas or across the entire market, with the support of channel, pricing, and promotion strategies.
- *Monitoring of customer reaction.* If a new product doesn't fare as well as expected, the company faces decisions about changing the marketing mix (including the product), repositioning the product, or pulling it. Google watches product usage closely and has been known to discontinue new products quickly if they fail to attract many users.[10] You can learn many valuable lessons even when customers don't react as positively as you'd hope.

In many cases, companies make decisions about new products and life-cycle movement to avoid or minimize **cannibalization**—allowing a new product to eat into sales of one or more existing products. Some cannibalization is inevitable in high-tech markets, where life cycles are relatively short because competitors race to launch the next breakthrough product. Companies often believe that if they don't cannibalize their own products, rivals will seize the opportunity to grab both sales and customer relationships. In some cases, marketers may reposition a product for other uses, segments, or markets if cannibalization is a concern.

PLANNING TIP

Should you cannibalize your own product before a competitor grabs the opportunity?

For instance, General Electric (GE) has manufactured cutting-edge ultrasound equipment for more than thirty years. Not long ago, it developed a portable ultrasound scanner specifically for China as part of its marketing plan to increase market share in Asia. As the company improved ultrasound scan quality year after year, buyers outside China became interested in this versatile piece of equipment. In response, GE expanded distribution worldwide and wound up turning a niche into a large and highly profitable segment that it could defend against other suppliers. Rather than cannibalizing sales of other GE ultrasound equipment, the portable system led to new profit opportunities.[11]

Product Lines and the Product Mix

The product strategy in your marketing plan should also cover the management of each **product line** (products that are related in some way) and the overall **product mix** (the assortment of all product lines offered). You should analyze the existing mix as part of the current situation; after examining each product and line individually, you can make decisions about the length and width of your lines and mixes. One way to grow your business is by putting an established brand on a new product that's added to the existing product line, creating a **line extension**. Another way is to plan a **brand (or category) extension**, putting an established brand on a new product in a different category for a new customer segment.

Because of the high cost of developing entirely new products, many products introduced these days are actually extensions. PepsiCo's Frito-Lay snack division has more than four dozen extensions (counting flavor variations, packaging variations, and region-specific products) in development at any one time to support its competitive position in India, for example.[12] Depending on your market, resources, and product category, you may want to consider the development of a limited-time or limited-edition product. PepsiCo does this, as do other marketers. (Take a look at PepsiCo's home page by going to www.pepsico.com or by scanning this QR code.)

Limited-time and limited-edition products. Limited-time products are marketed during a specific period; limited-edition products are produced once, in small quantities. PepsiCo, for instance, releases a different summer-only soda flavor in Japan every year—hoping that novelty seekers will rush to stores for a taste of such limited-time flavors as "salty watermelon." Since 1982, McDonald's has been putting its McRib sandwich on the menu in selected locations for only a few weeks every year. Fans flock to their local McDonald's when it becomes available because they don't know when it will be on the menu again. Burger King recently launched a limited-time bacon sundae, featuring vanilla soft-serve ice cream with sweet and salty toppings including bacon.

Limited-edition products have become commonplace in nonfood categories. Limited-edition Nike Air Yeezy II shoes designed by Kanye West sold out quickly, and Aston Martin sold all 88 of the luxury Dragon88 cars it produced during 2012, the Chinese year of the dragon. Limited-time and limited-edition products attract attention because they are novel, scarce, and suggest both urgency and exclusivity. Customers feel fortunate (and may even gain status) when they manage to buy something seen as desirable yet in limited supply—even if they wind up paying a high price for it. Many buyers comment about such products on Facebook, on Twitter, or in other social media, building word-of-mouth momentum in a way that marketer-controlled media can rarely match. In some cases, the product may be offered as a way to spotlight the brand's or the firm's unique capabilities, meaning that financial objectives are secondary to marketing objectives. Limited-time or limited-edition products aren't right for every marketer, however: Firms shouldn't divert resources from their main product(s) in order to chase a flavor or fashion fad without a compelling business analysis.[13]

Shortening or narrowing lines and mixes can help you concentrate your resources on the most promising products and segments for survival, maintenance, or growth. Longer product lines and wider product mixes typically require more resources to develop and sustain, but they help deep-pocketed companies grow and pursue ambitious objectives. In addition, long lines or wide mixes can be important to companies that operate in many markets, because marketers can plan to use extensions in order to appeal to specific segments in each area.

PLANNING BRANDING

Branding is the use of words, designs, and symbols to give a product a distinct identity and differentiate it from competitive products. After customers learn to associate a brand with the value created by a particular set of product elements (such as features, benefits, and quality), they simplify the decision-making process by routinely buying that brand rather than stopping to evaluate every alternative on every shopping occasion.

PLANNING TIP

Pay attention to brand symbols and sounds because they are as recognizable as brand names.

In creating your marketing plan, consider which of the following approaches to brand names you will choose for your product:

- *Company name and individual brand,* such as Courtyard by Marriott, Marriott Marquis.
- *Individual name* for a product, for a category, or for targeting a segment. Infiniti and Nissan are separate brands, under Nissan's ownership, that are geared toward different segments of car and truck buyers.
- *Private-label brand* used by one retailer or wholesaler, such as Costco's Kirkland brand.
- *Multiple brands,* by *cobranding,* in which two or more organizations put their brands on one product; or by *ingredient branding,* in which an ingredient's brand is featured along with the product's brand. All brands gain by association with the others, and loyal users of one brand may be encouraged to try other products by the other brands.

Unilever uses individual brand names (Knorr soups, Omo laundry detergent) but shows the company brand on packaging, so that customers who like an individual product will associate it with the parent company and possibly try more Unilever products.[14] Nestlé does the same thing, for the same reason. One risk, however, is that a negative experience with one of the company's products might cause a customer to avoid other products that carry the company brand.

Brands should be recognizable and memorable. They should also be legally protectable in the physical world and the digital world, and be suitable for international markets if and when the company expands globally. Be sure brands have some meaning for the target market and are appealing (whether expressed in words, images, or sounds). Online brands are not immune to these basic branding guidelines. Amazon.com and Google have become strong, distinctive, and valuable brands through constant, consistent performance and support of the marketing-mix, whereas online brands without clear differentiation or marketing reinforcement have struggled or been acquired by others. Google regularly appears at or near the top of experts' lists of the world's most valuable brands.[15]

With a strong brand, you gain long-term advantages such as greater customer trust and loyalty, stronger competitive position, and the ability to set a higher price or enjoy higher profit margins. During the recent financial crisis in Europe, Michelin was able to hold the line on tire prices and even increase future sales and profit targets because of its brand's strength. "When you have a crisis, a strong brand is what consumers turn to," observes the head of marketing.

"It's true that a Michelin tire is a little more expensive than another brand, but you have safety and quality guarantees, and that's what we have to communicate."[16]

Branding decisions made during the planning process are closely tied to product positioning and other marketing activities for building customer relationships through brand equity, as the next two sections explain.

Branding and Positioning

Every consumer or business product faces some competition in the marketplace, from direct competitors (Huggies disposable diapers compete with Pampers disposables), substitutes (Huggies disposables compete with cloth diapers), or both. The brand not only identifies a particular product, it reminds customers of the value that sets the product apart from all others and makes it both distinctive and competitively superior. The company can influence but not control

customer perceptions; however, it can control product features, benefits, design, and other points of differentiation that customers care about. Consistency counts: If a marketing-mix strategy or implementation conflicts with the positioning, customers can become confused about what the brand stands for.

American Express has prospered by emphasizing benefits that its customers value highly and that have been at the heart of its brand positioning throughout the decades. Lately, the company has injected more personality into its customer dealings by avoiding strictly scripted service conversations. (To see the American Express home page, click to www.americanexpress.com or scan the QR code here.)

> **American Express.** This financial services firm positions itself as the world's most respected provider of reliable, convenient, secure payment services supported by top-quality service, day in and day out. This positioning extends far beyond individual credit card transactions: It's about cultivating long-term relationships, regardless of when and where customers use a card and whether they request service online, via apps, by phone, via Twitter, or in some other way. "Deep, service-based relationships are what keep us constant even as our business changes," says the chief marketing officer.
>
> Instead of training its customer care staff to save money by ending service conversations as quickly as possible or to follow a structured script during phone calls, American Express strives to engage and understand its customers, for relationship-building purposes. Customer service employees are empowered to listen, be helpful, and be creative, guided by what they see in each customer's account details and history of credit-card usage patterns. "Problems are actually a very small percentage of why customers interact with American Express," observes the head of customer service. "What we've learned is that the power of that interaction gives us an opportunity to expand the perception of the brand in a very positive way."[17]

The Power of Brand Equity

PLANNING TIP

High brand equity can help defend share when a product is mature or faces fierce competition.

The stronger the brand, the more it encourages customer loyalty and boosts **customer lifetime value**, the total amount a customer spends on a brand or with that company during the entire relationship. For instance, Amazon doesn't have to make much profit on its Kindle tablets and e-book readers, because it can count on profiting from the many e-books and other content

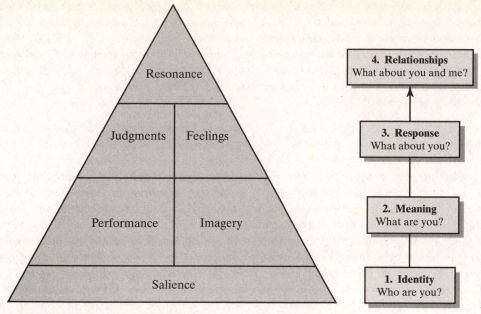

EXHIBIT 6.8   Pyramid of Brand Equity

Source: Kevin Lane Keller, *Strategic Brand Management,* 2d ed. (Upper Saddle River, NJ: Pearson Prentice Hall, 2006), Fig. 2.5, p. 76.

(and products) that customers will buy from Amazon for years after they acquire a Kindle.[18] The Kindle and Amazon brands both get a boost, which increases **brand equity**, the extra value customers perceive that enhances their long-term loyalty to the brand.

As shown in Exhibit 6.8, simply making the brand salient isn't enough to build equity. Strong brand equity occurs at the top of the pyramid, where a brand resonates with customers through an ongoing relationship in which they are loyal to it, have positive attitudes toward it, and feel actively engaged with it. All marketing-mix elements have the potential to contribute to equity, which is why each year's marketing plan should set relationship objectives and contain programs to move customers toward the top of the brand-equity pyramid.

Address brand awareness, preference, and equity in your marketing plan because a strong brand can insulate your organization against competitive threats and become a driver for long-term growth and prosperity. Luxury brands, in particular, should seek to build positive feelings and trust, which in turn will help reduce customers' perceptions of risk in buying and will reinforce loyalty over time.[19]

When your plan covers a new product or an extension, think about whether your brand has a positive image consistent with the targeted segment's needs, expectations, and perceptions. Consider the Swiss food-and-beverage giant Nestlé, which markets a broad portfolio of food and beverage brands. Its highly successful single-serve coffee machines and capsules carry the Nespresso brand, tapping into some of the equity of the company brand and its well-known Nescafé instant coffees. The Nespresso brand's stylish boutiques and premium positioning have helped to reinforce positive perceptions of the company brand, as well. With such strong brand equity and a long

connection with coffee products, Nestlé has been able to expand its Nescafé-branded products to restaurants and office facilities that buy coffee machines.[20] (Visit Nestlé's global home page at www.nestle.com or use the QR code on page 109 to see the site.)

In the end, it's customers who decide what a brand means to them and how they feel about it. You can influence salience, performance, judgments, and resonance, but you don't have direct control over how customers think about, feel about, or act toward your brand.

Summary

In a marketing plan, product strategy covers decisions about features, benefits, and related services; quality and design; packaging and labeling; product development and management; and branding. Products can be tangible goods, services, places, ideas, organizations, or people. Features are the attributes that enable the good or service to perform its intended function and deliver benefits—the need-satisfaction outcomes customers want from a product. Product-related supplementary services deliver valued benefits to satisfy customer needs as part of the product strategy.

Product quality means how well the product satisfies customers, and it's closely linked to design. Packaging and labeling deliver value to customers (by providing benefits such as storing products, keeping them safe, and explaining ingredients and usage) and to organizations (by polishing brand image, communicating features and benefits, and attracting interest). The marketing plan should include planning for the product life cycle (introduction, growth, maturity, and decline), for new-product development, and for managing both product lines and the product mix. Branding gives a product a distinct identity and differentiates it from competitive products. Moreover, it supports the chosen positioning for a product in a targeted segment and helps build customer relationships for long-term loyalty and brand equity.

Your Marketing Plan, Step by Step

Now that you're ready to plan your marketing mix, use the following questions as starting points for making decisions about product and brand strategy. Document your answers in your marketing plan.

1. Using your knowledge of the market and your targeted segment, identify at least one specific customer need that each of your products (goods or services) is intended to satisfy. What features will each product include, and what benefits will these features deliver? How will these benefits create value for customers by satisfying needs? Be as specific as possible.

2. Take a closer look at the features you've identified. What basic functionality must this product's features deliver to meet customers' needs and their minimum quality expectations? Are any features too expensive to include in a competitively priced product or otherwise inconsistent with your marketing plan objectives? What alternatives might be appropriate

in this situation? What is the quality of competing products, and should you seek competitive advantage through superior quality?

3. What supplementary services, if any, would enhance the value of your offering? Will you plan to offer supplementary services to any customers, to all customers, or to selected segments? Why and how? What are the financial implications of these services?

4. Which competitors (if any) compete on the basis of innovative design or packaging? Can or should you design or redesign your product and/or packaging to improve your competitive standing or to enhance the aesthetic appeal of your product? What legal requirements must you follow in designing and labeling your

product? What packaging or labeling requirements do channel members have for products of this type?

5. Does your new product appeal to some of the same customers as one of your existing products? Can or should you avoid cannibalizing sales of your existing product(s), given your competitive situation? Think about the product's life cycle as you consider this issue.

6. Will you brand with a company name, individual name, private-label brand, or multiple brands?

Why? Could you better differentiate your product by modifying your brand or cobranding with another organization? Do your product plans fit with your brand's positioning and image? What can you do to make your brand more memorable, distinctive, recognizable, and appealing? Given your brand, your product plans, and the competitive environment, what can you do to boost brand loyalty and make a difference in customers' lives? What role should social media play in your branding decisions?

Endnotes

1. Richard Verrier, "Fandango and Moviefone Dial Up New Partnership," *Los Angeles Times,* May 23, 2012, www.latimes.com.

2. Stephen Betts, "Midcoast Wood Products Firm Finds Success in Catering to Customers' Wishes," *Bangor Daily News (Maine),* August 26, 2012, www.bangordailynews.com; Rupal Parekh, "Personalized Products Please but Can They Create Profit?" *Advertising Age,* May 21, 2012, p. 4; B. Joseph Pine II, "Beyond Mass Customization," *Harvard Business Review,* May 2, 2011, http://blogs /hbr.org.

3. Blair Kamin, "Building Comfort from Within," *Chicago Tribune,* June 8, 2012, www.chicagotribune.com.

4. Ira Boudway, "Fancy Swedish Helmets Coming to a Ski Slope Near You," *Bloomberg Businessweek,* June 7, 2012, www.businessweek.com; Deborah Arthurs, "Is the Airbag in Your Collar the Crash Helmet of the Future?" *Daily Mail (London),* May 1, 2012, www.dailymail.co.uk.

5. Jenni Spinner, "TerraCycle Launches Cigarette Package Recycling," *Packaging Digest,* June 4, 2012, www.packagingdigest.com.

6. Labonita Ghosh, "Green Drive Makes Coca-Cola & Pepsi See Red Once Again," *Economic Times (India),* February 23, 2012, www.economictimes.indiatimes.com.

7. Sheila Shayon, "UPS: Packaging Sustainability for Pearl Jam and You, Too," *BrandChannel,* June 11, 2012, www .brandchannel.com; Eve Troeh, "Brown Goes Green," *Marketplace,* December 19, 2011, www.marketplace.org.

8. Zack Whittaker, "Can RIM Survive Until Blackberry 10?" *ZDNet,* May 29, 2012, www.zdnet.com; Ashley Vance, "H.P. and Palm—P.D.A. Powerhouses Unite," *New York Times,* April 30, 2010, www.nytimes .com; Tom Krazit, "Can a Palm Pre Multitask Better than an iPhone?" *CNet,* May 7, 2009, www.cnet.com.

9. Miguel Helft, "Data, Not Design, Is King in the Age of Google," *New York Times,* May 10, 2009, p. BU-3.

10. Juan C. Perez, "Google to Discontinue Mini Search Appliance, iGoogle, Other Products," *PC World*, July 3, 2012, www.pcworld .com; Christina DesMarais, "Dead Google Products Pile Up," *Inc.,* November 28, 2011, www.inc.com.

11. Vijay Govindarajan, "Reverse Innovation and the Myth of Cannibalization," *Forbes,* April 29, 2012, www.forbes.com.

12. "PepsiCo's Frito-Lay Lines up 50 New Products to Counter Rivals," *Economic Times,* June 12, 2012, http://economictimes .indiatimes.com.

13. "Fans Line up for Limited Edition Kanye West Nikes," *WCIV News (Mount Pleasant, S.C.),* June 11, 2012, www.abcnews4.com; "Just in Time for Summer: Salty Watermelon Pepsi," *WCVB News (Boston),* June 1, 2012, www.wcvb.com; Nicole Carter, "The McRib's Magic Marketing Sauce," *Inc.,* October 25, 2011, www.inc.com; "Burger King Betting on Bacon Sundae," *WCBS News (New York),* June 12, 2012, www .cbsnews.com; "Beijing Auto Show 2012," *Jing Daily,* April 24, 2012, www.jingdaily.com.

14. "Can Unilever's Brand Fit All?" *Marketing,* January 21, 2009, p. 14.

15. Don Reisinger, "Apple Again the World's Most Valuable Brand; Google Third," *CNet,* May 22, 2012, www.cnet.com.

16. Rupal Parekh, "Meet the Woman Behind the Michelin Man," *Advertising Age,* June 11, 2012, www.adage.com.

17. Geoff Colvin, "Can I Help You?" *Fortune,* April 30, 2012, pp. 62–68; John Adams, "American Express Adds Geolocation, Analytics to Its iPhone App," *American Banker,* May 22, 2012, n.p.; Kunur Patel, "AmEx Tests New Ways to Transact in Social Media," *Advertising Age,* May 14, 2012, p. 36; Daniel Wolfe, "Amex Plants Its Digital Wallet in FarmVille," *American Banker,* May 23, 2012, n.p.

18. "The Customer Lifetime Value Equation: Will It Pay Off for Tech Companies?" *Knowledge@Wharton,* December 7, 2011, http://knowledge.wharton.upenn.edu.

19. Won-moo Hur, Minsung Kim, and Younghee Song, "Brand Trust and Affect in the Luxury Brand-Customer Relationship," *Social Behavior and Personality,* March 2012, pp. 331–338.

20. Louise Lucas and Haig Simonian, "Rivals Eye Nestlé's Captive Coffee Market," *Financial Times,* March 9, 2012, www.ft.com; Dermot Doherty, "Nestlé Selling New Coffee Machines as Recipe for Growth," *Bloomberg,* June 4, 2012, www.bloomberg.com.

Developing Pricing Strategy

In this chapter:

PREVIEW

Pricing decisions—formulated during Step 5 of the marketing planning process, as shown in Exhibit 7.1 —are vital because they directly produce revenue, whereas other marketing functions require investments of money, time, and effort. Another reason to give careful attention to pricing is that you can implement such decisions more quickly and at less cost than you can implement changes in the other three marketing-mix components. Depending on developments in the dynamic marketing environment, there will be times when you'll need the ability to change prices on short notice.

In this chapter, you'll learn about customers' perceptions of value and price, how demand operates, and the role of pricing in the marketing plan. Next, you'll see how to set pricing objectives and which internal and external factors can influence pricing decisions. Finally, you'll take a closer look at why and how your marketing plan should address price adaptation, recognizing that effective pricing is both art and science.

APPLYING YOUR KNOWLEDGE

Once you've completed this chapter, answer the questions in "Your Marketing Plan, Step by Step." Also look at the sample plan in this book's appendix and review the checklist as you think about your pricing strategy. Then document decisions about pricing in your marketing plan.

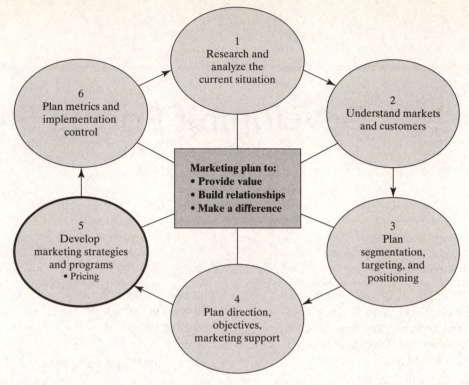

EXHIBIT 7.1 Marketing Planning: Step 5

CHAPTER 7 CHECKLIST   Planning Pricing Strategy

Internal Factors

✓ What do you want your pricing strategy to accomplish for the organization?
✓ How is pricing influenced by positioning, targeting, and the marketing mix?
✓ What are each product's costs, and how do they affect the price floor?
✓ How are different prices likely to affect revenues, sales, and breakeven?

External Factors

✓ How do customers perceive the product's value? Are customers price sensitive?
✓ What are the prices and costs of competing products, and how do they affect price ceilings?
✓ What legal, regulatory, and ethical issues must be considered?

Price Adaptation

✓ What price adaptations are appropriate for achieving pricing objectives?
✓ How do resources, capabilities, goals, and direction affect your flexibility to adapt prices?

UNDERSTANDING VALUE AND PRICING TODAY

PLANNING TIP

Research the key benefits that customers value in order to satisfy needs or solve problems.

In the current climate of economic uncertainty, value has assumed special importance in customers' buying decisions and marketers' plans. As noted in Chapter 1, customers assess the *value* of a product according to the difference between the total perceived benefits they receive and the total perceived price they pay (see Exhibit 7.2). The more weight customers give to benefits in relation to perceived price, the higher the value they perceive in that product. Therefore, as you formulate your marketing plan, prepare to research and analyze value from your customers' perspective; also consider how perceptions of value may be changing and how you will communicate value to your customers.

In practice, customers don't perceive product value in isolation; instead, they look at value in the context of the benefits and the prices of competing or substitute products as well as in the context of the marketing environment. Many customers routinely compare prices by researching online or by using price-comparison apps before they make buying decisions—which affects their value perceptions. Even if customers perceive all products as being priced the same (whether or not their perceptions match reality), no two customers place exactly the same value on the total perceived benefits. To enhance value, your plan should indicate whether you'll add to the perceived benefits (e.g., by improving quality or introducing new features) or reduce the perceived price (e.g., by lowering the purchase price or offering more affordable financing).

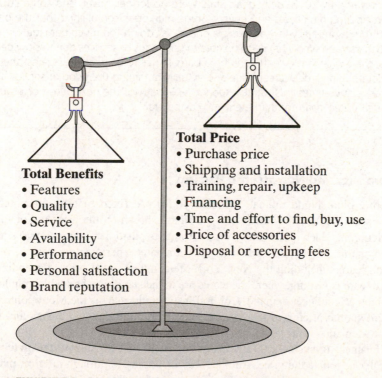

Total Benefits
• Features
• Quality
• Service
• Availability
• Performance
• Personal satisfaction
• Brand reputation

Total Price
• Purchase price
• Shipping and installation
• Training, repair, upkeep
• Financing
• Time and effort to find, buy, use
• Price of accessories
• Disposal or recycling fees

EXHIBIT 7.2   Perceptions of Total Benefits and Total Price

The evolving trend toward group buying and daily deals has changed the value equation in some areas, something to keep in mind as you prepare your plan. By focusing consumers on the purchase price, marketers that invite group buying and work with daily-deals sites face a number of challenges.

Group buying and daily deals. Group buying has been popular in China since 2005. Known locally as *tuangou*, the trend swept the country as consumers formed groups (in person, online, and via smartphone) to use their bargaining power to obtain discounts on everything from TVs to cars. Negotiations with stores and other channel members typically resulted in higher volume and lower margin for the marketer but big savings for the buyers. Meanwhile, daily-deals sites (such as LivingSocial.com) were on the rise in the United States and beyond, offering subscribers deeply discounted goods and services for very limited periods with just a couple of clicks. Soon, niche deal sites sprang up to serve highly targeted segments, such as dog-lovers, "green" buyers, and military personnel. Thousands of daily-deals sites operated by local and global players now serve China and other Asian nations, fueled by rapid adoption of smartphone technology and continued interest in bargain pricing.

Smaller businesses, in particular, originally saw daily-deals sites as a good way to introduce themselves to large numbers of new customers at one time, reasoning that satisfied customers would return to buy at regular prices. The focus on low price, however, risked overshadowing the benefits side of the equation, including the brand equity that comes from long-term loyalty. By 2012, daily-deals sites were no longer novel, and some struggled to attract participating businesses and buyers. Some marketers complained that the pressure to compete through unusually low daily-deals prices was doing too much damage to their profit margins. Others were simply happy to be able to sell goods or services during slow periods. For customers, the excitement of getting in on a bargain has to be weighed against the time and effort of determining a deal's real value and actually obtaining the good or service before the deal expires, a sometimes frustrating experience. What will the next phase of group buying and daily-deals sites mean for marketers and customers?[1]

Fixed, Dynamic, and Negotiated Pricing

Your marketing plan should indicate whether you'll use **fixed pricing**, in which customers pay the price set (fixed) by the marketer—the figure shown on the price tag or the menu—or **dynamic pricing**, in which prices vary from customer to customer or situation to situation. Most airlines use dynamic pricing, and a few sports teams are experimenting with it. Marketers for many baseball teams, including the New York Mets, adjust ticket prices depending on factors such as which team is visiting, where the teams are in the standings, and which pitchers are starting, all of which affect ticket demand. Cultural institutions such as the Metropolitan Opera also are adopting dynamic pricing to increase revenue from high-demand events and to sell more tickets for low-demand events.[2]

Some business-to-business (B2B) marketing plans call for **negotiated pricing**, in which buyer and seller negotiate the price. Another way of pricing is through **auction pricing**, where buyers submit bids to buy goods or services. This type of pricing may occur through a traditional auction (such as those conducted by Sotheby's), an online auction (such as those on eBay), or

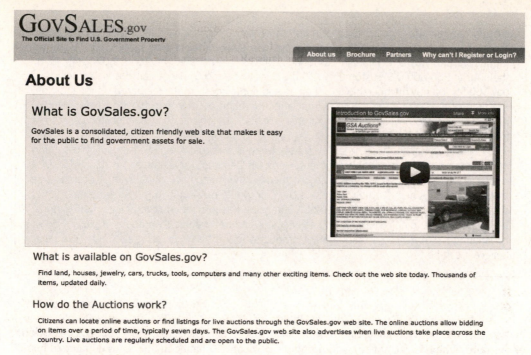

EXHIBIT 7.3   GovSales.gov Auction Site

other types of auctions. Organizations that rely on negotiated or auction pricing can't predict the precise price they will receive for each product, but they should be able to plan for a minimum acceptable price and profit. In marketing government surplus and seized goods, for example, the U.S. government uses online auctions, and it publicizes some auctions on its Facebook page (see Exhibit 7.3).

Customer Perceptions and Demand

When customers act on the basis of their perceptions of price and benefits, their purchases help create demand for a good or service (in combination with supply and other factors). If customers perceive the price to be too high in relation to the benefits, they simply won't buy, which means lower demand. If the total perceived benefits of your offering outweigh the total perceived price, customers are more likely to see the value and buy or rent from you, which helps to increase demand. In fact, rentals are becoming more common in untraditional categories, from couture fashions and workshop tools to fine jewelry and oil paintings. As you work on your marketing plan, consider the possibilities of pricing for rental instead of for purchase, which is what Zipcar does. (To see Zipcar's home page, visit www.zipcar.com or follow the QR code shown here.)

Hourly car rentals. Zipcar, Hertz, and Enterprise now offer hourly rentals (also known as car sharing) as an alternative to vehicle ownership and daily rentals. Zipcar pioneered this pricing model, starting with a few cars in Cambridge, Massachusetts, and now rents 9,000 vehicles by the hour to 500,000 U.S. customers in 15 big cities and on 250 college campuses. Its customers pay $60 for a yearly membership and then an additional hourly rental fee based on the location, the time of day, and other elements that affect demand. Rather than having to visit a rental kiosk, Zipcar customers arrange rentals online or via smartphone, then pick up the car from a neighborhood parking spot.

Hourly rental has become such an attractive business that the niche is rapidly blossoming into an important and profitable segment. Hertz On Demand, for instance, has nearly 100,000 customers who rent by the hour, without membership fees. "We don't want to cannibalize the car rental business," notes Hertz's CEO. "Our whole mission is to get incremental market size out of a new market: hourly rental." Enterprise has purchased several local hourly rental firms and is expanding rapidly, seeing its fleet size and geographic coverage as a plus. "Today, car-sharing has not been a mass market product offering," says Enterprise's CEO. "We really believe it can be."[3]

Careful research can help you determine customers' sensitivity to pricing and the level of demand for a product at different price points. This sensitivity is shown by the **price elasticity of demand**, which is calculated by dividing the percentage change in unit sales demanded by the percentage change in price. When a small price change significantly increases or decreases the number of units demanded, demand is *elastic*; if, for example, you reduced your price by 20%, and wound up selling twice the number of units, you'd know that demand for your product is highly elastic. When a price change doesn't significantly change the number of units demanded, demand is *inelastic*; if you slashed your price by half and your unit sales didn't change, you'd know that demand for your product is highly inelastic. Exhibit 7.4 indicates how different price changes affect demand under elastic and inelastic demand conditions.

Your marketing plan may need to account for testing different price points in order to see how specific segments react before you make a final decision on price. In general, customers tend to be less sensitive to a product's price when:[4]

- They are buying a relatively small amount.
- They are unaware of or can't easily compare substitutes and prices.
- They would incur costs or difficulties in switching products.
- They perceive that the quality, status, or another benefit justifies the price.
- They are spending a relatively small amount or are sharing the cost.
- They perceive the price as fair.
- They are buying products bundled rather than separately.

EXHIBIT 7.4   How Pricing Affects Demand

Change in Price	Under Inelastic Demand	Under Elastic Demand
Small increase	Demand drops slightly	Demand drops significantly
Small reduction	Demand rises slightly	Demand rises significantly

Customers' price sensitivity and perceptions of value also can be used to deal with imbalances of supply and demand, which is what some major U.S. cities are doing with metered parking rates. What lessons about pricing can you apply to your offerings?

Pricing big-city parking spaces. On both coasts, and in between, major cities are dealing with high demand for downtown parking spots by adjusting hourly meter rates so that drivers pay more to park in the busiest areas or at the busiest times. Los Angeles has hiked the fee for parking in a prime city location to $6 an hour or more during peak periods and has reduced the price for little-used spaces to 50 cents an hour during low-demand times. To keep pace with recent trends, the city analyzes supply and demand every month or two and changes rates accordingly.

Similarly, San Francisco has raised the price of its most in-demand parking spaces and lowered the price on emptier streets. The purpose isn't just to bring in revenue but also to affect consumer behavior by encouraging drivers to park in a less-busy area, increasing the possibility that at least one spot will be available on the most popular streets. New York City prices metered parking higher in the most congested Manhattan neighborhoods and also charges commercial vehicles more than personal vehicles to park. The result is higher city revenue and more efficient use of limited downtown parking space.[5]

Value-Based Pricing

Researching and analyzing how customers perceive the value of a product should be the first step in formulating an appropriate pricing strategy to build demand and meet internal objectives. Nagle and Hogan[6] note that this is not the typical approach to pricing. The most common way is to start with the product and its cost, set a price that covers the cost plus a particular percentage for profit, and then communicate the value to customers.

The membership retailer Costco does this, "based on the idea that a business can operate on a fair markup and still pay all of its bills," says one executive. Pricing "is determined by carefully examining true costs, and profits are maintained by stringently controlling costs."[7] Costco tries not to raise prices as product costs go up. As an alternative, as the cost of living goes up and depending on the rate of inflation, it will raise membership fees every five or six years.[8] Although cost-based pricing works well for Costco, it fails to take into account how customers perceive the value of the offering.

In contrast, the starting point for **value-based pricing** is research about customers' perceptions of value and the price they are willing to pay.[9] Then the company finds ways of making the product at a reasonable cost (**target costing**) in order to return a reasonable profit or to achieve other marketing plan objectives based on the value price. Increasingly, businesses are using target costing to incorporate the impact of sustainability, such as costs for recycling and renewable energy, when they work on product design.

Consider how IKEA, the global home furnishings retailer headquartered in Sweden, planned value-based pricing for its Uppleva product line. (IKEA's worldwide home page is at www.ikea.com; you can also follow the QR code to see it.)

IKEA Uppleva. With nearly 300 stores in 26 nations, IKEA is one of the world's best-known and most popular stores for home products, selling everything from bunk beds to bathroom accessories and beyond. Because the company designs and manufactures the furniture sold in its stores, it can keep a tight rein on the entire supply chain. IKEA's marketers start by analyzing the features and benefits that customers most value in a product category. Next, they formulate pricing for specific products based on this analysis and use target costing to control expenses during the manufacturing process. Products come packed flat for customers to assemble at home, another key way to keep prices down.

When researching the market for home entertainment centers, IKEA's marketers learned that customers were dissatisfied with existing products because the "electronics didn't match the style of the furniture, that there were too many remotes, too many cables, and so on," explains an IKEA executive. In response, IKEA teamed up with TCL, a Hong Kong–based electronics firm, to develop the Uppleva line of furniture, which integrates a flat-screen TV, Blu-ray DVD player, CD player, and speaker system—value-priced at about $1,000. The wiring and hardware are discreetly hidden, putting the focus on the sleek furniture and matching TV screen (available in various sizes). "This is a new way of working that integrates the electronics in the furniture," the executive says, noting that customers prefer a complete, one-price solution of built-in products instead of separate boxes perched on shelves and connected by a tangle of wires.[10]

From a strategic perspective, price decisions must be value based, profit driven, and proactive. In other words, simply reacting to the market is not an effective approach; you must proactively develop appropriate pricing strategies based on how customers perceive value and how your firm can profitably achieve its objectives through pricing.[11]

PLANNING PRICING DECISIONS

When planning pricing, first determine what the strategy is intended to achieve, given the marketing, financial, and societal objectives in your marketing plan (see Exhibit 7.5). Also investigate the various external influences (customers, competitors, channel members, and legal, regulatory, and ethical concerns) and internal influences (costs and breakeven, targeting and positioning strategy, product strategy, and other marketing decisions) that can affect your pricing decisions.

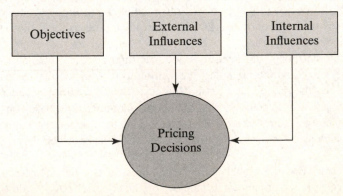

EXHIBIT 7.5   Influences on Pricing Decisions

Pricing Objectives

Because a product's price is the organization's source of revenue, you should establish specific objectives for all pricing decisions. These objectives must be consistent with each other and with the overall mission, direction, goals, and marketing plan objectives. Remember that you may have to trade off one pricing objective for another. Rarely can a company boost profitability while simultaneously raising its market share to a much higher level, for example.

In some industries, one additional percentage point of market share can translate into millions of dollars in higher sales, which is why certain companies put share ahead of profit when setting pricing objectives. Over the long term, however, companies cannot survive without profits. Exhibit 7.6 shows a number of pricing objectives that firms may set in their marketing plans.

External Pricing Influences

Many factors outside the organization—and outside its control—come into play when making decisions about pricing. In addition to customers, pricing can be influenced by competitors, channel members, and legal, regulatory, and ethical considerations. Because not every external influence is equally important for each product, targeted segment, or market, carefully analyze each within the context of other marketing plan decisions and the organization's situation.

CUSTOMERS   Perceptions of value, behavior, and attitudes all affect a customer's reaction to pricing. Customers are generally willing to buy a good or service if the price falls within a range they view as acceptable for that type of offering. This suggests that consumer marketers have some pricing latitude if they stay within the accepted range or change the product to change its perceived value. Even digital items such as virtual game characters with special powers have value and therefore can be priced. The price may be only a dollar or two, but revenues can add up as more people buy virtual products.[12]

Economic reverses may slow but don't eliminate *conspicuous consumption,* the purchasing of goods or services to convey the buyer's importance, wealth, or status, as luxury marketers have found. Many low- and middle-income consumers switch to generic or low-priced products when their incomes are squeezed, but consumers intent on signaling their status have continued loading up on luxury, for example, adding to the profits of France's LVMH. (Follow the QR to see LVMH's home page or go to www.lvmh.com.)

EXHIBIT 7.6   Sample Pricing Objectives

Type of Objective	Sample Pricing Objectives
Financial	• For profitability: Set prices to achieve gross profit margin of 27% on this year's sales. • For return on investment: Set prices to achieve full-year ROI of 13%.
Marketing	• For higher market share: Set prices to achieve a market share increase of 3% within six months.
Societal	• For charitable fund-raising: Set prices to net $5 per item for donation to chosen cause.

LVMH. Despite the recent recession, consumers worldwide are still spending an estimated $1.4 trillion every year on luxury experiences, luxury vehicles, and high-end products such as jewelry and handbags. Louis Vuitton Moet Hennessey (LVMH) has long been part of this luxury trend. The company markets carefully crafted, top-quality goods and services in such categories as clothing, luggage, and vacation resorts under dozens of exclusive brands.

In the past few years, LVMH has tripled the number of Louis Vuitton stores in China, where expensive designer brands are particularly prized as status symbols. In fact, buyers in China will pay up to 40% more for a Louis Vuitton item than buyers in Europe, reflecting high demand and the brand's special allure. LVMH supports its high-profile brands and upscale positioning through all of its marketing-mix decisions. For example, it ensures that the Louis Vuitton stores deliver the same high level of personalized service that customers expect from the luxury brand.[13]

In business markets, customers frequently search for the lowest price to minimize their organizational costs, and some switch suppliers constantly to pay less for parts, materials, components, or services. If you're targeting business or institutional buyers, remember that globalization has only increased choices and opportunities to obtain better prices. Rather than emphasizing low prices, you may want to join the many B2B marketers who build relationships by communicating benefits such as how the product saves money in the long run or how it enhances quality.

PLANNING TIP

Research how customers perceive the benefits and costs of competing products.

COMPETITORS   Customer behavior is one external clue to an acceptable price range (the ceiling, in particular). The competitive situation provides another external clue. By analyzing the prices, special deals, and probable costs of competing products, you get a better sense of the alternatives that are available to customers and get insight into your competitors' pricing objectives and strategies. To illustrate, as the economy struggled, McDonald's and other fast-food chains highlighted special low-priced menu items, which in turn increased the pressure to compete on the basis of price. More recently, however, the chains began trying to shift the emphasis from pricing to quality and variety. McDonald's added fresh and seasonal salads, and Taco Bell introduced the Cantina Burrito Bowl and other items to attract new customers and bring existing customers back more often. Over time, the chains are limiting the number of budget-priced items but are adding higher-priced items to broaden the range of price points across their menus.[14]

Pricing is a highly visible competitive tool in many industries, often exerting downward pressure on profits and limiting pricing options. Yet, no two companies have exactly the same objectives, resources, costs, and situations, which means competitors cannot simply copy each other's pricing. Marketers need not always match or beat competitors' prices, but they do have to ensure that their product's price fits into the value equation as perceived by customers and makes economic sense for the company.

CHANNEL MEMBERS   Companies that reach customers through wholesalers or retailers must take into account these intermediaries' pricing expectations and marketing objectives. Changes in a channel member's pricing can have a significant influence on its suppliers.

A sample progression of how a consumer product might be priced by the producer, wholesaler, and retailer is in Exhibit 7.7. In this sample, the producer charges the wholesaler $20 for the product and the wholesaler sells it to the retailer for $24, which is 20% above the producer's

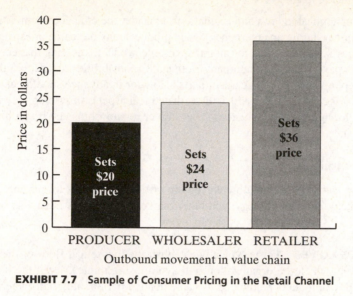

EXHIBIT 7.7   Sample of Consumer Pricing in the Retail Channel

price. The retailer sells the product to the consumer for $36, which is 50% above the price paid by the retailer and 80% above the price paid by the wholesaler.

Of course, the actual number of participants in the channel will vary according to product, industry, market, and segment, affecting the prices paid by intermediaries and the ultimate customer. Note that when a participant performs more functions or enhances the product in a unique way, it may be able to set a higher price (and make more profit) because its immediate customers perceive more value in the offering. Also consider the effect of the Internet and mobile marketing on your product's channel pricing. In many categories, wholesale and retail prices are coming down, thanks to more efficient transaction capabilities, convenient price comparisons, and more intense competition between online-only businesses and channel members with physical stores. Amazon.com's online dominance has affected the pricing decisions of book publishers and retailers, among other marketers.

LEGAL, REGULATORY, AND ETHICAL CONCERNS   Whether planning for domestic or international marketing, all companies need to comply with a variety of pricing laws and regulations. In the United States and many other areas, competing firms are not allowed to collude in setting prices and are not allowed to take other anticompetitive pricing actions. The United States also outlaws predatory pricing—the aggressive use of low pricing to damage a competitor or to reduce competition.

In addition, a company usually cannot charge different prices for essentially the same product at the same time in the same market unless the lower price is available through discounts or allowances that are open to all. However, different prices may be allowed if the company has different costs, is responding to competition, or is clearing outdated merchandise. Your marketing plan should also account for any legal limits on the highest price that can be charged for certain products; Canada, for instance, sets a ceiling on prices of prescription drugs. In some industries, including financial services, marketers must be sure pricing disclosures comply with special rules requiring particular formats or definitions. For transparency purposes, some marketers go beyond standard disclosures to offer additional information or to explain terms and conditions in simple language.

Apart from applicable laws and regulations, consider the ethical dilemmas in pricing. Is it ethical to raise prices during an emergency, when products may be scarce or especially valuable? Should a company set a high price for an indispensable product, knowing that certain customers will be unable to pay? What are a company's ethical responsibilities regarding full disclosure of prices for upkeep, updates, or replacement parts? How far in advance should customers be notified of planned price increases? As difficult as the ethical aspects of pricing may be, you should carefully think through the consequences for customer relationships and brand image when you prepare your plan.

Internal Pricing Influences

Within the organization, costs and breakeven are critical influences on pricing. Targeting and positioning strategy, product strategy, and other marketing decisions must also be factored into pricing plans.

COSTS AND BREAKEVEN   Costs typically establish the theoretical floor of the pricing range, the lowest price at which the organization will avoid losing money. Even the largest company can't afford to price products below cost for an extended period, although (where legal) it may do so to combat a competitive threat or to achieve another objective over a limited period. Cost containment is, in fact, a high priority for many companies today, not just to achieve quarterly profit targets but also to prepare for future market conditions.

For planning purposes, you'll need to know your costs and how to calculate the **breakeven point**—the level of sales at which revenue covers costs. Costs and breakeven are more easily calculated for existing products in existing market segments, because you can use historical results as a basis for future projections. For new products and segments, you'll usually rely on research-based forecasts and expert estimates of costs and sales volume (see Chapter 10). When detailed or timely information is unavailable, make an educated guess about costs as you plan.

PLANNING TIP

If you don't know your costs, estimate for now and start tracking costs for next year's plan.

The total cost of a product consists of *fixed costs*—overhead expenses such as rent and payroll, which do not vary with volume—plus *variable costs*—expenses such as raw materials, which do vary with volume. Fixed costs for an airline include airport space; variable costs include fuel and meals. Airlines look carefully at every cost, down to the penny. Why? Because pennies add up for businesses that provide services to large numbers of people every day, day after day. Delta Airlines estimates that a 1¢-per-gallon increase in jet fuel translates to an extra $40 million in fuel costs over a full year.[15] This is why marketing plans must include product cost details.

Once you know your product's costs, you can calculate the average cost of producing a single item (total costs divided by production) at various output levels, corresponding to different assumptions about demand. This reveals cost changes at a number of output levels and indicates how low the company might price the product at each level to at least cover its costs. Next, calculate the breakeven point to see how many units must be sold to cover total costs. The formula for the breakeven volume is as follows:

$$\text{Breakeven volume} = \frac{\text{Fixed cost}}{\text{Price} - \text{Variable cost}}$$

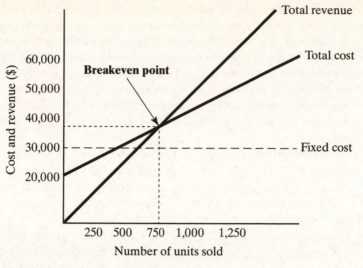

EXHIBIT 7.8 Breakeven Analysis

Exhibit 7.8 illustrates a sample breakeven analysis for a company that manufactures decorative bowls. In this example, the price per unit is $50, the variable cost per unit is $10, and the fixed cost totals $30,000. Thus, the calculation is as follows:

$$\text{Breakeven volume} = \frac{30,000}{50 - 10} = \frac{30,000}{40} = 750 \text{ units}$$

When the company sells 750 units at $50 each, its revenue will be $37,500, the point on the graph in Exhibit 7.8 where the total cost and total revenue cross. Selling more than 750 units will result in profit.

TARGETING AND POSITIONING STRATEGY   A product's price must be appropriate for the organization's targeting and positioning strategy. To illustrate, because Dollar General targets the segment of price-sensitive shoppers, charging high prices would be inconsistent with its targeting (and would alienate customers). Conversely, if the luxury goods manufacturer Louis Vuitton put low price tags on its handbags, the target segment of affluent consumers would question the products' positioning as symbols of status, style, and quality. In fact, Vuitton refuses to mark down its handbags for clearance, on the basis that low pricing would conflict with the positioning.[16]

PRODUCT STRATEGY   Marketers should not only examine every pricing decision in the context of costs, targeting, and positioning, they should also set prices in line with their product strategy. In particular, pricing can be used to manage the product's movement through the life cycle:

- *Introduction.* Some companies use **skim pricing**, pricing a new product high to establish a top-quality image or to highlight unique value and more quickly recover development costs in line with profitability objectives. Apple does this with its iPad tablet computers. Other marketers prefer **penetration pricing**, pricing products relatively low to penetrate

the market more quickly. Chobani used penetration pricing to launch its Greek yogurts in supermarket chains, instead of pricing them high and distributing them through health-food stores. The result: Chobani built a $1 billion business in only five years.[17] These two approaches are compared in Exhibit 7.9. (Visit Chobani's home page at http://chobani.com or follow the QR code to see it.)

- *Growth.* Pricing is important for competitive strategy during the growth stage, when rival products challenge the new product or service. During growth, companies also use pricing to stimulate demand while moving toward the breakeven point.

- *Maturity.* With sales growth slowing, companies can use pricing to defend market share, retain customers, pursue profitability, or expand into additional channels. In Indonesia, Unilever holds market-leading positions in tea, personal-care products, and other categories. Now that these products are mature, Unilever is introducing lower-priced versions to attract new customers and defend share among current customers.[18]

- *Decline.* Pricing can help clear older or outdated products to make way for new ones, stimulate sales to prevent or at least slow a product's decline, or maximize profits. Yet prices do not necessarily drop during decline: Scarcity may make a product more valuable to certain customers and therefore justify a higher price.

Moreover, pricing is vital for managing the strategy of products in a single line and in the overall mix. After researching customers' perceptions, marketers may set different prices to signal the value of the features and benefits of different products and to differentiate among multiple lines and brands in the product portfolio. The U.K. supermarket chain Tesco, for example, offers various private-label food brands such as Tesco Finest, Everyday Value, and Tesco Standard, using pricing to signal quality and value.

Sometimes a marketing plan calls for pricing one product to encourage purchases of other products in the line or mix. The classic case involves razors and replacement blade cartridges, such as those marketed by Gillette. (To see Gillette's home page, go to www.gillette.com or scan the QR code on page 127.)

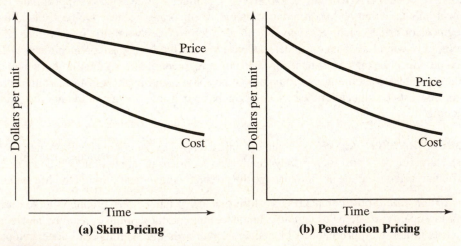

(a) Skim Pricing   **(b) Penetration Pricing**

EXHIBIT 7.9   **Skim Pricing and Penetration Pricing**

Source: Roger J. Best, *Market-Based Management,* 6th ed. (Upper Saddle River, NJ: Pearson Prentice Hall, 2013), Fig. 8-16 on p. 285 and Fig. 8-17 on p. 286.

Gillette. Gillette recently began emphasizing that its ProGlide razor blade cartridge will last up to five weeks. What's surprising is that for decades, Gillette focused much more on razor technology and the benefits of close, comfortable shaves than on the life of a blade cartridge. But now, with the price of blade cartridges rising, competing on the basis of the *number* of blade edges is not as effective as educating consumers about the long life of a single cartridge. "One of the things we wanted to do was to help reframe the value perception of our brand," says a Gillette official.

This message got buyers to pay attention to how many shaves they can get before they have to replace the cartridge in the razor they use—whether it's Gillette or a competing brand. Meanwhile, viral videos featuring low-cost blades, sometimes sold through subscription offers, have kept the spotlight on cartridge prices and have put competitive pressure on Gillette. Because Gillette's market share in razor cartridges slipped slightly during the recent economic turmoil, the company (owned by Procter & Gamble) is particularly eager for consumers to understand exactly how much value its replacement cartridges actually represent.[19]

OTHER MARKETING DECISIONS   The marketing plan's direction will strongly influence the organization's pricing strategy. For survival, the organization's prices should cover costs at the very least; for bankruptcy, organizations can use pricing to liquidate stock and raise money quickly. For aggressive growth, the company may decide to set prices that return slim or no-profit margins in the short run.

Pricing is also influenced by decisions about suppliers and logistics. In terms of promotion strategy, higher-priced products aimed at higher-income customer segments are often promoted in different media and with different messages than lower-priced products aimed at lower-income segments. Finally, pricing is a big challenge for companies that market through personal selling, especially when customers expect to negotiate prices with salespeople. This is why many companies train sales personnel in profitability requirements and set a floor for price negotiation to prevent sales that generate little or no profit.

Adapting Prices

If internal factors suggest the price floor and external factors suggest the price ceiling, price adaptation helps companies modify and fine-tune prices within an acceptable range—or even beyond. Marketers may use price adaptation to make the following types of changes in support of their objectives:

- *Discounts.* Many companies offer quantity discounts for buying in volume and seasonal discounts for buying out of season. Business customers also may earn a cash discount for prompt payment; intermediaries may earn a functional discount when they perform specific channel functions for a producer.
- *Allowances.* Wholesalers and retailers may receive discounts, extra payments, or extra product allocations for participating in special promotions. Some companies offer trade-in allowances for businesses or consumers who bring in older products and buy newer ones.
- *Bundling or unbundling.* You may enhance customer perceptions of value by bundling one product with one or more goods or services at a single price. Unbundling can be used if the bundle price is perceived as too high and individual products will sell well on their own. Unbundled pricing of airfares has caused some complaints, however, because

customers resent having to pay extra for everything from checked luggage to seats in exit rows.[20] Keep such reactions in mind when you decide whether to bundle or unbundle.

- **Product enhancement.** Enhancing the product to raise its perceived value can help the company maintain the current price or perhaps increase the price.
- **Segment pricing.** Pricing may be adapted for certain customer segments, such as a children's menu (segmenting by family composition), a senior discount (segmenting by age), or a delivery charge (segmenting by need for service). State Farm and other auto insurance firms offer college students a discount on insurance premiums if they have good grades, for example.[21]

Specific pricing tactics can help marketers achieve specific marketing or financial objectives. Loss-leader pricing, for instance, with popular or new items priced near cost, is a common way to build store or website traffic. Objectives for customer acquisition might be supported by short-term pricing cuts or by tactics that temporarily enhance value, such as low interest rates during select periods. The chosen adaptation depends on the company's resources and capabilities, its goals and strategic direction, and its marketing plan objectives.

PLANNING TIP

Consider which adaptations are traditional—and nontraditional—in your industry or channel.

Be sure your plan accounts for the short-term and long-term effects of price competition. If every company matches or beats the price of its rivals and a price war ensues, customers will soon perceive few if any differences between offers and will become less brand-loyal. Smaller brands sometimes touch off price wars to capture customers' attention and encourage switching. This happened in Tasmania not long ago, when United dropped the price of gasoline and bigger brands followed suit to avoid losing customers.[22] At the very least, your marketing plan should anticipate the possibility of a price war and include your thoughts about how to respond.

Summary

From a customer's perspective, value is the difference between the total perceived benefits and the total perceived price of a product. Marketers care about customers' price perceptions because they influence demand. Price elasticity indicates customers' price sensitivity. Marketers can use fixed, dynamic, negotiated, or auction pricing. Value-based pricing rather than cost-based pricing is preferred as the basis of a pricing strategy that will drive demand and satisfy company objectives.

As you plan pricing strategy, determine what you want to achieve in the context of the marketing plan's marketing, financial, and societal objectives. Next, factor in key external influences (customers, competitors, channel members, and legal, regulatory, and ethical concerns) and key internal influences (costs and breakeven, targeting and positioning strategy, product strategy, and other marketing decisions) when making pricing decisions. Finally, consider when and how to adapt prices.

Your Marketing Plan, Step by Step

Answer the following questions as you work on the pricing part of your marketing plan.

1. Look at the marketing plan objectives you've set. How will pricing move you closer to those objectives? What, specifically, do you want to accomplish through pricing? List at least two objectives for your pricing strategy, checking to be sure that they don't conflict with your other objectives or with your targeting and positioning decisions.

2. List the elements that contribute to your offering's total benefits and total price, as shown in Exhibit 7.2. Be sure to include elements that aren't obvious, such as the benefit of status. Now do the same for your top three competitors. How do their offerings and prices compare with yours? For planning purposes, how can you research customers' perceptions of your offer's value versus the value of competing offers?

3. What do you know about the price elasticity of demand for offerings such as yours? What public information can you find about the reaction when the prices of competing offers (or goods/services in this category) have increased or decreased? What are the current and projected trends of supply in your industry? What do you know or suspect about the price sensitivity of customers in your targeted segment(s)? What are the implications for your pricing decisions and your marketing mix?

4. What expectations or customs of channel members must you factor into your thinking about pricing for your offer? For instance, do wholesalers or retailers typically expect a certain profit margin from the sale of products such as yours? Should pricing be adapted to accommodate seasonal demand or promotions in your channel? What legal, regulatory, and ethical concerns apply to your pricing strategy?

5. Do you know or can you estimate your fixed costs, variable costs, and total costs? Are those costs likely to change during the period covered by your plan? If so, how and why? Using the formula for calculating breakeven volume, can you estimate the sales level you must achieve to cover your costs? How does this level relate to the objectives in your marketing plan?

6. If you're introducing a new good or service, will you use skimming or penetration pricing, and why? If your product is in a later stage of its life cycle, how will you use pricing? When, how, and how often should you adapt your price to achieve your pricing objectives? Be sure to calculate the effect of price adaptation on projected sales and profits. Also consider whether price or nonprice competition makes sense for your marketing situation. Finally, write a few lines about what you might do if a competitor slashes its price and you're forced to respond.

Endnotes

1. Brad Tuttle, "A Deal Just for You," *Time,* February 9, 2012, http://moneyland.time.com; Rachel Konig Beals, "Top Complaints About Daily Deal Sites," *U.S. News and World Report,* January 10, 2012, http://money.usnews.com; Tae-Hyung Kim, Kevin Lam, and Christopher Tsai, "The Groupon Effect in China," *Knowledge@Wharton,* January 3, 2012, http://knowledge.wharton.upenn.edu.

2. Will Leitch, "Mets Season Preview: What Is This Dynamic Pricing Thing the Mets Are Doing?" *New York Magazine,* March 28, 2012, www.nymag.com; Jennifer Maloney, "The Met Orchestrates Price Changes," *Wall Street Journal,* February 24, 2012, www.wsj.com.

3. Mark Clothier, "Zipcar Now Sees Enterprise in Rear Window," *Bloomberg,* June 5, 2012, www.bloomberg.com; Mark Clothier, "Can Hertz Outrun Zipcar in Hourly Car Rentals?" *Bloomberg Businessweek,* March 29, 2012, www.businessweek.com.

4. Thomas T. Nagle and John E. Hogan, *The Strategy and Tactics of Pricing,* 4th ed. (Upper Saddle River, NJ: Prentice Hall, 2006), p. 130.

5. Henry Goldman, "NYC Seeks Company to Run 90,000 Parking Spots," *Bloomberg News,* June 11, 2012, www.bloomberg.com; Michael Cooper and Jo Craven McGinty, "A Meter So Expensive, It Creates Parking Spots," *New York Times,* March 15, 2012, www.nytimes.com; "Downtown L.A. Parking Fees to Rise, Fall with Demand," *Los Angeles Times,* May 18, 2012, www.latimes.com.

6. Thomas T. Nagle and John E. Hogan, *The Strategy and Tactics of Pricing,* 4th ed. (Upper Saddle River, NJ: Prentice Hall, 2006), Chapter 1.

7. "From the Editor's Desk," *The Costco Connection,* March 2009, p. 5.

8. Personal communication with Costco, August, 2012.

9. Dhruv Grewal, Anne L. Roggeveen, Larry D. Compeau, and Michael Levy, "Retail Value-Based Pricing Strategies: New Times, New Technologies, New Consumers," *Journal of Retailing,* March 2012, pp. 1–6.

10. Kim McLaughlin, "IKEA Plans TV Sales as Home-Entertainment Range Started," *Bloomberg,* June 15, 2012, www.bloomberg.com; Emma Rowley, "IKEA to Sell TVs and Sound Systems," *The Telegraph Online (UK),* April 17, 2012, n.p.; Mark Wilson, "IKEA's Biggest Product Launch in Years," *Fast Company Design,* April 23, 2012, www.fastcodesign.com.

11. Thomas T. Nagle and John E. Hogan, *The Strategy and Tactics of Pricing,* 4th ed. (Upper Saddle River, NJ: Prentice Hall, 2006), pp. 8–9.

12. Nick Wingfield, "Virtual Products, Real Profits," *Wall Street Journal,* September 9, 2011, www.wsj.com; Rob Walker, "Immaterialism," *New York Times Magazine,* May 3, 2009, p. 28.

13. Michael Witt, "Will Chinese Consumers' Love for Luxury Eventually Wane?" *Economic Times (India),* June 8, 2012, www.economictimes.indiatimes.com; Georgia Wilkins, "Luxury Knows No Bounds," *Sydney Morning Herald (Australia),* June 7, 2012, www.smh.com.au; Michael Wright and Peter Evans, "Asia Remains Engine for European Luxury Goods," *Wall Street Journal,* May 31, 2012, www.wsj.com.

14. Bruce Schreiner, "Fast-Food Chain Taco Bell Going More Upscale with New Menu Introductions," *Minneapolis Star-Tribune,* June 6, 2012, www.startribune.com; Brad Tuttle, "McDonald's Dollar Menu Shakeup," *Time,* March 8, 2012, www.time.com.

15. Kelly Yamanouchi, "Airlines Keep Adapting to High Fuel Costs," *Atlanta Journal-Constitution,* March 4, 2012, www.ajc.com.

16. Carol Matlack, "The Vuitton Machine," *Business Week,* March 22, 2004, pp. 98+.

17. Katy Steinmetz, "Smooth Operator: How Chobani Spread Greek Yogurt Across America," *Time,* June 25, 2012, pp. 70–71.

18. Raras Cahyafitri, "Unilever Maintains Market Dominance," *Jakarta Post,* May 30, 2012, www.thejakartapost.com.

19. Scott Cendrowski, "How Long Does a Razor Really Last?" *Fortune,* June 7, 2012, http://management.fortune.cnn.com; Adam Gordon, "Gillette Finds Rhyme and Maybe Reason with Reduce-Reuse Message," *Forbes,* June 14, 2012, www.forbes.com; Alexander Chernev, "Rethinking Gillette's Pricing with Dollar Shave's Disruptive Innovation," *Bloomberg Businessweek,* April 10, 2012, www.businessweek.com; Ben Popken, "Does Dollar Shave Really Save?" *Smart Money,* April 20, 2012, www.smartmoney.com.

20. Bill Saporito, "Skyway Robbery!" *Time,* June 13, 2011, pp. 90–91.

21. Penny Gusner, "The Good Student Car Insurance Discount," *Fox Business,* June 14, 2012, www.foxbusiness.com.

22. Matt Smith, "Petrol Price War Arrives," *Mercury (Tasmania),* May 31, 2012, www.themercury.com.au.

Developing Channel and Logistics Strategy

In this chapter:

PREVIEW

Decisions about how, when, and where to distribute your goods and services—whether digitally, in stores, or via overnight delivery—are all part of Step 5 of the marketing planning process (see Exhibit 8.1). In this chapter, you'll explore connections and flows in the value chain and learn to analyze how various participants add value to the offering. You'll also explore the major influences on channel strategy and the decisions you must make about channel functions, levels, and members. Finally, you'll look at decisions to be made in formulating logistics strategy, including how to approach transportation, storage, inventory management, and other functions vital to marketing.

APPLYING YOUR KNOWLEDGE

After reading this chapter, review the channel and logistics entries in this book's sample plan. Next, answer the questions in "Your Marketing Plan, Step by Step," at the end of this chapter, and consider the issues mentioned in this chapter's checklist. This will help you make decisions about your distribution and logistics, which you should document in your written plan.

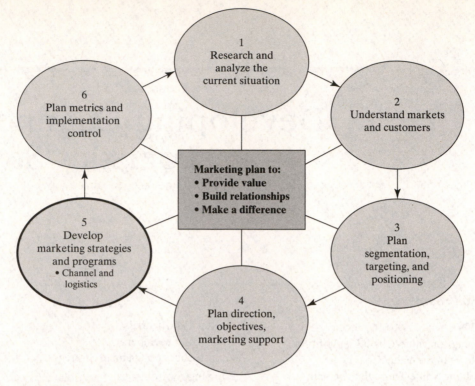

EXHIBIT 8.1 Marketing Planning: Step 5

CHAPTER 8 CHECKLIST   Channel and Logistical Issues

Channel Issues

✓ How do goals and objectives, resources, direction, need for control, and marketing-mix decisions affect channel choices?

✓ Which channels and members perform the best, and at what cost to the organization?

✓ How do product characteristics and life cycle, positioning, targeting, market issues, and competitive factors affect channel choices and costs?

✓ How do customers expect or prefer to gain access to the product, and what is the impact on channel decisions?

Logistical Issues

✓ What logistical functions must be performed and by which channel members?

✓ How do production- and sales-related objectives affect logistical plans?

✓ How are logistics affected by customer needs/preferences, channel/company capabilities, product plans, and marketing plan objectives?

PLANNING FOR VALUE-CHAIN FLEXIBILITY

All goods and services are marketed as part of a **value chain**—also known as a *supply chain*—a series of interrelated, value-added functions that get the right product to the right markets and customers at the right time, place, and price. For the product to reach its intended market, each function must be performed—and the choice of who should handle each function will be documented in the marketing plan.

PLANNING TIP

Think ahead: Altering channel arrangements can be difficult and time consuming.

The marketer (shown as "producer" in Exhibit 8.2) manages supplier relationships and logistics on the inbound side to obtain the inputs (such as parts, shipment dates, and cost figures) needed for creating goods and services. On the outbound or demand side, the marketer manages logistics and **channels** (also called *distribution channels*), the functions that allow it to meet demand by making a product available to customers in each market. During the planning process, marketers need to analyze how value is added at each connection in this chain, from inputs on the inbound side to finished products moving outbound to the point at which customers pay and take possession, and then decide whether to handle the functions internally or to contract for outsiders to do the work.

To illustrate, Godiva, a gourmet chocolate marketer, buys chocolate, vanilla, nuts, and other ingredients from suppliers around the world (the suppliers add value inbound, as depicted in Exhibit 8.2). The company produces its luxury chocolates in its own facilities and then uses temperature-controlled shipments to deliver the chocolates to its own stores, to other retailers, and to consumers who buy directly from Godiva's catalog or website. The ability to operate its own stores is especially important in China, where Godiva supports its image by being one of the few chocolatiers to sell through upscale boutiques rather than through grocery stores.[1]

As you plan, remember that the value chain you have today may not be the same as the one you'll need tomorrow, depending on internal and external developments. Whether you're developing a marketing plan for a retailer, a manufacturer, or another kind of marketer, be aware that you have the long-term option of changing the players in your value chain and/or changing the way each adds value. You might want to bring some functions in-house to gain more control or for other purposes. Apple did this when it opened its very successful chain of Apple Stores so that it could control every aspect of the in-store experience, from merchandise display to service support. Now Walmart and some other retailers authorized to sell Apple products are creating special "store within the store" departments to display only Apple products and related accessories.[2]

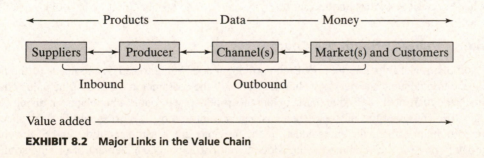

EXHIBIT 8.2 **Major Links in the Value Chain**

Consider whether an outside player might give you the flexibility to manage certain value-chain functions more efficiently or effectively than your organization. For example, some businesses are choosing an Amazon Marketplace storefront instead of setting up their own e-commerce website. As another example, some record labels are coping with the transition from physical distribution of CDs to distribution of electronic music files by hiring an outside firm to manage the digital side. Universal Music Group has contracted with INgrooves for digital distribution in North America, a function that includes formatting digital music for specific download systems and getting it to streaming services, online retailers, and other channel members.[3] Although such distribution arrangements may change in the future, right now they help the record labels keep up with technological changes in the way customers buy music.

Flows in the Value Chain

PLANNING TIP

Diagram the value chain to see where value is added and to find areas for improvement.

Channel and logistics strategy involves managing three value-chain flows. The *flow of products* refers to physical items such as raw materials and product packaging (on the inbound side), finished products (on the outbound side), plus other items that move from outbound to inbound (such as products returned for repair). The *flow of data* refers to information such as the number of items ordered (moving inbound or outbound), customer requirements and feedback (passed along from channel members or directly from customer to producer), and other information that adds value through effectiveness and efficiency. The *flow of money* refers to payments for supplies (on the inbound side), reseller or customer payments for finished goods (on the outbound side), and other money movements between participants. Map the flows in your value chain so your marketing plan will cover the movement of all three flows in both directions, and note places where flows may skip some participants.

The inbound side of the value chain is always business to business (B2B). For example, Dancing Deer, which makes cakes, cookies, and brownies, is a business customer to the suppliers that sell it chocolate, butter, and other ingredients. After producing its baked goods, Boston-based Dancing Deer makes them available to customers through its website and through selected specialty stores, all part of the outbound channel. New product information and other details flow between producer and suppliers as well as between producer and its outbound channel partners. Dancing Deer also uses Facebook and other social media to exchange information with customers. Finally, money flows from producer to suppliers and from markets/customers to channel partners to producer. (To view Dancing Deer's home page, follow this QR code or visit www.dancingdeer.com.)

Adding Value Through the Chain

As you plan, take into account how each participant adds value to satisfy the needs of the next link (the immediate customer) as well as the needs of the customer at the end of the value chain. Thus, the department stores that market Godiva's products will put its chocolates on display and have sufficient quantities in stock when customers want to buy. The price paid by each successive participant reflects the value added by the previous link; customers at the end of the chain ultimately pay for the combined value added by all participants, an element of pricing strategy that was discussed in Chapter 7.

Think creatively about the functions that must be performed at every stage of the chain, which participant will perform each function, and how each participant will be paid. This is true for services as well as for physical goods. The marketing plan for the Metropolitan Opera's HD Live broadcasts shows how a nonprofit New York City cultural institution has been adding value (and offsetting costs) through innovative decisions about distribution.

Metropolitan Opera HD Live. For decades, the only way audiences could experience a performance of the Metropolitan Opera (nicknamed "the Met") was to go to its New York City opera house. Then, starting in 1931, the Met began broadcasting its Saturday matinees live on coast-to-coast radio, a distribution decision that remains in force to this day. In 2006, Peter Gelb, the Met's newly appointed general manager, thought about the longevity and popularity of that weekly radio program. Seeking a way to reach a wider audience and boost revenue without raising ticket prices in the 4,000-seat opera house, Gelb had the idea of broadcasting operas live to movie theaters nationwide. "If only a small percentage of Saturday radio listeners would walk over to their local cinema, I knew we would have an audience," he remembers thinking.

Since then, the Met has been transmitting some opera performances live, in high defini-tion (HD), to 1,700 theaters in 54 nations, including Russia and China. Instead of reaching only the 68,000 ticket holders who filled the Met for 17 performances of *Don Giovanni*, the opera reached a worldwide audience of 216,000 with a single performance in HD Live, not count-ing the 50,000 additional viewers who saw it in later ("encore") showings. The average ticket price at the Met's opera house is about $122, while the average ticket price at a local theater showing HD Live performances is about $20. This distribution decision is paying off: The Met earns a net profit from HD Live broadcasts, rebroadcasts, and DVD sales, which helps cover costs in its $300 million yearly budget.[4]

The Metropolitan Opera pioneered a new method of distribution by signing up a network of local theaters to receive its HD Live transmissions (the outbound side of the value chain). The HD Live series has been so successful that other cultural organizations are adopting this distribution arrangement. Now movie theater companies are diversifying by setting up cutting-edge satellite networks to transmit a wider range of live events to individual theaters around the country, rather than relying on physically transporting film.[5] Although your marketing plan may not have the same flows as the Met or the same technology as theaters, you can see how careful and creative value-chain planning can make a difference.

PLANNING CHANNEL STRATEGY

How can channel strategy help your organization achieve its marketing plan objectives? Although many aspects of this strategy are invisible to customers, it plays a major part in the marketing mix of every business. You must decide which channel functions will be covered, who will handle each function, how many channel levels to use, and how many and what type of channel members to choose. (In addition, you'll face decisions about logistics, as discussed later in the chapter.)

Channel Functions

As you know, the channel as a whole must perform a variety of value-added outbound functions such as matching the volume, amount, or offer to customer needs; providing intermediaries and customers with product and market information; contacting and negotiating with customers to maintain relationships and complete sales; and transporting and storing products prior to purchase.

During planning, identify the channel functions needed for each product, determine which functions intermediaries should handle, and estimate the compensation each channel member should receive for the value it adds. Some producers prefer to assume many or all of the functions themselves because they want more control over customer contacts, pricing, or other elements; others delegate selected functions to reduce costs and focus resources on other tasks. Even within the same industry, a channel strategy that works for one company may not be suitable for its competitors.

Channel Levels

How many channel levels are needed or desirable? The higher the number of channel levels, the more intermediaries are involved in making the product available (see Exhibit 8.3). Each channel level adds value in some way by having the product in a convenient place for purchase, for instance, or by providing information and demonstrations. In exchange, each level expects to profit from the sale to the next level or to the final customer, costs that must be factored into the ultimate selling price.

A *zero-level channel* refers to a direct channel linking seller and buyer. This was once the primary strategy for catalog merchants. Today, a wide variety of marketers prefer direct contact with buyers. For instance, entrepreneurs who embrace gourmet food trucks are using a zero-level

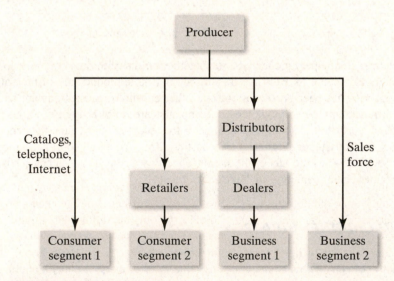

EXHIBIT 8.3   Channel Levels

Source: Gary Armstrong and Philip Kotler, *Marketing: An Introduction,* 11e (Upper Saddle River, NJ: Pearson Prentice Hall, 2013), p. 300, Fig. 10.4.

channel to reach their targeted customers, learning firsthand which items are popular and what else to stock. Despite limitations, this channel brings a new twist to an old way of doing business and shows the value of bringing creativity to distribution decisions.

Gourmet Food Trucks. Low overhead and the ability to go where customers are—those are compelling reasons for food-truck entrepreneurs to take to the streets selling gourmet menu items. From Portland, Maine to Paris, France and beyond, food trucks are the preferred distribution method for entrepreneurs who don't want the cost and operational hassle of a restaurant. Instead, they drive specially equipped trucks to downtown locations, campuses, parks, and other places where customers congregate, cooking up a limited menu of distinctive items. In Paris, for example, Cantine California sells fresh organic tacos and stylishly decorated cupcakes, drawing devoted crowds. Some food trucks announce the day's itinerary via Twitter or Facebook, whereas others drive a regular route that customers come to know.

 Food trucks must comply with all local, state, and federal guidelines for food preparation, not to mention rules for where they can park and how long they may remain in one place. In Paris, food trucks can park only in assigned spots on assigned days. In New Orleans, food trucks can't operate anywhere in the popular French Quarter, nor can they park and serve food in one place for longer than 30 minutes. So Brigade Coffee has found a legal way around such restrictions by teaming up with a local restaurant that lets the coffee truck park in its lot and operate under its catering license.[6]

Sometimes complex or novel products need considerable support from channel members, which may mean using a one-level, two-level, or even three-level channel for certain markets or segments. In a *one-level channel,* the seller works with a single type of intermediary to build strong channel relations and facilitate product, data, and financial flows through the value chain. Some products, such as automotive parts, are customarily distributed through two- or three-level channels. Apple uses multiple channel levels, marketing through selected retailers and catalog merchants as well as through its own stores. If the product covered by your market plan is new, you'll need to find ways of breaking into established channels to reach your targeted segments, which isn't always easy with an unproven product or brand.

> ***PLANNING TIP***
>
> Add or eliminate levels depending on the product, buying patterns, and other factors.

Multichannel Marketing

Increasingly, consumers are varying their buying behavior, sometimes buying from a firm online and at other times buying in its stores or by smartphone. *Multichannel marketing* puts the emphasis on providing a range of choices for customers who buy through different channels at different times or for different reasons. Therefore, your marketing plan should include steps to research and accommodate customers' preferences concerning how, when, and where they want to buy.

 Traditional retailers, in particular, are working hard to adapt their strategies based on the multichannel marketing trend, especially as mobile marketing grows in popularity. Here's what the House of Fraser has done with multichannel marketing in recent years. (Take a look at its home page by scanning the QR code or by going to www.houseoffraser.co.uk.)

House of Fraser. The House of Fraser, which operates dozens of U.K. stores, recognizes that "multichannel customers are three to four times more valuable than the single channel customer each year," according to the e-commerce director. As a result, the House of Fraser revamped its website, launched a mobile-commerce site, and upgraded in-store ambiance and services to differentiate itself from other department stores. The goal was to invite customers to shop in any way they choose, with the tools they need to personalize the experience.

Now in-store shoppers can scan QR codes to get more details about products or look at in-store TV screens to see product demonstrations. If they shop online, they can arrange to have purchases shipped to a local House of Fraser store for pickup. The company is also testing ".com" stores where customers can walk in to browse online offerings, order, pay, and pickup at their convenience. Mobile marketing, however, is the linchpin of the company's multichannel strategy because it "allows you to merge offline and online environments, and that is the store of the future," the e-commerce director says.[7]

Just because customers are buying through a specific channel at one point, don't assume that will be the case for the long term. This is where your marketing plan needs flexibility. During Facebook's meteoric rise, some marketers rushed to open virtual storefronts on the social media giant's pages. Gamestop had 3.5 million Facebook fans and expected to sell a lot of video games through Facebook. After only six months, Gamestop closed that storefront because "we just didn't get the return on investment we needed from the Facebook market," says the head of marketing and strategy. JC Penney also closed its Facebook storefront, as did Banana Republic and a few other retailers, finding that customers preferred to shop on the full-offering websites.[8] The lesson: Know your market, and be ready to change channel arrangements if they're not contributing to your marketing, financial, and societal objectives.

Reverse Channels

In some industries or countries, a company's marketing plan also must allow for reverse channels  to return products for exchange, repair, or recycling, especially when legal or regulatory guidelines apply. Some firms are taking advantage of reverse channels to use discarded packaging and products as inputs for new products. For example, Terracycle has a marketing plan for collecting cigarette butts and transforming them into shipping pallets for industrial use.

At times, companies plan for reverse channels not only to help the environment but also to add to their positive public image. This is what Dell is doing. (You can see Dell's home page at www.dell.com or by scanning this QR code.) What ideas from Dell's experience can you use as you develop your marketing plan?

Dell Recycles. Dell, which is headquartered in Austin, Texas, is using a number of reverse channels to prevent electronic waste from piling up in landfills. Its website invites customers to click to print a label in order to send it old computers, monitors, empty Dell toner cartridges, and other items for responsible recycling. Dell also has a deal with thousands of nonprofit

Goodwill Industries stores across the United States to accept used computers dropped off by consumers. Dell then refurbishes any equipment that is reusable for resale by Goodwill and disposes of equipment that cannot be rescued. Although only a small percentage of computers can be recycled through refurbishing, the Dell–Goodwill partnership keeps 1.25 million pounds of electronics out of local landfills each year. Dell also has reverse channels for recycling obsolete and unwanted computers worldwide. In some cases, it offers an incentive to encourage recycling behavior. For instance, Dell offers a discount coupon to customers in India who return old laptop batteries from Dell products for recycling at its local outlets.[9]

Channel Members

How many and what type of channel members will be needed at each channel level? Customers' needs and habits are important clues to appropriate channel choices and to identifying creative new channel opportunities for competitive advantage. Financial considerations are another key factor. Channel members have certain profit expectations, and customers have their own perceptions of a product's value; both affect the marketer's pricing strategy and profit potential. In addition, the choice of channel members depends on the product's life cycle, the positioning, and the targeted segment (see Exhibit 8.4).

EXHIBIT 8.4 Intensive, Selective, and Exclusive Distribution

	Value to Marketer	Value to Customer	Planning Considerations
Intensive distribution (in many outlets for maximum market coverage)	Increase unit sales, market impulse items, cover more of each market, reduce channel costs per unit sold	Convenient, wide access to frequently used or impulse products; price may be lower due to competition	• Will service be adequate? • Will product be displayed and sold properly? • Will conflict arise between outlets?
Selective distribution (in a number of selected outlets)	Cover specific areas in each market, reduce dependence on only a few outlets, supervise some channel activities, control some channel costs	See product and receive sales help in more outlets within each market; obtain some services as needed	• What is the optimal balance of costs, control, and benefits? • Will outlets be convenient for customers? • Do sales reps understand the product and customers' needs?
Exclusive distribution (in a few outlets for exclusivity within each market)	Choose specific outlets to introduce an innovative item, support positioning, build closer channel relationships, better supervise service, etc.	Receive personalized attention; access to delivery, alterations, customization, and other services	• Will channel costs be too high? • Will product be available to all targeted segments? • Will price be too high, given channel profit requirements? • Will outlets be committed marketing partners?

At introduction, an innovative new product may be offered in a very limited number of outlets (*exclusive distribution*) in order to reinforce its novelty and enable store staff to learn all about features and benefits. In maturity, the company may try to keep sales going by getting the product into as many outlets as possible (*intensive distribution*). In decline, companies may sell through fewer channel members (*selective distribution*) to keep shipping costs down.

Plan to examine ongoing relations with channel members periodically to be sure your objectives are being achieved and to determine whether channel members and customers are being satisfied. As an example, Marlin Steel Wire Products, which makes wire baskets for export to global markets, identifies the relatively small number of distributors that account for most of its sales. Then it can concentrate its efforts on supporting and evaluating these high-volume distributors.[10]

Influences on Channel Strategy

All the channel decisions discussed earlier are influenced by a number of internal and external factors, which are summarized in Exhibit 8.5. The major internal factors for marketers to consider during this part of the planning process include the following:

- *Direction, goals, and objectives.* The channel strategy must be consistent with the organization's chosen direction, its higher-level goals, and its marketing plan objectives. Companies with green marketing objectives need to plan appropriate channels for getting products to green-oriented customers as well as plan reverse channels for reclaiming recyclable products or parts. Some major retailers, including Target and Costco, are switching to sustainably sourced seafood, for instance, in line with their societal objectives and their customers' preferences.[11]

- *Resources and competencies.* If the company has the resources and competencies to handle certain channel functions, it may do so while keeping costs in line by hiring others for different functions. The Starbucks-owned brand Seattle's Best Coffee has partnered with Coinstar to place upscale coffee vending machines in grocery stores and other retail locations. Coinstar brings its equipment expertise to the deal, and Seattle's Best brings its distinctive coffee products. The target: a "mass market audience" that values the convenience of good-tasting coffee in a hurry.[12] (Visit the Coinstar home page at www.coinstar.com or scan the QR code here.)

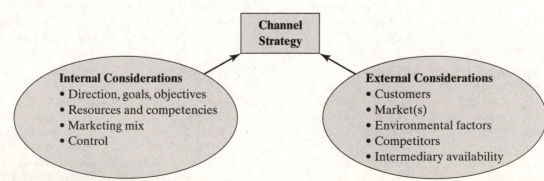

EXHIBIT 8.5 Influences on Channel Strategy

- *Marketing mix.* Channel decisions must work with the organization's product, pricing, and promotion strategies. In some cases, manufacturers will share the cost of advertising a branded product with their channel partners, showing support for the channel and increasing exposure for their brand in a way that's consistent with its image and positioning.
- *Control.* Does the company want or need tight control over channel functions for quality or image reasons? Can the company afford this kind of control, or must it give up some control in exchange for other benefits, such as lower costs or wider coverage in certain areas? Some high-end fashion brands, such as Prada, prefer to operate separate boutiques within department stores so that they can control displays, prices, and other aspects of the retail experience. Others, including Chanel, don't insist on separate boutiques. "Our partners understand the value of the brand and work with us well on service models, sales associate training, and store space and design and location," says Chanel USA's president.[13]

The major external factors influencing decisions about channel strategy are as follows:

- *Customers.* Channel choices should be consistent with what customers want, prefer, expect, or will accept. The growth of in-store medical clinics indicates that shoppers find it convenient to get a flu shot or have a sore throat treated in a local drug or discount store. CVS Caremark already operates more than 500 MinuteClinics inside its drug stores, with more in the works as demand increases for affordable, easy access to treatment for minor illnesses—and the ability to fill prescriptions on the spot, if needed.[14]
- *Market(s).* Companies are finding new ways to reach far-flung markets. For example, Western Union is expanding its money-transfer services into new domestic and global markets by partnering with banks, check-cashing firms, mobile-phone network providers, and other channel members. As a result, customers of Garanti Bank in Turkey can now transfer money (in euros or in dollars) to any Western Union office worldwide. In Kenya, Western Union has partnered with Ericsson to provide money-transfer services via customers' mobile phones.[15]
- *Environmental factors.* Channel choices should reflect the marketer's analysis of political-legal, economic, social-cultural, technological, and other factors in the business environment. Be especially aware of restrictions on certain product categories or segments. For instance, alcoholic beverages are subject to rules regarding where and when they may be marketed, which clearly affects channel decisions. Cross-border channel management is particularly challenging, although the U.S. government offers help to businesses that encounter problems in international trade (see Exhibit 8.6).
- *Competitors.* How can the company use channel strategy to gain a competitive edge? Walmart, the world's largest retailer, finds that smaller stores are highly effective for competing against dollar stores—and highly profitable in specific markets. The Walmart Express stores, which are smaller than 15,000 square feet, operate as convenience stores, with selected food and pharmacy items and sometimes gas pumps.[16] Competitive challenges due to *showrooming*—customers examining merchandise in stores but buying from online retailers—have also caused some changes in channel strategy. Target stopped carrying Amazon's Kindle, reportedly because of concerns about showrooming, and implemented an app that rewards shoppers with points (exchangeable for discounts) when they scan products with their smartphones while standing in a Target store.[17]

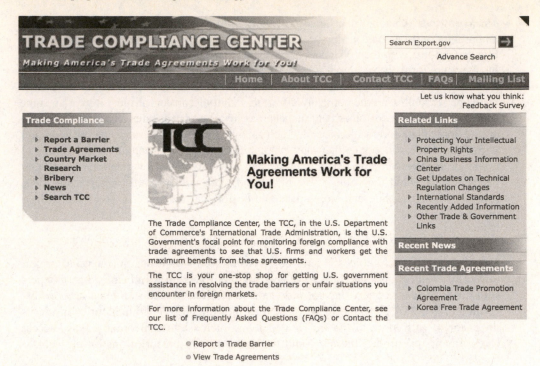

EXHIBIT 8.6   U.S. Trade Compliance Help at Export.gov

• *Availability of intermediaries.* What intermediaries are available in each market, what are their strengths and weaknesses, and what is their reach? Marketers with frequently purchased consumer products often seek distribution through large retail chains, for instance, but each chain has its own locations, strategy, and so on. A decade ago, organic food companies had relatively limited choices; now mainstream supermarkets and discounters stock a wide array of organic foods, increasing distribution opportunities.

PLANNING FOR LOGISTICS

PLANNING TIP

Estimate the total cost of logistics for each service level before making a final decision.

The mechanics of managing the flows through the value chain from point of origin to point of production and then outbound to point of sale or consumption are addressed by **logistics**. You want a logistics strategy that's responsive to customer needs yet meets your internal financial targets. This is a delicate balancing act: Companies don't want to overspend to get supplies and products, information, and payments to the proper place on time. Simply stockpiling parts or finished products takes up space and costs money. On the other hand, companies risk losing customers if they take too long to fill orders, have too few units or the wrong assortment on hand to fill orders, have a confusing or complex ordering process, cannot easily track orders and shipments, or make it difficult for customers to return products.

Still, responding to customers' needs entails some costs (for delivery, inventory, order confirmation, etc.). Thus, when planning for logistics, you should weigh the total cost of logistics against the level of customer responsiveness that is appropriate to meet your marketing plan objectives.

Logistical Functions

Consider four main logistical functions when preparing a marketing plan (see Exhibit 8.7):

- *Storage.* Where will supplies, parts, and finished products be stored, for how long, and under what conditions? Sometimes suppliers agree to warehouse goods; sometimes the marketer warehouses goods until needed to fill customer orders. More storage facilities will increase costs but also increase response times. Walmart locates its huge distribution centers no more than one day's drive from each cluster of stores so that it can replenish shelf stock quickly. In addition, each outlet has refrigerated storage and other special storage arrangements for perishable, tiny, outsized, or fragile products. If you're planning for a new firm, you may want to check on warehouse rentals or see whether suppliers can manage storage for you.

- *Inventory.* How many parts, components, and supplies must be available for production? How many finished goods are needed to meet customer demand and organizational objectives? How do projected inventory levels affect storage and transportation decisions? Lower inventory means lower costs but may cause delays in filling customers' orders if products are out of stock. After a major earthquake and tsunami in Japan disrupted the operations of many automotive suppliers and closed some ports and airports, automakers such as Honda and Toyota scrambled to find new suppliers and to replenish inventory. Similarly, a shortage of resins has led General Motors and other automakers to investigate substitutes from DuPont and other suppliers, with the objective of keeping assembly lines going as planned.[18]

- *Order processing and fulfillment.* Who will be responsible for taking orders, confirming product availability, packing products for shipment, tracking orders in transit, preparing invoices or receipts, and handling errors or returns? How will these tasks be accomplished and relevant information be tracked, and in what time frame? Such tasks are as vital for intangible offerings as they are for tangible products. Apple's App Store makes things simple for developers who sell applications (games, organizing tools, etc.) for iPhones, iPods, and Macs. The founder of Instapaper, an app that assembles user-selected articles into a daily "paper," distributes his app via the App Store because Apple handles payment and all other functions seamlessly.[19]

- *Transportation.* How will supplies, parts, and finished products be transported inbound and outbound? Who will pay? Where and when will goods or materials be picked up and

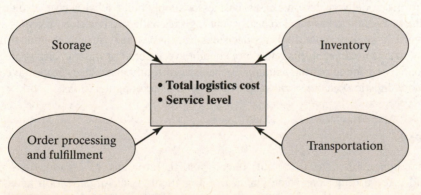

EXHIBIT 8.7 Logistics Decisions

delivered? For door-to-door pickup and delivery, marketers often use truck transport. When schedules are flexible and products are heavy or bulky, they may choose less-costly rail or water transport; when deadlines are short and products are perishable or precious, marketers may use fast (but expensive) air transport. Think about this when you prepare your marketing plan, because such decisions can involve significant outlays and some lead time.

Influences on Logistics Decisions

One factor that can influence your planning for logistics is the organization's approach to social responsibility, as Give Something Back's experience indicates. (Take a peek at its home page by visiting www.givesomethingback.com or by following the QR code here.)

> **Give Something Back.** After seeing how Newman's Own raised money for charity by marketing food products, Mike Hannigan and Sean Marx started Give Something Back (GSB) in 1991 to market office supplies and donate the profits to charity. Now GSB is the largest independently owned office-supply firm in California, with multiple distribution centers and a retail website that competes with Staples and other big rivals. Although GSB offers many of the same items as its competitors—and free next-day delivery, just like competitors—it stocks thousands of environmentally friendly products, as well. Looking ahead, it has set the aggressive goal of increasing sales to $100 million within five years.
>
> Being socially responsible has affected GSB's logistics strategy. Recently, the firm decided to start a free electronic waste pickup service for customers. "We send a fleet of trucks out every morning full of stuff, and they come back empty," explains Hannigan. "So we'll fill them with e-waste and bring it back to our warehouse. It's leveraging [assets]—our trucks and people—without additional cost, to allow customers to do something that they wanted to do anyway."[20]

Cost constraints are another key factor to consider. Online businesses often provide a choice of delivery options with associated prices, allowing customers to decide how much they're willing to spend for faster delivery. In some cases, businesses simply build delivery costs into the price of their products. Finally, be prepared to justify your logistics budget to decision makers.

Even on a smaller scale, logistics decisions can make a real difference in any marketing plan. Note that the marketing plan need not contain every detail of the logistics strategy, but it should contain a general outline, explain the balance of total costs versus responsiveness, and indicate how logistics functions will support your other marketing decisions.

Summary

Products reach markets at the right time, place, and price through the value chain, a series of interrelated, value-added functions and the structure of organizations performing them. Each organization adds value to satisfy the needs of the next link as well as of the customers at the end of the chain. The marketer manages suppliers and logistics on the inbound side to obtain inputs, then manages channels and logistics to meet demand on the outbound side. Plan for the movement of products, information, and money in both directions along the value chain. Service marketers also need to understand all the flows in the chain, determine how value is added and by which participant, and manage flows to balance supply and demand.

Channel strategy covers decisions about which channel functions must be performed and by which participant, how many channel levels to use, how to manage multichannel marketing, and how many and what type of channel members to choose. Influences on channel strategy include direction, goal, and objectives; resources and core competencies; other marketing-mix decisions; control issues; customers' needs and preferences; market factors; environmental factors; competitors; and intermediary availability. Logistics involves managing the mechanics of products, data, and information flows throughout the value chain, based on objectives that balance total costs with customer responsiveness levels. The four main logistics functions are storage, inventory, order processing and fulfillment, and transportation.

Your Marketing Plan, Step by Step

To get started on planning for channel and logistics, answer the following questions. Document what you decide in your written plan.

1. If you're planning for an existing good or service, study and map the product, information, and money flows through the value chain. If you're planning for a new offering, map the value-chain flows you would like to have. Identify any special needs or situations that would affect any of the flows at one or more links in the chain. If possible, approximate the value-chain flows of two major competitors to spot possible areas where your organization can improve or gain an edge.

2. Consider the demand side of the value chain. Based on your knowledge of your target markets and customers, how, when, and where do consumers or businesses expect or prefer to gain access to your offering? What demand peaks and valleys should your value chain accommodate? How does the demand side affect the supply side of your value chain, including suppliers, production, and preparation for handoff to channel partners?

3. Looking at your entire value chain, what functions must be performed inbound and outbound? Which will your organization handle and which will you have outsiders handle—and why? Especially if your marketing plan is for a new product, think about the learning curve you'd face in managing these functions on your own, and weigh that against the cost of having someone else handle some functions.

4. How many channel levels will you plan for? Is your type of offering usually marketed directly to customers or through intermediaries? If you want to use one or more channel levels, identify the types of intermediaries in each and note how each will make your offering available to the ultimate buyer, a consumer or a business customer. What about multichannel marketing? Also, will you need reverse channel(s)? Explain why or why not in your plan.

5. Will you choose intensive, selective, or exclusive distribution? Why is your choice appropriate for your offering, your organization, your market, and your customers? What criteria will you use to evaluate channel members (potential or existing)?

6. Before you finalize your channel decisions, reexamine your ideas with the following factors in mind: your organization's direction, goals, objectives, resources, capabilities, and need for control; the marketing mix you're recommending in your marketing plan; your customers' preferences and requirements; the markets you're targeting; environmental and competitive factors; and availability of intermediaries.

7. Now plan for logistics. How will you balance the need to be responsive to customers with the need to meet internal financial targets? List each of the four main logistical functions; next to each, write a few sentences about the main issues to be considered and how you will address each. Reread your notes with an eye toward cost. Also look at how your logistics will help you achieve the financial, marketing, and societal objectives already recorded in your marketing plan. Do you see any conflicts?

Endnotes

1. Marielle Segarra, "Business Is Sweet," *CFO Magazine,* September 1, 2012, www.cfo.com; Dermot Doherty, "Godiva to Double Number of Stores in Chinese Market," *Bloomberg Businessweek,* June 12, 2012, www.businessweek.com.

2. Stephanie Clifford, "Electronics Retailers Scramble to Adapt to Changing Market," *New York Times,* June 18, 2012, www.nytimes.com.

3. Antony Bruno, "If You Can't Beat 'Em," *Billboard,* September 3, 2011, p. 16.

4. Zachary Woolfe, "I'm Ready for My Close-Up, Mr. Puccini," *New York Times,* April 29, 2012, pp. AR-1, AR-13; Sean Gregory, "Tenors on the Big Screen," *Time,* May 11, 2010, www.time.com; Warwick Thompson, "Star Manager Gelb's Live Broadcasts Make $11 Million for Met," *Bloomberg,* March 4, 2012, www.bloomberg.com.

5. Richard Verrier, "Movie Theaters Diversify Offerings Beyond Films," *Los Angeles Times,* June 12, 2012, www.latimes.com.

6. Micheline Maynard, "Why Food Trucks Have It So Tough in New Orleans," *Forbes,* June 12, 2012, www.forbes.com; Julia Moskin, "Food Trucks in Paris?" *New York Times,* June 3, 2012, www.nytimes.com; Josh Ozersky, "Why Food Trucks Aren't Going Away," *Time,* June 13, 2012, www.time.com.

7. David Moth, "42% of Smartphone Owners Go Online to Check Prices In-Store," *E-Consultancy,* June 19, 2012, http://econsultancy.com; David Moth, "House of Fraser: Digital Is Key to Personalizing In-Store Experience," *E-Consultancy,* June 13, 2012, http://econsultancy.com.

8. Ashley Lutz, "Gamestop to J.C. Penney Shut Facebook Stores," *Bloomberg,* February 22, 2012, www.bloomberg.com.

9. Joe Turner, "Now, You Can Ditch Your Old Gadgetry," *Virginian Pilot,* January 15, 2012, p. 1; "Dell Launches Laptop Battery Recycling Programme," *Times of India,* June 6, 2012, http://articles.timesofindia.indiatimes.com; Robert Klara, "Where Your Gadgets Go to Die," *Adweek,* January 16, 2012, p. 20; Dell website, www.dell.com.

10. Carolyn M. Brown, "7 Tips for Rating and Evaluating Your Suppliers and Vendors," *Inc.,* December 30, 2010, www.inc.com.

11. Allison Aubrey, "Sustainable Seafood Swims to a Big-Box Store Near You," *National Public Radio,* January 20, 2012, www.npr.org.

12. Alicia Lavay, "Stir It Up! The Case For Vended Coffee," *Vending Times,* August 31, 2012, www.vendingtimes.com; Dale Buss, "With Coinstar and K-Cup Expansion, Starbucks Puts a Premium on Convenience," *BrandChannel,* June 11, 2012, www.brandchannel.com.

13. Rachel Dodes and Christina Passariello, "Luxury Brands Stake Out New Department Store Turf," *Wall Street Journal,* May 4, 2011, www.wsj.com.

14. Christina Veiders, "In-Store Clinics Primed for New Growth: Report," *Supermarket News,* February 27, 2012, www.supermarketnews.com.

15. Paul Wafula, "Kenya: Western Union, Ericsson in Deal to Boost Mobile Money Services," *Business Daily (Nairobi),* February 28, 2012, http://allafrica.com; "Garanti, Western Union in Cooperation," *Hurriyet Daily News,* May 26, 2009, www.hurriyet.com.

16. Susanna Kim, "Walmart Said It Plans to Roll Out More Smaller Stores," *ABC News,* May 28, 2012, http://abcnews.go.com; Anne D'Innocenzio, "Walmart Sees Early Success in Walmart Express," *Bloomberg BusinessWeek,* May 23, 2012, www .businessweek.com.

17. Brad Tuttle, "Scan This! Target Encourages Shoppers to Scan Items with Smartphones Nationwide," *Time,* May 25, 2012, www .time.com.

18. Dee-Ann Durbin and Tom Krisher, "Crises Make Automakers Rethink Lean Parts Supplies," *Bangor Daily News,* April 22, 2012, http://bangordailynews.com; Craig Trudell and Mark Clothier, "DuPont Sees Boost to Polymers from Automakers Seeking Resins," *Bloomberg,* April 19, 2012, www .bloomberg.com.

19. "The App Economy," *National Public Radio,* January 31, 2012, www.npr.org.

20. Carolyn Said, "Give Something Back Plans to Give Even More," *San Francisco Chronicle,* February 14, 2011, www.sfgate .com; Cameron Scott, "Doing Good by Doing Well," *San Francisco Chronicle,* June 5, 2009, www.sfgate.com; Eve Kushner, "Mike Hannigan: Give Something Back," *The Monthly,* December 2006, http://themonthly .com/feature12-06-mike.html.

Developing Marketing Communications and Influence Strategy

In this chapter:

PREVIEW

Preparing your strategy for communications and influence is part of Step 5 in the marketing planning process (see Exhibit 9.1). This chapter explains the elements of communications and influence, including the latest social media, word-of-mouth techniques, and buzz marketing. You'll also learn about choosing the target audience, setting objectives and budget, examining relevant issues, selecting specific communications tools, and preparing for research before and after a promotion or campaign, especially for evaluation purposes. Finally, you'll take a closer look at planning for the five main tools marketers use to communicate with audiences and the need for coordinating all messages in all media.

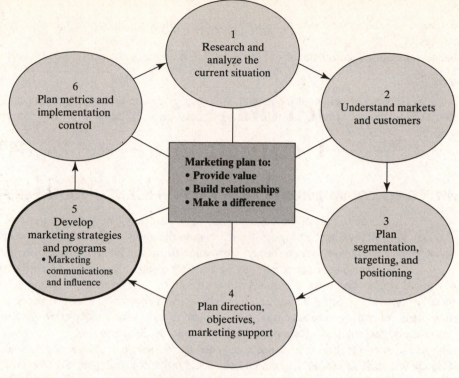

EXHIBIT 9.1   Marketing Planning: Step 5

APPLYING YOUR KNOWLEDGE

Read this chapter and take a look at the marketing communications section of this book's sample plans (in the appendix and online). Once you've answered the questions in "Your Marketing Plan, Step by Step" at the end of this chapter and consulted the following checklist, you'll be ready to decide on steps for marketing communications and to record them in your marketing plan.

CHAPTER 9 CHECKLIST   Planning Marketing Communications

Audience Analysis

✓ What is the profile of a typical audience member?
✓ How do the audience's behavior, characteristics, and media usage affect media and message choices?

Objectives and Budget

✓ What are your marketing communications intended to achieve?
✓ Is the budget sufficient to achieve the objectives with the chosen tools and media?

Issues

✓ What legal, regulatory, and ethical issues affect the audience, geographic region, media, or messages?

✓ What social, cultural, competitive, and technological issues must be considered?

Research

✓ What does research reveal about the market, audience, and communication preferences?

✓ How can you pretest communications and research postimplementation awareness and response?

PLANNING TO COMMUNICATE WITH AND INFLUENCE AUDIENCES

PLANNING TIP

Maintain a dialogue with customers for feedback and open communication.

You're part of the audience for many marketing messages, so you already know that the purpose of such communications is to influence the decisions you make as a consumer. **Customer-influence strategies** are strategies for engaging customers through marketing communications and for influencing how they think, feel, and act toward a brand or offering.[1] In the past, marketing communications were usually one-way messages from the organization to its customers and prospects; today, marketing plans generally aim to encourage dialogue and to build relationships through communications in messages and media that engage audiences and invite interaction.

The rise of **social media**, online media designed to facilitate user interaction, has added a powerful new dimension to today's communications and influence strategies. Social media such as YouTube, Facebook, Twitter, Pinterest, and blogs promote engagement because their content is largely or entirely created by their users, who post written messages, videos, podcasts, photos, and so on, and also respond to posts and comments by other users. Many marketers have a presence on social media, and they encourage conversations with customers. However, because usage is free and users post what they wish, marketers lack the kind of control over social media that they have over the content of a TV ad they pay to produce and air, for instance.

Social Media, Word of Mouth, Buzz, and Influence

Interaction among users of social media can spark positive or negative **word-of-mouth (WOM) communication**, people telling other people about a company, a brand, an offering, or something else they have noticed. Information spread by WOM (or *word-of-mouse* online) has more credibility because it comes from a personal source rather than being controlled by a company or an agency. As a result, the outcome of WOM is unpredictable and often cannot be accurately measured.

A video or an ad or another type of message goes *viral* when it gains a large audience through people sending it (or a link to it) to others online. This, in turn, can influence how consumers or business customers think about and feel and act toward the subject of the viral message—the company, offer, issue, or person mentioned or depicted in it. Forwarding a viral message and viewing a video that friends recommend are two actions that indicate a level of interest and that can influence attitudes and behavior, such as encouraging agreement with the view expressed in the message or prompting the purchase of the featured brand. When the "Old Spice Guy" online videos first went viral, millions of people watched Isaiah Mustafa (wearing only a towel) talk up the Old Spice brand. The viral videos boosted the brand's image and sales, and made Mustafa instantly recognizable as the face of Old Spice.

Businesses and nonprofits use social media to reach audiences and influence what members say and feel about, and act toward, a brand, an offering, or an idea. Here's how the Centers for Disease Control and Prevention, a U.S. government agency, uses social media—sometimes with a dash of humor—to get the word out about preparing for emergencies. (You can visit its emergency preparedness page at http:// emergency.cdc.gov or scan this QR code to see the page.)

Centers for Disease Control and Prevention. The U.S. Centers for Disease Control and Prevention (CDC) has found social media such as blogs, Facebook, and Twitter to be effective for public outreach in many situations. Ordinarily, a CDC blog post receives a few thousand views, but in the spring of 2011, the CDC's health communication specialists came up with an idea that made a huge impact on its ability to engage audiences. Given the pop culture prevalence of zombie themes, they decided to create a YouTube video, tweets, and blog entries to call attention to what people should do to prepare for emergency situations such as a zombie apocalypse (or more likely scenarios like flu pandemics and hurricanes).

The CDC's communications captured the imagination of the media, medical personnel, and everyday people, adding a light touch to the serious topic of being ready for emergencies. In less than a week, the CDC's blog page was viewed more than 3 million times, and soon it had sparked 1,000 reader comments. Following up on that success, the CDC created a graphic novel showing how to prepare for a zombie apocalypse (including real tips on emergency preparedness) and released it just before Halloween—again receiving a torrent of media attention and WOM response. Today, the CDC's Facebook page has more than 220,000 "likes," and the agency continues to mention zombies from time to time, always mixing a serious message with the tongue-in-cheek zombie talk.[2]

With **buzz marketing**, the company seeks to generate more intense WOM, knowing that the buzz may fade as quickly as it starts. Sometimes marketers provide communicators with incentives to build buzz, such as samples or coupons (or, occasionally, payments). Buzz marketing, whether face to face, electronic, or through publicity, has been used to stimulate WOM in support of all kinds of marketing tactics, including new product introductions, new store openings, and Super Bowl ads.

As you work on your marketing communications and influence strategy, start by defining your target audience. Then establish objectives and a budget, analyze pertinent issues, and select appropriate tools. Your final step before implementation will be to plan research to test communications and to evaluate the effectiveness of your campaign(s).

Choose the Target Audience

The target audience might consist of customers and prospects, or when image building is part of the marketing plan, it may consist of employees, community leaders, local officials, and a number of other key stakeholders. Some communication strategies used to achieve market share and sales objectives can be characterized in terms of "push" or "pull" (see Exhibit 9.2).

In a **push strategy**, you target intermediaries, encouraging them to carry and promote (push) the product to business customers or consumers. In a **pull strategy**, you encourage consumers or business customers to build demand to pull the product through the channel. The decision to use push or pull must fit with channel decisions and be appropriate for the product, its

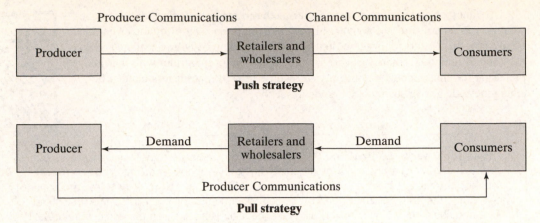

EXHIBIT 9.2   Push and Pull Strategies

Source: Gary Armstrong and Philip Kotler, *Marketing: An Introduction,* 11th ed. (Upper Saddle River, NJ: Pearson Education, 2013), p. 364, Fig. 121.

pricing, and its positioning. When Chobani began marketing yogurt as a tiny start-up in upstate New York, it relied more on push than pull. Within a couple of years, however, the company added pull, partly to support its push efforts and partly to increase market share.

> **Chobani.** Hamdi Ulukaya introduced the new Chobani brand of Greek-style yogurt in 2007. His initial objective was to obtain U.S. distribution, so he concentrated on sales to big supermarket chains—a vital push strategy for a start-up food company. Ulukaya also realized that his limited budget wouldn't stretch to cover an effective pull campaign at the outset. In 2009, however, he set aside a small budget for consumer-oriented communications, and by 2011, he was investing more than $13 million in consumer marketing, both to support his channel partners and to continue boosting market share in an increasingly competitive business. That year's multimedia consumer campaign combined commercials, billboards, and social media featuring highly positive WOM comments from real brand fans.
>
> In 2012, Chobani became an official sponsor of the U.S. Olympic team and kicked off a $12 million campaign promoting its children's Greek yogurt, Chobani Champions. That campaign featured Jennie Finch, who pitched for the medal-winning U.S. Olympic softball teams in 2004 and 2008, giving Chobani Champions to her two young children. "We wanted a 'consumer-up' campaign to tap into and extend the 'Chobani love' that is rapidly spreading across the country," explained the head of the ad agency that created the TV ads. By tapping into the brand's existing buzz, Chobani's communications increased overall sales and helped defend against challengers such as Dannon that want to wrench share from market-leader Chobani. Now Chobani is using a push strategy to enter Australia, with pull to follow once the company completes its local plant expansion and has sufficient distribution.[3]

When you plan for reaching your audience, look beyond generalities and develop a profile of a typical audience member in as much detail as possible, including gender; age; lifestyle; media, product, and payment preferences; attitudes; timing of buying decisions; and so on. Digging for such details reveals nuances to help shape what the messages should say and how, when, and where to say them.

Knowing that many consumers and business customers are heavy users of cell phones, a growing number of firms are using **mobile marketing** to make information, directions, coupons, and other messages available to customers through text messages, e-mail, QR codes, apps, and websites optimized for handset screens. This is especially important with multichannel marketing strategies that encourage customers to choose how they want to interact with the brand and to make purchases at any given time.

Large or small, marketers can use mobile marketing to reach targeted audiences and to achieve specific objectives, if they understand buying patterns and media usage. The Girl Scouts of the USA, for example, offers a free "cookie finder" app that alerts users to when and where they can buy Girl Scout cookies in their area. Because cookies are only sold during limited periods and then only in certain locations, people who want to buy need to know where to go to stock up. As a result of this app, the Girl Scouts have enjoyed higher cookie sales and stronger support of local troops.[4] (For more information, visit the Girl Scout Cookie page at http://www.girlscoutcookies .org/ or follow the QR code here.)

Set Objectives and Budget

You can use marketing communications to move your target audience through a series of responses corresponding to beliefs, behavior, and feelings about your product, brand, or company. As Exhibit 9.3 shows in simplified form, marketers of high-involvement products such as cars start by influencing the audience's beliefs; then they strive to influence feelings, with the ultimate goal of influencing behavior. Not all offerings are high-involvement products, however. For soft-drink marketers, communications can be a way to encourage positive emotions toward the brand (feelings), which in turn might lead to an impulse purchase (behavior) and finally lead customers to decide they like the taste and find it satisfying (belief). Research will help you determine whether customers see your goods or services as high-involvement and how that will affect your communications decisions.

If you want to acquire new customers, then your audience must be aware of your offer (influencing beliefs). One communication objective might be to "achieve 25% awareness of Product A among the target audience within four months," with the exact percentage and timing dependent on the marketing objective, the promotion investment, and knowledge of the customer's buying process. Related objectives might be to "have 900 prospects request an information package about our services before June 30" and "generate 300 qualified leads for the sales staff by October 15."

Marketing research provides critical background for setting objectives. If research shows that the segment is aware of the product but has no strong preference for it (feelings), the objective might be to "achieve 18% preference for Product E among the target audience within 3 months." If research indicates that customers like the product enough to try it (behavior), the aim might be to "achieve 9% trial of Product C among the target audience within 6 months" or "have 200 customers request samples of Product B during September." Using communications to enhance image, the objective might be to "make 55% of the target audience aware of the corporation's philanthropic donations by December 31" or to "double the percentage of the target audience having positive attitudes toward the corporation within 12 months."

| Communications | $\longrightarrow$ | Influence beliefs | $\longrightarrow$ | Influence feelings | $\longrightarrow$ | Influence behavior |

EXHIBIT 9.3   High-Involvement Model of Response

Consider a number of factors when devising a marketing communications budget, including the overall marketing budget, the objectives to be achieved, environmental forces and trends, choice of advertising or other tool(s), the number of markets to be covered, the competitive circumstances, the potential return on investment, and so on. No company has unlimited resources, so be realistic about the situation, have definite short- and long-term objectives in mind, and budget creatively in your marketing plan. See Chapter 10 for more about budgeting.

Examine Issues

Your communications strategy can be affected by a variety of legal, regulatory, technological, ethical, cultural, and competitive issues. For example, it's illegal for companies in the United States, United Kingdom, and some other nations to make false claims for a product or to describe a food as "low fat" if it does not meet certain criteria. Communications for products such as prescription drugs must comply with strict rules; sometimes messages must include health or product-use warnings, and companies must safeguard customer privacy in particular ways. Companies that communicate ethically and follow voluntary industry ethics codes are more likely to build trust with target audiences and to polish their image.

This is an especially challenging issue when social media are involved, because legal and regulatory guidelines are still evolving. The U.K. Advertising Standards Authority recently ruled that Nike didn't follow the rules when it had two athletes (both brand spokespeople) post tweets without identifying them as ads, for example. Nike argued that including a hashtag with the brand's ad slogan and a Nike web address should have alerted Twitter users that these were marketing tweets and that its sponsorship of the athletes was well known. The regulators disagreed, saying the tweets weren't "obviously identifiable" as marketing communications, and suggested that sponsored tweets include a disclosure such as #ad.[5]

The U.S. Federal Trade Commission has also been looking at proper disclosure techniques for social media, given the space limitations of tweets and the size of mobile-phone screens.[6] Exhibit 9.4 shows the logo of the FTC's Bureau of Consumer Protection Business Center, where you can find out more about marketing regulation.

You should consider competitive issues, as well. How can you use communications to play up a meaningful point of difference that sets your offering apart from those of rivals? How can you counter campaigns from competitors with much larger budgets and better-established brands or products? Are new technologies available to pinpoint target audiences more accurately regardless of competitive campaigns? How can you attract attention despite a cluttered marketing environment? Explain your thoughts about these issues in your marketing plan.

Choose Communication Tools

There are five basic categories of marketing communication tools you can consider for your marketing plan (see Exhibit 9.5). Following is a brief overview; highlights of planning for each will be examined later in the chapter. Note that social media can be used in combination with

EXHIBIT 9.4   Federal Trade Commission Bureau of Consumer Protection Business Center

EXHIBIT 9.5 **Major Communications Tools**

Tool	Use	Examples
Advertising	Efficiently get messages to a large audience	TV and radio commercials; Internet, magazine, and newspaper ads; paid search engine links; product and company brochures; billboards; transit ads; mobile, text, and e-mail ads
Sales promotion	Stimulate immediate purchase, reward repeat purchases, motivate sales personnel	Samples; coupons; premiums; contests, games, sweepstakes; displays; demonstrations; trade shows and incentives
Public relations	Build positive image, strengthen ties with stakeholders	Event sponsorships; news releases, briefings, and podcasts; speeches and blogs; public appearances
Direct marketing	Reach targeted audiences, encourage direct response	Mail, e-mail, telemarketing campaigns; printed and online catalogs; direct response TV, radio, and mobile marketing
Personal selling	Reach customers one-to-one to make sales, strengthen relationships	Sales appointments; sales meetings and presentations; online chat sales help

any or all of these basic tools—and that marketers cannot control the message once it has been initiated in a social media context.

- *Advertising.* Advertising is cost-effective for communicating with a large audience, and the marketer is in complete control of message and media. Marketers often use advertising to introduce and differentiate a product, build a brand, polish the organization's image, communicate competitive superiority, or convey an idea.
- *Sales promotion.* This marketer-controlled tool can be used to target consumers, businesses, or channel members and sales representatives. It's particularly useful for accelerating short-term sales results, combating competitive pressure, provoking product trial, building awareness and reinforcing other communication activities, encouraging continued buying and usage, and increasing the offer's perceived value. A variety of goods are being marketed through sales promotions at house parties, as discussed in a later example.
- *Public relations.* Public relations (PR) has more credibility than other promotion tools because the audience receives the message through media channels perceived to be more objective than sources controlled by the organization. However, you can neither control what the media will report nor guarantee that the company or product will get any media coverage. Consider PR when you want to present the product and company in a positive light, build goodwill and trust, and inform customers, channel members, and other stakeholders about the product and its benefits.
- *Direct marketing.* A highly focused, organization-controlled tool, direct marketing facilitates two-way interaction with a specific audience, allows for pinpoint targeting, and accommodates offers tailored to individual needs and behavior. You can easily measure the outcome and compare it with objectives to determine effectiveness and efficiency.

Direct marketing helps start, strengthen, or renew customer relationships; increase sales of particular products; test the appeal of new or repositioned products; or test alternative marketing tactics such as different prices.

- *Personal selling.* Personal selling is an excellent organization-controlled tool for reaching business customers and consumers on a personal basis in order to open a dialogue, learn more about needs, present complex or customized information, or obtain feedback. Companies selling expensive goods or services or customizing products for individual customers frequently rely on personal selling.

Plan Research

PLANNING TIP

When pretesting, allow time for testing changes before launching the campaign.

If you have the time and money, your marketing plan should allow for pretesting and postimplementation research to evaluate communications. The point of pretesting is to find out whether the target audience understands the message and retains information about the brand or product. It also shows whether your audience responds as expected: Do beliefs, attitudes, or behavior change as a result of communications?

Depending on pretesting, you may want to fine-tune the format, content, delivery, timing, duration, and context of communications before the bulk of the campaign is implemented. Kellogg's pretests its digital ads for cereals to be sure the creative approaches resonate with the target audience; it also tests the timing and relation to surrounding content to better match online ad messages to the audience's interests and receptivity.[7] (To visit the Kellogg's home page, go to www.kelloggs.com or use this QR code.)

Postimplementation research will show whether the communications strategy accomplished its objectives and which activities were particularly effective in supporting your marketing plan. As you select your communications tools, think about how you'll measure and evaluate performance. Chapter 10 will explain more about metrics, which must be chosen during the planning stage to ensure that you can actually measure what your marketing plan accomplishes.

USING COMMUNICATION TOOLS TO ENGAGE AUDIENCES

Marketing plans usually cover the use of various tools in one or more campaigns to engage audiences and achieve communications objectives; the details and explanations are generally shown in an appendix or other documents rather than in the body of the plan. Before selecting specific tools and planning programs, use your audience analysis to understand customers' interests, habits, and preferences. If possible, prepare a SWOT (strengths and weaknesses, opportunities and threats) analysis of what your competitors are doing to communicate with and exert influence on customers. As you plan, apply the principle of integration and consider the overall effect when you use any combination of advertising, sales promotion, PR, direct marketing, and personal selling.

Look carefully at how you can weave social media into your communication plan. Air France, for example, has more than 800,000 Facebook "likes." It plans formal marketing campaigns but also leverages its social media presence to engage customers by going beyond corporate messages. The airline recently launched an app that allows passengers to create photo albums as they travel and to share the results with their Facebook friends. Adding sales promotion to the mix, Air France invites its Facebook friends to vote for their favorite passenger-created albums, involving them with the brand and rewarding them for participating. It has a Pinterest page with images from its in-flight magazine and other images, a YouTube channel with more than 1 million views, and a Twitter account with both news and customer service assistance. All these elements enhance Air France's image as an authentic company that is interested in and engaged with its passengers.[8] (Visit Air France's corporate home page by going to http://corporate.airfrance.com/en or via this QR code.)

Advertising

For the purposes of developing a marketing plan, advertising's two basic decisions concern the message (what content will be communicated?) and the media (what vehicle or vehicles will deliver the message, and when, where, how, and how often?). These decisions must be in keeping with the target audience's characteristics, needs, behavior, and receptivity; the budget allocated for advertising; relevant issues affecting communications strategy; and the objectives set (e.g., awareness or purchase of the product). Audiences are attracted to creative messages, but messages that are too extreme or outlandish won't be effective.

Your messages and media have to work together: If, for example, your plan calls for product demonstration, a visual medium like the Internet or television will be the best choice—but only if the budget allows and the chosen vehicle reaches the target audience. The ad's wording, format and design, graphics, sound, and other medium-specific elements will communicate the appeal of the message.

A message with an **emotional appeal** relies on feelings (fear, love, anger, happiness, or another emotion) to motivate audience response. Messages that rely on a **rational appeal** use facts and logic to stimulate response by showing how the product solves a problem or satisfies a need. B2B ads, in particular, have traditionally been based on rational

> **PLANNING TIP**
>
> Be sure a message's creative execution will work in each medium under consideration.

appeals linked to the specific benefits that business buyers seek. To attract attention, humanize companies, and engage customers—especially in social media—today's B2B campaigns sometimes include a touch of emotional appeal. Yet, as the editor of *BtoB* magazine points out, "Even if [the campaign] has emotional pull and humor, it needs to be business-relevant as well."[9]

Each medium has characteristics that convey the message in a different way; the Internet offers sight, sound, motion, and interactivity, whereas print ads can offer color, longer life, and the ability to communicate more details. To achieve marketing communication objectives, even the most creative message must be presented in a specific medium or vehicle (such as a certain magazine or website) that will reach the target audience. When planning for advertising, bear in mind that you may need a combination of media to convey your message(s), especially now that audiences have such a diversity of choices for how, when, and where they access media and are often exposed to multiple messages in multiple media—simultaneously.

In-store TV is becoming popular because the message reaches buyers when and where they make decisions, and the cost is reasonable.

In-store TV. Kroger is among the U.S. supermarkets with an in-store TV network. Harrods, the well-known U.K. luxury department store, has a 150-TV network plus five media walls where advertisers can display their messages. In-store TV has also arrived at hundreds of McDonald's restaurants, interspersing the company's catchy ad jingles with brief programs featuring lifestyle news, profiles of local high school and college athletes, and other content—including commercials for non-McDonald's products.

Even the TVs for sale in stores can be used for promotional purposes. When Sony Pictures was readying the theater release of *The Amazing Spider-Man,* it arranged for Walmart to show an unreleased scene on the TV sets in its electronics departments for two days only. The time and place made sense: Walmart was putting hundreds of *Spider-Man* licensed items on sale and families were crowding into its stores for summer vacation shopping.[10]

Two key decisions in planning media choices are how many people to reach during a certain period (known as **reach**) and how often to repeat the message during that period (known as **frequency**). Reaching more people is costly, as is repeating the message multiple times. When you plan, you have to determine how to allocate the budget by balancing reach with frequency,

based on knowledge of the target audience. Some marketers are advertising at the movies in order to reach target audiences during specific periods. Kia Motors did this when it launched its Soul subcompact car. Why? "The mindset of people watching movies is much different than the mindset of people watching TV," says Kia's director of advertising. But to extend reach, the company also uses sales promotions and public relations, including sponsoring giveaways and musical events, to reach the Millennial-generation audience it's targeting.[11] (To visit Kia's home page, go to www.kia.com or scan this QR code.)

The choice of where to advertise—in geographic terms—depends on where the product is available or will be introduced during the course of the marketing plan (see Exhibit 9.6). In terms of timing, a message or campaign might run continuously (reminding the audience of benefits or availability), during periods of seasonal or peak demand (when the audience is interested in buying), or steadily but with sporadic intensity (along with sales promotions or other marketing activities). Ethical Bean Coffee Company in Vancouver uses transit advertising embedded with QR codes to reach commuters on their way to or from work. When commuters scan the QR code with a smartphone, they reach a page where they can order a cup of coffee to be ready at a specific time at one of Ethical Bean's train station cafés.[12]

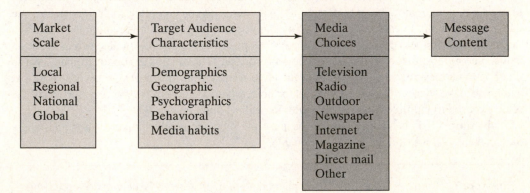

EXHIBIT 9.6   The Media Mix

Source: Kenneth Clow and Donald Baack, *Integrated Advertising, Promotion, and Marketing Communications,* 3rd ed. (Upper Saddle River, NJ: Pearson Prentice Hall, 2007), p. 260, Fig. 8.5.

Finally, look at whether you should use **keyword search advertising**, also known as **paid search**, a form of online advertising in which the company pays to have its site listed in the search results for specific words or brands. Sony recently changed to year-round use of paid search instead of paying for keyword ads during product launch periods. "People search all year round, so from now on we're looking at being 'always on,'" a marketing executive explains.[13]

Sales Promotion

It takes time to build a brand, cultivate customer loyalty, or reinforce commitment among channel members, but sales promotion can help by reducing perceived price or enhancing perceived value for a limited time. Among the sales promotion techniques that marketers can plan to use when targeting customers and prospects are sampling, couponing, rebates and refunds, premiums, sweepstakes and contests, bonus packs, and loyalty programs. Among the techniques that marketers can use when targeting channel members and salespeople are allowances and incentives, sales contests, training and support, and point-of-purchase materials. Exhibit 9.7 describes the purpose of each and highlights issues to be considered during planning (see page 160).

PLANNING TIP

Consider sales promotion for internal and external marketing.

Objectives for sales promotion activities targeting customers and prospects may include building awareness, encouraging product trial or usage, encouraging speedy response, reinforcing loyalty, supporting advertising or other communications, and defending against competitors. Objectives for sales promotion activities targeting channel members and sales representatives may include enhancing product knowledge, building commitment, reinforcing focus and loyalty, encouraging speedy response, supporting channel and other communications, and defending against competitors.

Many marketers include sales promotion in their marketing plans as a way of accelerating response over a set period, with clearly measurable results (such as counting the number of coupons redeemed and the number of units sold). However, overuse can lead customers or channel members to be more price sensitive when buying certain types of products, posing a potential threat to brand equity and profitability. Some sales promotions, such as sampling via house parties, are becoming popular because they're not only cost-effective, they're also a good way to touch off a wave of buzz.

Sampling via House Parties. The objective is not to sell anything at these house parties, except the brand and a positive experience. When Sony introduced its Move motion-sensing videogame controller, its marketers decided to demonstrate the benefits by letting consumers try one for themselves. They invited game enthusiasts to host house parties with the Move as the focus, offering the opportunity to win controllers, cameras, party goods, and more. The parties were supported by websites, Facebook posts, and Twitter messages. Party hosts provided Sony with demographic information about attendees, allowing marketers to improve targeting of future promotions.

Thai Kitchen has used house parties to let consumers cook and sample its food products, and then spread the word to their friends and relatives—which they do, thousands at a time, boosting sales significantly. The Schwan Food Company has used house parties to promote sampling of its frozen Freschetta pizza. Kimberly-Clark has used house parties to distribute coupons for its Pull-Ups diapers, with the highlight being a special live-streamed concert by Ralph's World. Watch for more house parties as brands seek out unusual sales promotions that attract consumer attention.[14]

EXHIBIT 9.7 Sales Promotion Techniques

Technique and Purpose	Issues
Sampling—Allows prospects to examine and experience product without risk	• Does the budget allow for sampling? • How, when, and where will samples be distributed?
Couponing—Reduces the perceived price of a product	• Will coupons be redeemed by loyal customers rather than prospects? • Can coupons be distributed and redeemed via mobile devices?
Rebates and refunds—Reduce the perceived price and lower the perceived risk	• Is the organization prepared for the mechanics? • How will returning money to customers affect financial objectives?
Premiums—Offer something extra for free or for a small price to enhance product's value	• How will the premium affect the plan's financial objectives? • Will the premium be unattractive or too attractive?
Sweepstakes, contests, and games—Attract attention and build excitement about a product or brand	• What legal and regulatory rules apply? • Does the budget allow for prizes, operational mechanics, and communications support?
Bonus packs—Bundle two or more products together for a special price, lowering the perceived price	• Does the budget allow for special packaging? • Will customers perceive sufficient added value?
Allowances and incentives—Give retailer or wholesaler financial reasons to support the product	• Will intermediaries offer their customers special prices as a result? • Will intermediaries overorder now and order less later?
Sales contests—Reward salespeople for selling a certain product	• Will the product receive adequate attention after a contest is over? • Will the budget cover the cost of prizes and administration?
Training and support—Educate salespeople about product and support the sales effort	• How often is training needed? • How much support does a product or channel member need?
Point-of-purchase materials—Use signs, other methods of in-store promotion	• Will retailers use the materials? • Does the budget allow for providing different intermediaries with different materials?

Public Relations

The purpose of PR is to open the lines of communication and develop positive relationships with one or more of the organization's stakeholder groups. Target audiences (the *public* in public relations) usually include some combination of customers and prospects, employees and job applicants, channel members, suppliers, government officials, local community groups, special interest groups, and the financial community.

Some of the objectives that you may set for PR are as follows:

- *Understanding stakeholders' perceptions and attitudes.* PR can help take the public's pulse and identify concerns about products and operations, social responsibility, and other issues. Whether feedback comes in through letters, e-mails, phone calls, or interaction with company personnel, you can learn what your audiences care about and see your organization through the public's eyes—and then plan to respond.
- *Manage image.* Shaping and maintaining the company's or brand's positive image generates goodwill and sets the stage for strong relations with target audiences. One way to do this is by having management and employees participate in community events, charitable causes, and other local activities. PR is also used to minimize image damage if the company makes a mistake or is involved in a crisis such as suspected product contamination.
- *Communicating views and information.* Sometimes PR is used to correct public misperceptions or to clarify a company's stand or action on a particular issue.
- *Building brand and product awareness.* Through news conferences, special events, and other techniques, PR can spotlight a brand or a product line.

Many marketers combine PR with other communication tools to extend reach and spark WOM. At the start of this chapter, you read about the Centers for Disease Control and Prevention generating publicity by talking about zombies in its materials for emergency preparedness and then following up with blog entries to keep the buzz going. A little later in the chapter, you saw how Kia combines sponsorship and advertising in campaigns. How can you use a combination of tools in your marketing plan?

Direct Marketing

In direct marketing, the organization reaches out to customers and prospects through mail, broadcast and print media, the Internet, and other media. This communications tool is cost-effective for targeting and for the use of customized messages, offers, and timing—even one recipient at a time if enough information is available about each individual's needs and characteristics. Because the audience responds directly to the organization, you can easily measure results and see whether objectives have been met—and can change the message or medium fairly quickly if necessary. Your marketing plan should summarize the objectives, the expected response, how results will be measured, any use of research, relevant issues, and the connection with other communications objectives. To be effective, the direct marketing message must be relevant to the target audience and not be perceived as junk mail or spam.

PLANNING TIP

Research the audience's needs and receptivity as you plan content, media, message, and timing.

Many direct marketing programs aim for an immediate sale; other objectives may be building awareness, influencing perceptions and attitudes, continuing customer relationships, obtaining leads for sales staff, and encouraging prospects to take the next step toward buying. Not-for-profit organizations such as Teletón typically set objectives such as generating contributions and signing up volunteers. (You can get more information about Teletón from its home page at www.teleton.org.mx, or follow the QR code here.)

Teletón. Teletón, a charity in Mexico that operates 11 rehabilitation centers for children with disabilities, uses direct marketing to reach donors during its annual radio and TV telethon, plus commercials on Spanish-language TV networks in the United States. More than three-quarters of Teleón's donations are received by phone, although it also solicits donations online and through keyword text messages that charge the contribution to the donor's cell-phone account. In addition, Teletón engages donors through its presence on Facebook, Twitter, and YouTube. It has also released an app for use in making donations and for staying informed about the nonprofit's latest news. Since the organization began, it has raised more than $240 million to help children.[15]

Personal Selling

Personal selling is appropriate if the target audience requires customized goods or services, needs assistance assessing needs, makes large purchases, or requires individual attention for other reasons. This is an important tool for pharmaceutical firms, equipment manufacturers, and many other B2B marketers, as well as for some marketers that target consumers. The one-to-one nature of personal selling (in person or by phone) supports strong customer relationships; therefore, the emphasis may not be on making an instant sale but on building connections for the future.

Decisions you'll face in planning for personal selling include the following: whether to hire salespeople or to work with an outside sales agency; how to recruit, train, manage, motivate, and compensate sales staff; how many salespeople are needed; and how to organize the sales force (for example, by product, market, or type of customer).

A number of decisions about structuring the sales process draw input directly from the marketing plan:

- *Identifying and qualifying prospects.* Based on earlier segmentation and targeting decisions, management identifies the audience for personal selling activities and determines how prospects will be qualified for sales contact.
- *Planning the presales approach.* Details from earlier market and customer analyses inform the approach that a salesperson plans in contacting prospects.
- *Making sales contact.* Based on the prospect's needs and the firm's positioning, the salesperson opens a dialogue with a prospect, determines specific needs, and explains how the offering will provide value.
- *Addressing objections.* Using knowledge of the product, the prospect's needs, and the competition, the salesperson responds to specific concerns and questions raised by the prospect.
- *Closing the sale.* The salesperson completes the sale, arranges payment, and schedules delivery with an understanding of pricing and logistics strategies.
- *Following up after the sale.* To continue building the relationship, the salesperson must understand the customer service strategy, the customer's needs, and applicable communications support, such as frequent-buyer programs.

Generally, having sales personnel on staff or on contract is costly, which is why many products aren't marketed in this way. Expensive and novel products, however, may require personal selling to educate customers about the value they represent and to provide support before, during, and after the sale. Think about these issues as you write your marketing plan.

Integrated Marketing Communication

For maximum effect, plan to coordinate the content and delivery of all marketing communications for your offering, brand, and organization to ensure consistency and to support your positioning and direction. This approach is known as **integrated marketing communication**.

Integration not only avoids confusion about the brand and the benefits, it also reinforces the connection with the sports or lifestyle activities and sparks instant recognition when people in the target audience are exposed to the firm's logo or product name. The total effect of your communications makes an impact by differentiating your products and communicating their value in a crowded competitive arena. Integration also contributes to the level of influence you may be able to exert on your audiences, whether that influence is to make a favorable brand impression or to encourage buying of certain products.

Several factors make carefully planned and coordinated communications even more crucial to marketing success.[16] These include maturing markets, a decline in the effectiveness of mass-media advertising, consumers' perceptions of brand parity, an increase in consumers' choices and information sources, global competition, and changes in channel power. In any case, whether you use a combination of advertising, sales promotion, PR, direct marketing, and personal selling, or only one of these tools, integration of all messages in all media will help you leverage and focus your efforts to better effect.

Summary

Planning marketing communications and influence strategy involves the use of advertising, sales promotion, PR, direct marketing, and/or personal selling to engage target audiences and influence how they think and feel about and how they act toward a brand or an offering. A growing number of marketers use social media, word of mouth, and buzz to connect with audiences and influence them. A push strategy addresses the channel as the target audience; a pull strategy addresses customers as the target audience; a strategy that combines push and pull targets both customers and the channel. Start by choosing and analyzing the target audience, setting your objectives and budget, and examining key issues such as legal, regulatory, technological, and competitive circumstances. Depending on the plan's overall objectives, communications may be used to move the target audience through responses corresponding to beliefs, behavior, and feelings about the product or brand. After deciding on the communications tools for your campaign, allow for pretesting and postimplementation research to evaluate and fine-tune the strategy and specific programs. Integrated marketing communication means coordinating the content and delivery of all messages and media to ensure consistency and to support the positioning.

Your Marketing Plan, Step by Step

Answering the following questions will help you think through the decisions you face in planning communications and influence strategy. After you've considered all these issues, document what you decide in your written plan.

1. Who, specifically, is your target audience? What do you know about these people that can help you communicate with them? Look at the primary and secondary research, segmentation data, and other information you've gathered so far for your marketing plan as you write a paragraph or

two about your target audience. How can you learn more about your target audience's media usage, lifestyle, preferences, and other details that relate to communications and influence?

2. What do you want to accomplish by communicating with your target audience(s)? Will you use a push strategy, a pull strategy, or a combination? You'll need separate objectives when you target customers in a pull strategy and when you target intermediaries in a push strategy. Look at Exhibit 9.3 as you establish objectives for influencing your audience's response to your communications. List at least two specific objectives for communicating with and influencing each audience. How do these objectives support the marketing, financial, and societal objectives in your overall plan? If possible, look at the outcome of previous communications strategies to see whether objectives were achieved and if not, why not. Also estimate the communications budget needed to meet your objectives in the coming year, knowing you can fine-tune the budget later in the planning process.

3. What legal, regulatory, ethical, cultural, competitive, and technological issues are likely to affect your ability to reach your audience or to use certain messages or media? Write a few sentences summarizing the communications opportunities and threats presented by the issues you've identified, based on research and your firm's previous experience, if any. How are competitors communicating with your target audience, and what are the strengths and weaknesses of their communications and influence strategies? Write a brief SWOT analysis of your main competitor's communications and influence strategy, and draw conclusions about the implications for your strategy.

4. With your objectives and budget in mind, which communications tools are most appropriate for engaging your target audience, based on your audience analysis? Write a few sentences about each of the five main tools, indicating why you will or won't include it in your communications strategy, and explaining your rationale for your choices. Now dig deeper to consider how you will use your chosen tools. Outline the highlights of your marketing communications strategy, and indicate how you'll integrate your messages and media. Will you time your communications so that some start while others are already in the marketplace? Will you change communications during the coming year? If competitors launch extensive campaigns, what can you do to keep your message in front of your audiences?

5. Will you pretest your communications? What postimplementation research will you plan for evaluating the outcome of your strategy? How will you know whether your target audience receives your communications, understands them, and takes action? How will you know whether you've influenced the audience's thinking, feelings, and behavior? Be sure to explain your answers in your plan.

6. What role will social media play in your communications and influence strategy? How can you use social media to engage customers in a way that they value? Which social media are most appropriate for your product or campaign, and why? What will you do to link social media to other communication tools in your campaign? Who in your company will be responsible for social media interaction and how much will you need to budget for this?

Endnotes

1. See Michael Levens, *Marketing Defined, Explained, Applied* (Upper Saddle River, NJ: Pearson Prentice Hall, 2010), p. 167.

2. Sydney Lupkin, "Government Zombie Promos Are Spreading," *ABC News,* September 7, 2012, http://abcnews.go.com; Elizabeth Wiese, "The CDC Zombies Return with a New Comic Book," *USA Today,* October 19, 2011, www.usatoday.com;

Betsy McKay, "CDC Advises on Zombie Apocalypse . . . and Other Emergencies," *Wall Street Journal,* May 18, 2011, www.wsj.com.

3. Brent Balinsky, "Chobani Confident Australian Success Will Continue," *Manufacturers' Monthly (Australia),* September 18, 2012, www.manmonthly.com.au; Sarah E. Needleman, "Old Factory,

Snap Decision Spawn Greek-Yogurt Craze," *Wall Street Journal,* June 21, 2012, p. B1; Stuart Elliott, "Jennie Finch Pitches for Child's Version of Chobani Yogurt," *New York Times,* June 14, 2012, www.nytimes .com; Stuart Elliott, "Chobani, Greek Yogurt Leader, Lets Its Fans Tell the Story," *New York Times,* February 16, 2011, www .nytimes.com; Gillian Tan, "Chobani Hoping Foray Down Under Proves Fruitful," *Wall Street Journal,* May 30, 2012, www .wsj.com.

4. Marci Weisler, "Abandon or Monetize? How Brands and Marketers Can Maximize Their App ROI," *MediaPost,* June 21, 2012, www.mediapost.com.

5. "Nike's Twitter Football Advertising Campaign Banned," *BBC News,* June 20, 2012, www.bbc.co.uk.

6. Kenneth Corbin, "Mobile Tech, Social Media Force FTC to Revisit Advertising Guidelines," *CIO,* May 31, 2012, www.cio.com.

7. Ryan Joe, "Kellogg Company: 'We Don't Care About Clicks,'" *Direct Marketing News,* June 21, 2012, www.dmnews.com.

8. Jane L. Levere, "Customers Do the Selling for Travel Firms," *New York Times,* June 21, 2012, www.nytimes.com.

9. Rance Crain, "Why Business-to-Business Advertising Is Increasingly Also Aimed at Consumers," *Advertising Age,* June 18, 2012, www.adage.com.

10. Michelle Kung, "'The Amazing Spider-Man' to Debut Footage in Walmart Stores," *Wall Street Journal,* June 7, 2012, www.wsj .com; Maisie McCabe, "Harrods Launches Media Division," *MediaWeek,* August 23, 2011, www.mediaweek.co.uk; "Why In-Store TV Advertising Works," *Marshall Insights Newsletter (USC Marshall School of Business),* November 19, 2010, www .marshall.usc.edu; Greg Braxton and Joe Flint, "Would You Like TV with That Big Mac?" *Los Angeles Times,* October 17, 2011, www.latimes.com.

11. Karl Greenberg, "Kia Back at Vans Warped Tour," *MediaPost,* June 13, 2012, www .mediapost.com; Jon Fine, "Where Are Advertisers? At the Movies," *Businessweek,* May 25, 2009, pp. 65–66.

12. Emily Glazer, "Target: Customers on the Go," *Wall Street Journal,* May 15, 2011, www.wsj.com.

13. "Sony Expands Search Budget for an 'Always On' Strategy," *New Media Age,* April 23, 2009, p. 6.

14. Stacy Finz, "House Parties Push Products," *San Francisco Chronicle,* August 6, 2011, www.sfgate.com; Shahnaz Mahmud, "Brands Use House Parties to Collect Data," *Direct Marketing News,* January 1, 2011, www .dmnews.com; Leslie Patton, "House Parties with a Commercial Twist," *Businessweek,* February 3, 2011, www.businessweek.com.

15. Anna Marie de la Fuente, "'Sabado' Night Fever," *Daily Variety,* March 1, 2012, p. 10; "Hispanic Donors; Playing Up Family Ties in Appeals," *Nonprofit Times,* May 2009, www.nptimes.com; "Teleton MexAmerica Raises Largest One Day Amount to Date," *Science Letter,* March 24, 2009, n.p.; Teletón website, www.teleton.org.mx.

16. See Kenneth E. Clow and Donald Baack, *Integrated Advertising, Promotion, and Marketing Communications,* 3rd ed. (Upper Saddle River, NJ: Pearson Prentice Hall, 2007), p. 15.

Planning Metrics and Implementation Control

In this chapter:

PREVIEW

No marketing plan is complete without an explanation of how and how often you will measure the outcome and what happens if actual results are not what you expected. Thus, the final step in marketing planning is to prepare for tracking results and controlling implementation (see Exhibit 10.1). In this chapter, you'll learn about four tools for determining performance: metrics to gauge movement toward achieving objectives, forecasts of future sales and costs, budgets allocating financial resources, and schedules identifying the timing of marketing tasks. Also, you'll learn how to plan for marketing control to identify, analyze, and correct variations from the expected results.

APPLYING YOUR KNOWLEDGE

After you read this chapter, review the metrics and control entries in this book's sample plan and then answer the questions in "Your Marketing Plan, Step by Step" at the end of this chapter. Also look at this chapter's checklist. Finally, document your ideas and metrics, including any contingency plans you develop, in your written plan.

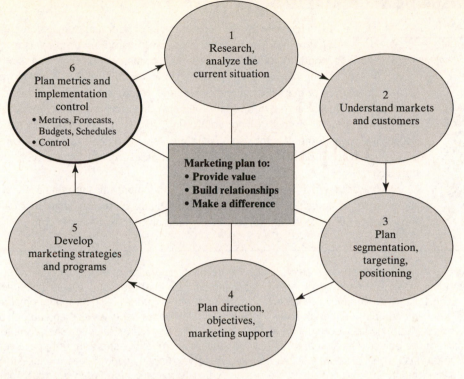

EXHIBIT 10.1 Marketing Planning: Step 6

CHAPTER 10 CHECKLIST   Planning a Marketing Audit

Marketing Strategy

✓ Does the mission focus on market and customer needs?

✓ Are marketing-mix strategies appropriate in light of the situation analysis?

✓ Do all objectives support the organization's long-term goals and mission?

✓ Do employees understand the marketing plan and have the skills, resources, and time to implement it?

Marketing Operations and Results

✓ Is the organization ready to track and report results and trends to marketing decision makers?

✓ Does the organization have good relationships with customers, channel members, salespeople, suppliers, and partners?

✓ Can the organization benchmark against industry or world-class standards?

✓ How are performance problems analyzed, and how is control applied?

Stakeholder Relations

✓ How are stakeholders' comments, feedback, and priorities obtained, analyzed, and incorporated into marketing decisions?

✓ How do customers and other stakeholders perceive the brand/product/company, and how have their perceptions and attitudes changed over time?

MEASURING WHAT MATTERS

PLANNING TIP

You can't manage what you don't measure, so plan to track progress toward results.

How will you measure the desired outcomes of your marketing strategies and programs? How will you measure progress toward long-term goals week by week or month by month? The time to establish checkpoints and standards for measuring performance is during the planning process. Whether you're developing a marketing plan for a single brand or a number of marketing plans because you're active in multiple markets and offer numerous product lines, you'll need to track progress toward your objectives. Then, once implementation is underway, you can monitor the established measures and analyze results over time to diagnose any variations and make changes in order to get back on track toward future success.

Measuring what matters is how Apple, with annual sales topping $100 billion and a yearly ad budget of almost $1 billion, maintains its market share momentum. (Follow this QR code to see Apple's home page or go to www.apple.com.)

Apple. When Apple writes a marketing plan for the next generation of iPad or iPhone, or for a brand new product, it accounts for every detail and builds in checkpoints to be sure everything leading up to the introduction happens on time and within budget. Apple monitors market demand and competitive market share for its product categories and uses its marketing plans to guide the timing and coordination of all activities. Achieving higher sales in a shorter period is one of the objectives that supports Apple's image and competitive strength, not just its revenue targets. When CEO Tim Cook announced that the company had reached the milestone of selling nearly 70 million iPads in the product's first two years, he pointed out that Apple needed 24 years to reach the same level of unit sales after launching its Mac computers.

Apple pays particularly close attention to measures of customer service because of the implications for long-term brand loyalty and customer retention. Its retail stores receive daily feedback about how customers rate their services, and if problems arise, each unit takes immediate action to get back on track. Good marketing plans and good implementation have helped Apple build iPhone sales very quickly in new segments (such as among buyers of pre-paid phone services) and growing markets (such as in China). The company knows to plan for slightly overall slower sales in the months leading up to the launch of a new model of iPhone or iPad while having the staffing and inventory in place for successful launches once a product is ready. By tracking unit sales by store and product line, as well as by channel and market, and by examining market-share changes over time, Apple can see how its marketing plans are bringing it closer to its global share goals. Just as important, the company is ready to adjust its plans in response to economic conditions, legal and regulatory changes, and other factors that might influence effective implementation.[1]

Marketing plans typically include four main tools for measuring progress toward the desired results: (1) metrics, (2) forecasts, (3) budgets, and (4) schedules (see Exhibit 10.2).

PLANNING METRICS

Metrics are numerical measures of specific performance-related activities and outcomes that are used to see whether the organization is moving closer to its objectives and goals. Metrics focus managers and employees on activities that make a difference, set up performance expectations

EXHIBIT 10.2 Tools for Measuring Marketing Progress

Tool	Application
Metrics	Used to establish measures for specific performance-related outcomes and activities so that results can be tracked over time
Forecasts	Used to predict future sales and costs as checkpoints for measuring progress
Budgets	Used to allocate funding across programs in specified periods and then to track expenditures during implementation
Schedules	Used to plan and coordinate the timing of tasks and programs

that can be objectively measured, and lay a foundation for internal accountability and pride in accomplishments. Exhibit 10.3 shows the main categories of metrics often used to assess marketing performance. Note that the marketing plan need not include all metrics for all activities—but

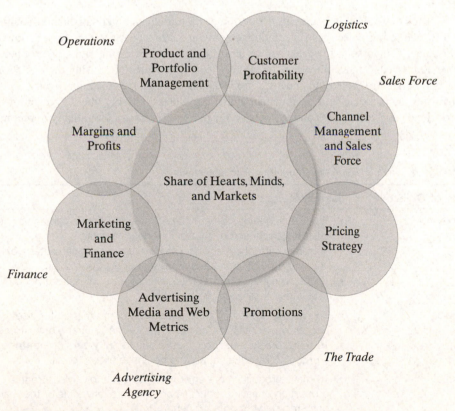

EXHIBIT 10.3 Main Categories of Marketing Metrics

Source: Paul W. Farris, Neil T. Bendle, Phillip E. Pfeifer, and David J. Reibstein, *Marketing Metrics*, 2nd edition (Upper Saddle River, NJ: FT Press, 2010), p. 5, Fig. 1.1.

it should show the most important metrics and explain the connection between those measurements and the organization's objectives, because accountability is vital.

Many organizations monitor key results using a **marketing dashboard**, a computerized, graphical, or digital presentation that helps management track important metrics over time and spot deviations from the marketing plan.[2] Like a car dashboard, the marketing dashboard helps marketers see the situation at a glance, based on a limited number of data inputs, so that they can make decisions quickly in order to improve effectiveness or efficiency.[3] For example, Discover Financial Services uses a marketing dashboard to track sales and other key metrics, and then uses the data to analyze the impact of communications and to plan for future campaigns.[4]

Identifying Metrics

PLANNING TIP

Include metrics for one-time, short-term, and ongoing programs.

How can you identify suitable metrics? One approach is to work backward from the mission, goals, and objectives to find specific outcomes and activities that signal progress (think both short-term and long-term progress). For example, companies pursuing growth need metrics to measure changes in customer relationships and sales. Such metrics might include measurements of customer acquisition, customer retention, customer satisfaction, customer lifetime value, and sales trends by customer or segment. Exhibit 10.4 shows some sample metrics for a number of marketing plan objectives.

Metrics that reveal increases in the customer base and customer satisfaction—which are related to marketing objectives for relationships—can serve as early indicators of future sales performance. Conversely, lower scores on these metrics are warning signs of problems that must be addressed. Some companies, including Apple and Philips, are using the *Net Promoter Score,* popularized by Bain & Company's Fred Reichheld, to gauge customer loyalty. This metric identifies the percentage of customers that are "promoters" (highly likely to recommend the firm to friends and colleagues) and the percentage that are "detractors" (unlikely to recommend

EXHIBIT 10.4 **Sample Metrics for Marketing Plan Objectives**

Type of Objective	Sample Metrics
Marketing	• To acquire new customers: Measure number or percentage of new customers acquired by month, quarter, and year. • To retain current customers: Measure number or percentage of customers who continue purchasing during a set period. • To increase market share: Measure dollar or unit sales divided by total industry sales during a set period.
Financial	• To improve profitability: Measure gross or net margin for a set period by product, line, channel, marketing program, or customer. • To reach breakeven: Measure the number of weeks or months until a product's revenue equals and begins to exceed costs.
Societal	• To make products more environmentally friendly: Measure the proportion of each product's parts that are recyclable or that have been recycled during a set period. • To build awareness of a social issue: Research awareness among the target audience after the program or a set period.

the firm). Users find value in tracking changes in this score over time, setting objectives for improvement, and investigating why detractors won't recommend the company. Philips regularly announces its scores so that investors and other stakeholders can see the results and watch its progress.[5]

In terms of financial outcomes, common metrics are return on investment (ROI) and gross or net profit margins for each marketing activity, products and lines, channels, promotions, and price adjustments, among other measures. If you use metrics related to both marketing and financial objectives, you'll get a much better idea of how much progress you're making and which areas of your plan might need tweaking. Consider the experience of startup PetFlow.com, which grew into a $30 million business in less than three years. (You can see its home page by scanning the QR code or visiting www.petflow.com.)

PetFlow.com. Entrepreneurs Alex Zhardanovsky and Joe Speiser used their insight into consumer behavior to establish a niche business in the lucrative $50 billion U.S. market serving the needs of pet owners. They realized that consumers would pay for the convenience of shopping for pet food online and arranging for regular deliveries on a subscription basis, as a way to avoid the hassle of remembering to buy and then lugging home big containers of pet food. Unlike many pet supply e-tailers, PetFlow is focused only on pet food because of the long-term potential for repeat business. PetFlow.com took its first orders in July 2010. Every day, the entrepreneurs tracked the number of customers who clicked to buy and the amount of each transaction. They also tracked the number of customers who scheduled future deliveries to be paid for and shipped automatically—and the number who stopped such automatic deliveries.

By paying attention to marketing and financial metrics, PetFlow's owners used their marketing plan to fuel meteoric growth in customer relationships and revenue. In less than a year, the company was selling $13 million worth of pet food, more than half of it to customers who subscribed to future deliveries. Double-digit sales growth has continued every year. Thanks to metrics, PetFlow's owners know that they spend about $50 to sign up a new customer. They also know they're retaining more than 98% of the customers who subscribe to automatic shipments—very important for future profitability. Why? Because PetFlow's owners can more accurately plan for inventory—down to specific brands and products that subscribers buy—they can better manage costs and profit margins over time.[6]

A second way to identify metrics is by looking for key components or activities related to customer buying behavior, using research gathered during the situation analysis. This means finding measurements that signal customer movement toward a purchase. When the U.K. retailer Marks & Spencer decided to open M&S Bank as a partnership with HSBC, it knew, thanks to metrics, that its brand had the superior strength and widespread respect absolutely critical for expanding into a different business. "M&S is one of the most trusted brands on the U.K. high street, and we've achieved this by continually listening and responding to the needs of our 21 million customers," the CEO says.[7] Although many firms measure brand preference as an indicator of future buying behavior, this metric is not right for all organizations. Once customers start buying, the company can use metrics to measure sales by transaction or segment, customer or segment purchase frequency, sales by channel or intermediary, and so forth. Exhibit 10.5 presents sample metrics keyed to some basic stages in the buying process.

Businesses that rely on personal selling usually set up metrics to measure the sales pipeline, such as number of prospect inquiries, number of qualified leads generated, number of

EXHIBIT 10.5 **Metrics Based on Customer Behavior**

Behavior	Sample Metrics
Customer becomes aware of an offering.	Measure customer awareness of offering and competing offers, by segment.
Customer learns more about an offering.	Measure number of information packets downloaded, number of hits on website or YouTube video, number of people who visit store.
Customer has a positive attitude toward the offering.	Measure customer attitudes toward the offer and competing offers, by segment; feedback from hotlines, social media, letters, e-mails, channel, etc.
Customer tries the offering.	Measure number of people who receive free samples or who redeem coupons for trials.
Customer buys the offering.	Measure sales by transaction, segment, channel, payment method; conversion from trials and information requests.
Customer is satisfied.	Measure customer satisfaction by offering and by segment; satisfaction feedback from hotlines, social media, letters, e-mails, channel, etc.
Customer becomes loyal.	Measure customer retention and churn; size and frequency of repeat purchases; utilization of frequent buyer program.

meetings with qualified leads, number of bids accepted, percentage of prospects converted to customers, and number of orders received. Channel productivity may be judged using metrics such as number or percentage of customers or sales generated per channel or intermediary, cost and profits per sale by channel or intermediary, speed of order fulfillment, and percentage of stock-outs. Of course, the exact metrics depend on each organization's situation and priorities.

Nonprofit organizations frequently use metrics to quantify the immediate and long-term results of marketing initiatives. Common metrics are donations received (to show effectiveness and efficiency of fund-raising by program and source), number of people being helped (to demonstrate use of service by segment or location), and public image (to gauge awareness among and attitude of stakeholders).

PLANNING TIP

Determine whether last year's metrics make sense for this year's plan.

To be effective in implementing and evaluating your plan, choose both internal and external metrics and metrics that look forward as well as look backward. Exhibit 10.6 shows some examples.

Marketing Metrics for Digital and Social Media

Metrics for digital and social media marketing are still evolving. At the dawn of the Internet age, marketers had limited options for measuring what was happening online and had to settle for vague measures such as number of clicks on an ad, which revealed nothing about progress toward a purchase or a customer relationship. When planning for e-mail, marketers could measure how many people opened it and how many clicked for more information. Ultimately, marketers really wanted to know how many of those people clicked to buy; with direct marketing, they can measure that result quite easily in a digital environment. With the rise of mobile marketing, companies

EXHIBIT 10.6 Internal versus External Metrics and Forward- versus Backward-Looking Metrics

Performance Perspective	Forward-Looking Metrics	Backward-Looking Metrics
Internal (company) metrics	Company metrics applied during an operating period, such as: • Product defects • Late deliveries • Inventory turnover	Company metrics reported at the end of an operating period, such as: • Sales revenue • Percent gross profit • Return on assets
External (market) metrics	Market metrics applied during an operating period, such as: • Brand awareness • Customer satisfaction • Intent to repurchase	Market metrics reported at the end of an operating period, such as: • Market share • Customer retention • Revenue per customer

Source: Roger J. Best, *Market-Based Management,* 6th ed. (Upper Saddle River, NJ: Pearson Education, 2013), p. 47, Fig. 2-8.

can use metrics such as how many recipients redeem a mobile offer (like a coupon) and which offers are most effective in achieving objectives (sales, relationships, etc.).

Knowing that awareness and engagement are prerequisites to donations and volunteer support, many nonprofits set objectives for social media and measure results by counting the number of "likes," followers, and retweets. Once they have followers or fans, they can communicate about specific campaigns. The nonprofit MUST Ministries in Kennesaw, Georgia, recently set a one-day objective of having 150 pairs of shoes donated to help people in homeless shelters. It tweeted about the challenge, and its communication partner Beremedy posted the shoe challenge on its Twitter account, as well. Within 24 hours, MUST had met the objective (and eventually received more than 500 donated pairs).[8]

Marketers have grown more sophisticated about measuring digital and social media results in relation to target audiences and marketing objectives. Kellogg's associate director of global digital strategy says his company doesn't look at number of clicks, because "clicks have zero correlation to sales." Instead, Kellogg examines whether its digital ads are being seen by specific audiences at particular times when they are must receptive, and it measures how brand awareness and purchase intentions change as a result.[9]

A different example comes from the experience of BT, the British telecommunications firm. BT knows that responding to a customer service problem costs about $18 through traditional channels, whereas receiving and responding to a service problem via Twitter costs less than 50 cents per incident. BT therefore uses metrics to track the proportion of service issues it resolves via traditional methods and via Twitter, because of the huge difference in cost.[10]

Even before customers make a purchase, they have to have a positive attitude toward the brand and acquire a preference for it. These steps in the buying decision process are often the focus of marketing objectives in plans that cover digital and social media. The luxury car maker Audi had specific metrics in mind when its marketing plan called for using Twitter hashtags in its Super Bowl commercials. (Visit Audi's worldwide home page at www.audi.com/com/brand/en.html or follow the QR code.)

> **Audi.** Few TV events draw more viewers than the Super Bowl, which is why advertisers like Audi create specific marketing plans for ads and other promotions related to the big game. During one recent Super Bowl, Audi's immediate objective was to become the most-mentioned hashtag among Super Bowl tweets and to spark ongoing buzz in social media. The automaker saw this as a way to highlight the brand and encourage consumers to keep it in mind when thinking about a future car purchase. In fact, consumers and the company repeatedly tweeted messages containing Audi's hashtags throughout the year, resulting in ongoing dialogue long after the Super Bowl was over and giving Audi a lot of brand exposure. Whether Twitter dialogues will add up to future car sales is a question that Audi can't yet answer because of the difficulty of tracking whether someone who tweets about a car brand ultimately buys that brand. Still, Audi is developing new marketing plans for staying in touch with target audiences through multimedia promotional activities linked to the Super Bowl and other sports events.[11]

Using Metrics

Although metrics start with periodic measurements of marketing plan activities and outcomes, they are most valuable when viewed in the context of the following:

- *Expected outcomes.* How do the outcomes measured by metrics compare with the expected outcomes in the marketing plan? If the metric is dollar sales by segment, the marketer will compare actual segment sales over a given period with expected segment sales for that period in order to evaluate progress. Adobe Systems, which makes business software, uses metrics to compare the actual outcomes of its business-to-business (B2B) campaigns with expected outcomes. "I have to have an ROI (return on investment) target at the beginning of a campaign and show performance against goals," explains the head of global marketing.[12]

- *Historical results.* How do the outcomes measured by metrics compare with the actual outcomes in previous periods? Because marketers review previous results as part of their internal environmental analysis, they have the data to weigh current outcomes against previous outcomes, which can reveal unusual trends and suggest possible problems that could affect performance. JetBlue, Southwest, United Continental, and all of the carriers that participate in the American Consumer Satisfaction Index examine short- and long-term trends as reflected in the company and industry rankings in the yearly survey. The trends help these airlines to understand customer attitudes over time and to look at changes in their ratings compared with competitors.[13]

- *Competitive or industry outcomes.* How do the outcomes measured by metrics compare with competitors' outcomes or average outcomes for the industry? When comparable competitive or industry information is available, marketers can check these against their own organization's outcomes to gauge relative performance and to reveal strengths and weaknesses. Because competitors operate under different circumstances and have very different goals, costs, and outcomes, competitive comparisons are useful only in relative terms.

- *Environmental influences.* How do the outcomes measured by metrics appear in relation to environmental trends, such as an economic boom or a parts shortage? Marketers need to interpret metrics in the context of everything else affecting the organization. If metrics indicate that sales objectives are barely being achieved when an economic boom has dramatically boosted demand, the organization should reevaluate its metrics or create new ones to find out why sales aren't higher still.

Many companies check performance metrics on a monthly basis, although some check weekly, some daily, and some more often, when they have access to fresh data and know they can gain or lose a sale at the click of a mouse. Remember that metrics are merely tools to track the progress of programs after implementation, nothing more. Management must make decisions and take action when metrics show that the expected results aren't being achieved.

One of the most common metrics for measuring marketing success in financial terms is return on investment in marketing (ROMI):

$$\frac{\text{Net profit attributable to a marketing activity (\$)}}{\text{Marketing investment (\$)}}$$

ROMI can be applied to individual marketing activities as well as to the overall marketing investment made by an organization. If a sales promotion returns a net profit of \$20,000 and it costs \$6,000, the ROMI calculation would be:

$$\frac{\$20,000}{\$6,000} = 333\%$$

Remember that activities geared toward marketing and societal objectives may not demonstrate immediate paybacks. In fact, not every marketing plan outcome or activity can be measured, nor is every possible metric actually meaningful. For example, if a company lacks the budget to conduct valid attitudinal research, it cannot use customer attitudes as a metric. Another potential problem is that marketers will simply aim to meet each metrics target without watching the overall effect on strategic outcomes.[14]

PLANNING FORECASTS, BUDGETS, AND SCHEDULES

In addition to specifying metrics for measuring interim performance, your marketing plan should include forecasts, budgets, and schedules.

Forecasting Sales and Costs

Forecasts are future projections of what sales and costs are likely to be in the months and years covered by the plan. To do a good job of forecasting, companies must weigh external factors such as demand, threats, and opportunities as well as internal factors such as goals, capabilities, and constraints. Many marketers prepare forecasts for the best-case, the worst-case, and the most-likely scenario. Nonprofits may prepare forecasts of future contributions, overall need for services, and projected service use, along with future estimates of associated costs.

Forecasts can never be more than good estimates, and in fact you must allow for some forecast error because they are only projections. Still, forecasts should be as accurate as possible, because the organization relies on them when developing strategies and planning the resources needed to implement the marketing plan. Also note that when you change the assumptions underlying a forecast, you need to think about what that means for a forecast and for future forecasts.

Plan to review your forecasts often because internal or external shifts can influence sales, costs, and marketing performance at any time. Tim Berry, head of Palo Alto Software, brings his managers together every three weeks specifically to review results and forecasts and to work together on any changes they decide to make.[15] Forecasting must also account for the effect that marketing activities will have on the direction and velocity of sales. For example, you may forecast higher sales for a new product if you plan to use penetration pricing to encourage rapid adoption. On the other hand, if you use skimming pricing to skim profits from the market, your forecast for introductory sales volume may be lower than with penetration pricing.

Remember, relying on a forecast that underestimates sales could leave you with insufficient inventory or staffing to satisfy demand; on the other hand, relying on an overestimate could lead to overproduction and other costly problems. Toyota understands this, so it reviews its forecasts frequently, especially during volatile economic periods, to be sure it will produce the right cars in the right numbers for each target market.[16] The key point is: If you don't have the right number of products, you won't be able to achieve your objectives.

TYPES OF FORECASTS   The following are the most commonly used types of forecasts:

- *Forecasts of market and segment sales.* The company starts by projecting a market's overall industry-wide sales for up to five years, using the definition created during the market analysis. This helps size the entire market so that managers can set specific share objectives (as discussed in Chapter 5) and can estimate the share competitors will have in future years. If possible, the company also should forecast year-by-year sales in each targeted segment. Bombardier, based in Canada, forecasts sales of its planes and trains by segment, up to 20 years in advance. Every year, it adjusts the segment forecasts based on factors such as the current and projected global economic situation and the price of jet fuel, and then amends its marketing plans in line with these updated forecasts.[17]

- *Forecasts of company product sales.* Based on market and segment forecasts, market and customer analysis, direction decisions, and marketing strategies, the company now projects the number and dollar amount of product (or product line) sales for each market or segment. These projections are usually presented month by month for a year or for the period covered by the marketing plan and sometimes longer. Procter & Gamble develops forecasts market by market, brand by brand, and product line by product line. It also forecasts new product sales, specifically as a way of focusing marketing resources on the most promising new products in the development pipeline.[18] Tesla Motors, which makes electric cars, forecasts sales by the number of cars it will sell per year. It uses these forecasts to plan for opening new dealerships and attracting consumers to test-drive (and buy) its cars.[19] (Follow the QR to see Tesla's home page or visit www.teslamotors.com.)

- *Forecasts of cost of sales.* Here, management forecasts the costs associated with company product sales forecasts, based on data gathered for the analysis of the current situation and on data about cost trends. These forecasts may be adjusted after marketing budgets have been prepared.

- *Forecasts of sales and costs by channel.* When the company sells through more than one channel level or intermediary, it may want to project monthly unit and dollar sales by product by channel and, if feasible, costs per channel. These forecasts focus attention on channel cost efficiency and provide a yardstick for measuring and analyzing actual channel results and expenses. Multichannel marketing requires a good grasp of channel forecasts. Rue La La, an online retailer, forecasts the percentage of sales it will derive from mobile marketing, users of home or office computers, and users of tablet computers, in great detail, down to different days of the week and different seasons. The retailer learned, through analyses of sales history by channel, that most of the purchases made on holidays come through the mobile channel. Now it forecasts for up to 70% of all holiday purchases to be completed through mobile marketing and plans its marketing, technology, and customer support accordingly.[20]

Next, the marketer calculates the month-to-month and year-to-year change for the figures in each forecast to examine trends (such as how much growth in sales is being projected for the coming 12 months) and rate of change (such as how quickly costs are rising). Forecast projections and trend calculations can be used to check on target markets, review objectives, reallocate resources, and measure actual against expected results. Given the rapid rate of change in many markets, many companies update forecasts monthly or more often to reflect current conditions; many also collaborate with key suppliers and channel members for more precise forecasting.

SOURCES AND TOOLS FOR FORECASTING DATA   Often, companies obtain data for forecasting purposes from their value-chain partners. Marketers can also tap primary research sources such as studies of buying patterns and buying intentions that suggest demand levels by market, segment, category, or product. However, marketers must use judgment, remembering that customers may not buy in the future as they have in the past, nor will they necessarily make future purchases even though they might have told researchers they would do so. Trade associations, government statistics, and industry analysts' reports can be valuable secondary sources of data.

Some marketers predict future sales by applying causal analysis methods such as regression analysis, econometric models, and neural networks or by using time series methods such as smoothing and decomposition. They may also apply judgmental forecasting tools such as sales force estimates, executive opinion, the Delphi method, and online prediction markets, as shown in Exhibit 10.7. Because these tools may be subject to human error or bias, marketers generally use a combination of judgment and statistical analysis, updated with estimates from knowledgeable sources for increased accuracy.

EXHIBIT 10.7   Judgmental Tools for Forecasting

Forecasting Tool	Use
Sales force estimates	Composite projection based on estimates made by sales personnel; convenient, but accuracy depends on instincts, experience, and objectivity of salespeople
Executive opinion	Composite projection based on estimates made by managers; convenient, but accuracy depends on instincts, experience, and objectivity of managers
Delphi method	Composite projection based on successive rounds of input from outside experts, who ultimately come to consensus on estimates; time consuming, but sometimes helpful when forecasting new-product or new-market sales
Online prediction market	Composite projection based on combined judgment of employees or stakeholders who indicate their confidence in certain marketing predictions through online "trading" in a mock stock market; efficient, but may involve bias toward longer-term predictions

When forecasting, remember to take into account the possibility that competitive pressure might change. Also look at your forecasting from a channel perspective, to be sure it will meet your distribution arrangements or to change your plans to accommodate higher or lower forecasts. If you're forecasting sales of a new product, try to identify patterns from an existing product or industry that might help you project sales when your organization has no previous experience with such a product. Finally, be realistic about your forecasts.[21]

Budgeting to Plan and Track Expenses

Budgets are time-defined allocations of financial outlays for specific functions, programs, customer segments, or geographic regions. Budgeting enables marketing managers to allocate expenses by program or activity over specific periods and to compare these with actual expenditures. Some organizations insist that budget preparation follow internal financial calendars; some specify profit hurdles or particular assumptions about expenses and allocation; some mandate particular formats or supporting documentation; and some require budgets based on best-case, worst-case, and most-likely scenarios. A growing number of businesses are no longer fixing budgets annually but instead are adjusting budgets monthly based on market realities or are tying budgets to longer-term performance.[22]

PLANNING TIP

Combine bottom-up and top-down budget input when allocating marketing funds.

BUDGETING METHODS FOR MARKETING SPENDING   How much money should be budgeted for marketing programs? Smaller companies often deal with this question by using **affordability budgeting**, simply budgeting what they believe they can afford, given other urgent expenses. Affordability budgeting may work for start-ups in the early days, when many entrepreneurs have little to spend. However, this is generally not a good way to budget, because it doesn't allow for the kind of significant, ongoing investments often needed to launch major new products or to enter intensely competitive markets. In effect, budgeting based on affordability ignores the profit payback that comes from spending on marketing to build sales.

Ideally, the size of the marketing budget should be based on careful analysis of the link between spending and sales (and for not-for-profit organizations, donations). By building a sophisticated model of how sales actually react to different spending levels, the company can determine exactly how big the marketing budget must be to achieve its sales targets. Companies without such models tend to rely on rule-of-thumb budgeting methods that don't directly correlate spending with sales, such as the percentage-of-sales method, the competitive-parity method, and the objective-and-task method.

With **percentage-of-sales budgeting**, management sets aside a certain percentage of dollar sales to fund marketing programs, based on internal budgeting guidelines or previous marketing experience. Although this is simple to implement, one disadvantage is that sales are seen as the source of marketing funding rather than as the result of budget investments. Another disadvantage is that the company may have no justification (other than tradition) for choosing the percentage devoted to marketing. Finally, if the budget is continually adjusted based on month-by-month sales, lower sales may lead to a lower marketing budget—just when the company needs to maintain or even increase the budget to stimulate higher sales.

When companies use **competitive-parity budgeting**, they fund marketing by matching what competitors spend (as a percentage of sales or a specific dollar amount). Again, this is a simple method, but it ignores differences between companies and doesn't allow for adjustments to find the best spending level for achieving marketing plan objectives.

PLANNING TIP

Don't match what competitors spend, but be aware of their budget priorities.

With the widely used **objective-and-task budgeting method**, marketers add up the cost of completing all the marketing tasks needed to achieve their marketing plan objectives. In the absence of a proven model showing how sales levels respond to marketing spending, the objective-and-task method provides a reasonable way to build a budget by examining the cost of the individual programs that contribute to marketing performance—as long as the appropriate objectives have been set.

BUDGETS WITHIN THE MARKETING BUDGET Once the overall budget has been established, marketers start to allocate marketing funding across the various activities in the time period covered by the marketing plan. Then, when they implement the marketing plan, they can input actual expenditures for comparison with planned expenditures. The marketing plan usually includes the following:

- *Budgets for each marketing-mix program.* These budgets list costs for each program's tasks or expense items, presented month by month and then with year-end totals. Depending on the company's preferred format, marketing-mix budgets also may show expected sales, gross or net margins, and other objectives and profitability measures. Tracking expenses by program reinforces accountability and helps management weigh expected costs against actual costs—and against results.
- *Budgets for each brand, segment, or market.* Creating these types of budgets forces companies to understand their costs and returns relative to individual brands, segments, and markets.
- *Budgets for each region or geographic division.* Budgeting by region or geography focuses attention on the cost of marketing by location and allows easy comparisons between outlays and returns.
- *Budgets for each division or product manager.* These budgets help divisional and product managers track costs for which they are responsible, compare spending with results achieved, and pinpoint problems or opportunities for further investigation.
- *Budget summarizing overall marketing expenses.* This summary budget may be arranged by marketing program or tool, by segment or region, or by another appropriate organizing pattern. Typically, this budget shows month-by-month spending and full-year totals; in some cases, companies may project spending for multiple years in one summary budget. And this budget may include expected gross or net margins and other calculations based on sales and expenditures.

All these budgets serve as checkpoints against which actual spending can be measured. In this way, marketers can quickly spot overspending and can calculate margins and other profitability measures to check on progress toward financial objectives. Given the dynamic nature of the business environment, however, be ready to rethink budgets when unexpected developments cause complications. The enormous popularity of social media has many marketers, including General Motors and P.F. Chang's China Bistro, focusing on how and how much to budget for campaigns on Twitter, Facebook, and other sites. (Visit P.F. Chang's home page at www.pfchangs.com or scan the QR code to go there.)

Budgeting for Social Media. Marketers have been increasing the amount they budget for social media, even though the sites and technology are evolving and the ability to measure actual results is limited. At one point, General Motors was spending $10 million to advertise on Facebook. The company then cut that part of its ad budget only to later set a $30 million budget for building elaborate brand-specific pages on Facebook, where it has more than 8 million "friends."

> Procter & Gamble, seeking higher efficiency and more dialogue with customers, is steadily adding to its social media budget while decreasing the amount it spends on traditional media for each individual brand, such as Secret, Cover Girl, and Crest. P.F. Chang's China Bistro is increasing its Twitter advertising budget because it's seen excellent response, especially from mobile users. The restaurant company budgets campaign by campaign for specific objectives, such as building awareness and trial of a new lunch menu, and it measures each campaign's results with an eye toward tweaking future plans and budgets.[23]

Scheduling Marketing Plan Programs

The next step is to coordinate the timing of each activity through scheduling. **Schedules** are time-defined plans for completing a series of tasks or activities (milestones) related to a specific program or objective. Scheduling helps you to define the timing of tasks and to coordinate implementation so you can avoid conflicts and measure progress toward completion. To create a detailed program-by-program schedule, list the main tasks and activities for one program at a time and, through research or experience, assign each a projected start and end date. Schedules also identify who's responsible for supervising or completing each task in each program.

PLANNING TIP

Include the timing and progress of multiyear activities in your situation analysis.

Some companies create a series of schedules, based on best-case, worst-case, and most-likely scenarios for timing. As an example, Estée Lauder, the cosmetics firm, has stepped up its use of scenario planning in the face of rapid changes in economic conditions worldwide. The CEO asks brand managers three questions: "What must you have? What would you like to keep going? And what can you give up?"[24]

Marketing plans typically include a summary schedule showing the timing and responsibility for each planned program; the appendix or separate documents may show detailed schedules for each program along with Gantt charts, critical path schedules, or other project management tools. The point is to make the timing as concrete as possible so that you can quickly determine whether you're on schedule. Then you can use metrics to monitor key performance-related activities and outcomes.

CONTROLLING MARKETING PLAN IMPLEMENTATION

To implement a marketing plan most effectively, your organization must "own" the plan, support it, and adapt it as needed (see Exhibit 10.8). During the planning process, a manager (or, ideally, a team) inside the company should be responsible for laying out strategies and details, championing the plan internally, seeing that rewards are based on marketing performance, and involving senior management. The plan needs support during development and during implementation—support in the form of sufficient time, funding, and staffing, as well as internal marketing. Finally, be persistent and be ready to adapt the plan if metrics indicate that there is room for improvement.

Four types of marketing control can help gauge the effectiveness of plan implementation: annual plan, profitability, productivity, and strategic control. Because marketing plans are generally developed every year, the organization needs **annual plan control** to assess the progress of the current year's marketing plan. This type of control covers broad performance measures, performance toward meeting marketing plan objectives, and performance toward meeting marketing strategy and program objectives.

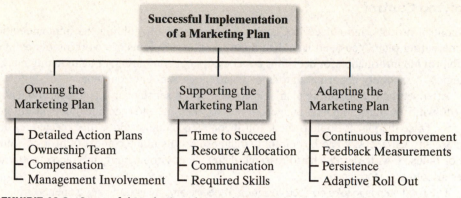

EXHIBIT 10.8 **Successful Marketing Plan Implementation**

Source: Roger J. Best, *Market-Based Management,* 6th ed. (Upper Saddle River, NJ: Pearson Education, 2013), p. 504, Fig. 15-9.

Profitability control assesses the organization's progress and performance based on key profitability measures. The exact measures differ from organization to organization, but often include ROI (or other return measures), contribution margin, and gross or net profit margin. Many companies measure the monthly and yearly profit-and-loss results of each product, line, and category, as well as each market or segment and each channel. By comparing profitability results over time, marketers can spot significant strengths, weaknesses, threats, and opportunities early enough to make appropriate changes.

Productivity control assesses the organization's performance and progress in managing the efficiency of key marketing areas such as the sales force, promotions, channels and logistics, and product management. Productivity is so important to the bottom line that some companies appoint marketing controllers to establish standards, measure performance, and boost marketing efficiency without compromising customer satisfaction or other objectives. Firms also measure the productivity of their product development and manufacturing activities as well as order fulfillment and other tasks, knowing that behind-the-scenes inefficiencies can damage customer relationships. Colgate-Palmolive's productivity control includes measuring the number of patents awarded and products launched in a year, as compared with previous years.[25]

Strategic control assesses the organization's effectiveness in managing the marketing function, customer relationships, and social responsibility and ethics issues—three areas of strategic importance. Whereas other types of control are applied monthly or more often, strategic control may be applied once or twice a year, or as often as needed to clarify the organization's performance in these strategic areas.

To assess the effectiveness of the marketing function and to gauge strengths and weaknesses, companies should conduct a yearly **marketing audit**, a detailed, systematic analysis of marketing capabilities and performance (see this chapter's checklist). After the audit, a summary of the findings should be included in the internal environmental analysis section of the marketing plan.

Applying Control

The control process, introduced in Chapter 1, is essential for guiding the implementation of any marketing plan. You need it to determine whether programs are working out as planned and to provide information for decisions about changing, continuing, or abandoning marketing strategies—especially important in today's volatile business environment.

After setting the marketing plan's objectives, you'll set standards and measurement intervals (drawn from marketing plan budgets, forecasts, metrics, and schedules) to measure interim progress. Once the plan is implemented, you'll compare actual results with expected results and diagnose any variances. It can be helpful to diagnose results in the context of historic, competitive, or industry-wide results and to research the macroenvironmental and microenvironmental issues affecting performance.

The final step is to take corrective action, if necessary, by making adjustments or by implementing a contingency plan formulated in advance. You may have to change the program, the strategy, or the implementation to achieve the planned results. Or, you may decide to change the standards or objectives by which you measure performance. This is appropriate when the variance is not a one-time occurrence and you understand the underlying influence(s) on performance. Although corrective action is the last step in marketing control, it serves as input for next year's situation analysis and for setting or reevaluating objectives at the start of the next control or marketing planning cycle.

Preparing Contingency Plans

Contingency plans are plans that organizations have ready to implement if one (or more) of their original strategies or programs is disrupted by significant, unexpected changes. For example, Lego, the Danish toy manufacturer, develops multiple contingency plans so that no matter what direction the economy moves in, the company is prepared.[26] Hospitals, banks, telecommunications firms, and other organizations that must operate without interruption are especially meticulous about contingency planning.

Marketers usually prepare contingency plans showing how their organization will respond in the case of emergencies such as: computer systems outages; prolonged power or telecommunications interruptions; natural disasters; the sudden bankruptcy of a major customer or supplier; contamination or other environmental disasters; a sudden technological breakthrough by a competitor; the major failure of a program or strategy; a price war or another extreme competitive development; and significant criminal, sabotage, or terrorist activities. The U.S. Federal Emergency Management Agency maintains a comprehensive website with suggestions for preparing a plan for emergency situations (see Exhibit 10.9).

Emergencies aren't the only reason for preparing contingency plans. Special circumstances such as the Olympic Games being held in your area will require you to be prepared as well. See the next page for a look at how London-area businesses such as Office Depot and Sainsbury's planned to continue operating during the 2012 Olympic Games.

Contingency plans should be outlined as marketing plans are being developed, then periodically reviewed and updated as the situation changes. When preparing a contingency plan, think creatively about the organization's options, priorities, and resources to come up with alternatives that minimize the impact of the disruption and allow the organization to recover as quickly as possible. Like Sainsbury's did, you should test the plan in advance to be

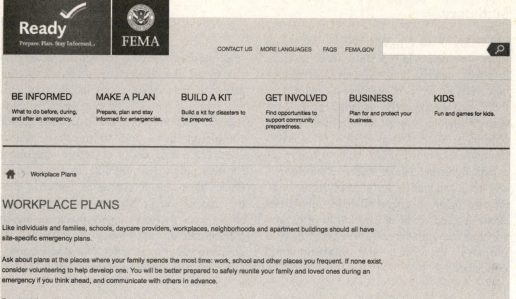

EXHIBIT 10.9   U.S. Federal Emergency Management Agency Helps Businesses Prepare for Emergencies

---

Planning for Disruptions During the Olympics. Months before the Olympic Games began in London during the summer of 2012, businesses were making plans to deal with the expected traffic disruptions. Local transportation authorities advised businesses to temporarily reduce their shipping schedules, avoid peak travel periods, and reroute shipments around street closures and congested intersections. Because the office supply retailer Office Depot started preparing a year in advance, it had contingency plans ready to implement. First, it suggested that customers inventory their supplies and preorder what they needed for delivery before the Olympics. Next, it rearranged its shipment schedule to offer late-night and early-morning deliveries during the Olympics. Finally, the retailer stepped up communications to keep customers informed of the changes, to answer questions, and to respond to last-minute service problems that might arise.

Sainsbury's, a supermarket chain, spent more than a year setting up detailed schedules for delivery, maintenance, and other functions—including testing its plans to identify areas for improvement. It gave engineers mopeds or motorbikes for flexibility in traveling to downtown stores that experienced mechanical or computer problems. It also stockpiled replacement parts and stationed engineers in several larger supermarkets in case freezer cases or other in-store equipment needed immediate repair. Thanks to careful planning, Sainsbury's kept all of its stores in and around London running smoothly during the Olympics.[27]

---

sure it will work and is as complete as possible. And use the lessons learned from dealing with any emergency as input for analyzing the current situation when preparing the next marketing plan.

Summary

Marketing plans typically specify four main tools for measuring performance: metrics, forecasts, budgets, and schedules. Metrics are numerical measures of performance-related activities and outcomes that marketers apply to determine whether they are moving closer to their objectives. Metrics focus employees on activities that make a difference, set up performance expectations that can be objectively measured, and lay a foundation for internal accountability and pride in accomplishments. Metrics should be examined in the context of expected outcomes, previous results, competitive/industry outcomes, and environmental influences.

A forecast is a future projection of what sales and costs are likely to be in the period covered by the plan. Budgets are time-defined allocations of financial outlays for specific functions, programs, customer segments, or geographic regions. Schedules are time-defined plans for completing tasks or activities (milestones) related to a program or objective—important for managing marketing plan implementation. Organizations use four types of marketing control: annual plan, profitability, productivity, and strategic control (including the marketing audit). If results are disrupted by significant, unexpected changes, the organization should have contingency plans ready for implementation.

Your Marketing Plan, Step by Step

Answering the following questions will help you think through plans for metrics, forecasts, budgets, schedules, and marketing control. When you have decided how you'll gauge interim progress and control implementation, note your ideas in your written plan.

1. Look at the financial, marketing, and societal objectives you previously set for your marketing plan. For each objective, list at least one metric for measuring progress toward achievement; also list an appropriate interval (such as daily, weekly, monthly, quarterly, yearly) for measuring progress. If you're planning social media marketing, what do you want to accomplish and how will you gauge results? Refer back to this chapter's exhibits for ideas as you choose suitable metrics.

2. Review your market and customer analyses. If you haven't already done so, forecast sales and costs for your market(s) and targeted segment(s). If possible, do this for each offering or product line, for the cost of sales, and for each channel. For background, read the opinions and forecasts of industry insiders, competitors, analysts, academic experts, and others knowledgeable about your type of offering found in secondary research collected from sources such as the following:
   a. Business and news media
   b. Academic, professional, and industry trade groups
   c. Government agencies
   d. Competitors' annual reports, websites, blogs, and public statements
   e. Financial analysts and industry consultants

3. Using the objective-and-task budgeting method, prepare a basic budget with estimated costs for all marketing activities in your plan. If possible, go into more detail to define budgets for each brand or offering and each marketing program or campaign. How can you link the investment represented by your budget(s) to the returns represented by your objectives?

4. Develop a basic schedule showing when each key marketing activity or program will begin and end. Also show who will be responsible for each activity. Note the overall pattern of activities and consider the circumstances under which you might need to revise your schedule. For example, if a particular activity doesn't end on time, will that affect the start or end date of another activity? How might departures from the schedule affect your ability to achieve your objectives on time?

5. What standard(s) will you use for determining whether progress has been made after the plan

is implemented? For instance, do you expect to move 10% closer to a particular objective every month? What historical, competitive, or industry-wide standards will you choose for a context in which to understand interim results? What environmental forces, if any, have special significance for each metric?

6. If interim measurements show that progress isn't being made at the rate you expect, indicate what corrective action you would consider taking (and when) to get back on track toward your most important objectives. What types of control are appropriate for your plan? Do you need contingency plans for extraordinary situations that might disrupt implementation? Outline the main points of a contingency plan you would develop to address one particular situation.

Endnotes

1. Jessica E. Vascellaro and Amir Efrati, "Google, Apple Tighten Grip on Smartphone Market," *Wall Street Journal,* June 18, 2012, www.wsj.com; Adam Satariano, "Apple Profit Rises 94% on Growing Global iPhone Demand," *Bloomberg,* April 24, 2012, www.bloomberg.com; Rob Markey, "Apple Stores in China," *Harvard Business Review Blog Network,* August 9, 2011, http://blogs.hbr.org; Peter Burrows and Adam Satariano, "Phil Schiller Still Key as Apple Develops Products," *Bloomberg,* June 10, 2012, www.bloomberg.com.

2. Paul W. Farris, Neil T. Bendle, Phillip E. Pfeifer, and David J. Reibstein, *Marketing Metrics,* 2nd ed. (Upper Saddle River, NJ: FT Press, 2010), p. 365.

3. Laura Patterson, "How to Create an Actionable Marketing Dashboard," *MarketingProfs,* March 2, 2012, www.marketingprofs.com; Laura Patterson, "Bridging the Gap: Unlock the Power of Your Marketing Dashboard," *Manage Smarter,* November 20, 2008, www.salesandmarketing.com.

4. Jeff Zabin, "Recessionary Times Call for Recessionary Marketing," *E-Commerce Times,* March 26, 2009, www.ecommercetimes.com.

5. Steve Denning, "Philips Is Committed to Customer Delight," *Forbes,* November 7, 2011, www.forbes.com; Steve Denning, "The 'Relative NPS' Trap," *Forbes,* November 2, 2011, www.forbes.com.

6. Carol Tice, "How One Startup Beat Walmart in Facebook Engagement," *Forbes,* July 2, 2012, www.forbes.com; Darren Dahl, "Among Online Entrepreneurs, Subscriptions Are All the Rage," *New York Times,* March 7, 2012, www.nytimes.com; Catherine Clifford, "PetFlow's Cash Cow: $1 Million in Monthly Sales," *CNN Money,* August 9, 2011, http://money.cnn.com; Elaine Pofeldt, "David vs. Goliath: PetFlow vs. PetSmart," *Fortune,* February 1, 2012, www.fortune.com.

7. Russell Parsons, "M&S Bank Has Brand Metrics but Doubts Remain," *Marketing Week,* June 13, 2012, www.marketingweek.co.uk.

8. Aine Creedin, "Nonprofit Succeeds in Twitter Challenge to 150 Shoe Donations," *Nonprofit Quarterly,* June 1, 2012, www.nonprofitquarterly.com.

9. Ryan Joe, "Kellogg Company: 'We Don't Care About Clicks,'" *DM News,* June 21, 2012, www.dmnews.com.

10. "Marketing in Social Media and the Complex Art of Measurement," *Guardian (UK),* June 21, 2012, www.guardian.co.uk.

11. Dale Buss, "Brands Climb onto NFL, NCAA Juggernauts for Football's Big Kick-Off," *BrandChannel,* September 5, 2012, www.brandchannel.com; David Griner, "Q&A: Audi's Social Chief Talks Hashtags and the Power of Twitter," *Adweek,* June 11, 2012, www.adweek.com; Farhad Manjoo, "Does Social Media Have a Return on Investment?" *Fast Company,* June 22, 2011, www.fastcompany.com.

12. Kate Maddox, "Forrester Conference Focuses on Digital, Social," *BtoB,* May 14, 2012, p. 3.

13. Susan Carey, "U.S. Airlines Scored Poorly in Consumer Survey," *Wall Street Journal,* June 19, 2012, www.wsj.com.

14. Gordon A. Wyner, "The Right Side of Metrics," *Marketing Management,* January–February 2004, pp. 8–9.

15. Tim Donnelly, "7 Tips for Improving Your Sales Forecasting," *Inc.,* May 31, 2012, www.inc.com.

16. Keith Naughton, "Toyota Increases U.S. Auto Sales Forecast on Consumer Confidence," *Bloomberg,* April 5, 2012, www.bloomberg.com.

17. Bertrand Marotte, "Bombardier Sees Slight Downturn in Commercial Market, Sustained Growth in Business Jets," *Globe and Mail (Canada),* June 19, 2012, www.theglobe-andmail.com.

18. Brad Dorfman and David Jones, "P&G Cuts Forecast, Will Focus on Big Businesses," *Reuters,* June 21, 2012, www.reuters.com.

19. Alan Ohnsman, "Tesla Ties Car Sales Goals to Apple-Style Store Strategy," *Bloomberg,* June 22, 2012, www.bloomberg.com.

20. Bill Siwicki, "Mobile Exceeds 50% of Sales on a Single Day at E-tailer Rue La La," *Internet Retailer,* May 8, 2012, www.internetretailer.com.

21. Tim Berry, "10 Ways to Validate a Sales Forecast," *Entrepreneur,* February 3, 2010, www.entrepreneur.com.

22. Loren Gary, "Why Budgeting Kills Your Company," *HBS Working Knowledge,* August 11, 2003, www.hbsworkingknowl-edge.hbs.edu.

23. Ben Kunz, "Why GM and Others Fail with Facebook Ads," *Bloomberg Businessweek,* May 22, 2012, www.businessweek .com; Lauren Coleman-Lochner, "Social Networking Takes Center Stage at P&G," *Bloomberg Businessweek,* March 29, 2012, www.businessweek.com; "Marketers: Digital Offers Us More for Less," *Advertising Age,* February 26, 2012, www .adage.com; Shira Ovide, "Twitter's Mobile Ads Begin to Click," *Wall Street Journal,* June 28, 2012, www.wsj.com.

24. Matthew Boyle, "The Budget Knives Come Out," *BusinessWeek,* October 13, 2008, p. 30.

25. Matthew Boyle, "Still the King of Dental Care," *BusinessWeek,* April 6, 2009, p. 48.

26. "Managing in the Fog," *The Economist,* February 28, 2009, p. 67.

27. Peter MacLeod, "Office Depot Says 'Business as Usual' During Olympics," *SHD Logistics,* June 28, 2012, www .shdlogistics.com/news; "The Olympic Challenge," *Direct Operations,* June 7, 2012, www.catalog-biz.com; Johanna Parsons, "Olympics: Get in Training," *Logistics Manager,* April 25, 2012, www .logisticsmanager.com.

APPENDIX

Sample Marketing Plan:
PretzL Elegance's Artisanal Chocolate Twists

PretzL Elegance, a hypothetical start-up company, is about to introduce a new line of premium-quality, all-natural, chocolate-covered pretzel twists sprinkled with artisanal salt. This entrepreneurial firm is entering the fast-growing snack market where global food giants, regional snack marketers, and niche snack manufacturers compete for attention and sales. It will differentiate itself on the basis of top-quality, all-natural prestige-branded snacks capable of meeting special dietary needs. The following abbreviated sample marketing plan shows how PretzL Elegance is preparing to launch its first two products, targeting two consumer segments and two business segments.

EXECUTIVE SUMMARY

Next January, PretzL Elegance (PLE) will introduce two varieties of chocolate-covered pretzel twists topped with artisanal salts. One will have a dark chocolate coating and the other will have a milk chocolate coating. By partnering with Lost Legends Luxury Chocolatier (LLLC), a famous U.K. chocolate firm, we'll be able to obtain superior, prestige-branded chocolate from certified sustainable sources while boosting our visibility and our credibility.

Our Artisanal Chocolate Twists will be positioned as premium, all-natural snacks for special occasions or as an affordable indulgence, with a fresh appeal to all five senses. They'll also be strictly peanut-free and gluten-free, adding to the appeal for consumers who must avoid certain ingredients. Each twist will be individually wrapped, reinforcing our upscale positioning, ensuring freshness and product purity, allowing for portion control, and offering the option of customized packaging for business customers.

Marketing priorities for the first year include building brand awareness among targeted consumer and business segments, securing appropriate distribution in the top 25 U.S. metropolitan-area markets, and achieving sales levels that will lead to profitability during the second year. Looking ahead, we plan to introduce a new flavor variety every February and November, periods when customers have snacking or gift-giving in mind.

CURRENT SITUATION

PretzL Elegance was founded last year by two entrepreneurs with extensive experience in the food industry. One owner is a nutritionist and baking enthusiast, the other was a specialty food wholesaler before cofounding PLE. Building on our expertise and industry contacts, we've developed a number of unique recipes; selected natural, high-quality ingredients; and perfected a process for making crispy chocolate-covered pretzel twists without peanuts or gluten. Our first two products will be introduced next January.

PLE's mission is to delight our customers and awaken all of their senses with the finest quality, all-natural snacks. Our use of rich, imported chocolate and special artisanal salts is one point of differentiation; another is that our snacks are safe for anyone who must avoid peanuts or gluten. A company with a conscience, we plan to make our snacks available to nonprofit groups at no cost so that they can resell the products for fund-raising purposes. We'll also partner with research and medical groups to educate consumers about food allergens.

We have an exclusive partnership and cobranding relationship with LLLC, a U.K. company with a worldwide reputation for producing superior chocolate from organically grown, ethically sourced cocoa beans. Thanks to this relationship, we were able to locate and import artisanal salts that complement dark and milk chocolates. Although start-up companies sometimes have difficulty arranging distribution because their products are unproven, our connection with LLLC is opening doors to fancy boutiques, fine restaurants, and other channel members and business customers.

We have contracted with a consultant for advice on complying with legal and regulatory requirements such as city and state rules governing food production facilities. Our snacks will be labeled in accordance with U.S. Food and Drug Administration guidelines, and we'll be ready to change our labels once new rules related to the Food Safety Modernization Act have been finalized. To be sure that people with food allergies understand exactly what our snacks contain, we'll list all ingredients and allergens prominently on labels and provide extensive information on our website.

Looking at the business environment, economic conditions are generally improving, and disposable income is beginning to increase. This is a positive sign for premium foods. Even if the economy remains uncertain, we anticipate good demand because affordable luxuries such as upscale snacks are perceived as personal rewards and special occasion treats. Businesses, however, tend to postpone purchases of extras during challenging economic periods, which could impair our ability to achieve sales objectives.

Food trends, which are changeable and unpredictable, will be a key element in our long-term success. We've chosen the increasingly popular flavor combination of chocolate and salty ingredients as the basis of our first two snacks. This combination is currently appearing at the high and the low end of the snack market. A number of small chocolate concerns are featuring truffles, bonbons, and other chocolate treats dusted with colorful specialty salts, and mainstream snack makers are also adding some chocolate/salty products. Preparing for the time when this combination is no longer trendy, we are already researching emerging trends and are planning to introduce new flavor combinations twice a year as a way of refreshing our product line and generating excitement about new flavors. As we prepare for production, we also need to closely monitor availability and prices of ingredients, because supplies and costs can fluctuate over time (depending on the weather, political developments, and other factors).

Competition

We face some competition from mainstream makers of salty snacks and chocolates. Multinationals such as Frito-Lay offer hundreds of flavor variations in a range of package sizes, and they have well-developed distribution networks for stocking supermarkets, convenience stores, and other grocery outlets. Frito-Lay has decided to move into higher-end (but not premium) snacks and to expand into other outlets. Makers of popularly priced chocolate products, such as Mars and Hershey, are also well-represented in grocery chains, and they continually introduce new products based on the latest flavor trends. However, PLE's Artisanal Chocolate Twists won't directly compete with such products, for the following reasons: (1) Our products will have more complex flavor combinations, higher-quality all-natural and artisanal ingredients, and more sophisticated packaging; (2) our prices will be higher; (3) our snacks won't be available through the same stores; and (4) our snacks won't contain peanuts or gluten.

Our direct competitors are fancy, high-priced salty snacks and chocolates made by local, national, or international companies and sold at department and specialty stores or online. For example, Godiva has added new products with sophisticated flavor combinations at higher price points, including two types of chocolate-covered pretzels. Nestlé is using its upscale Maison Cailler brand to build sales at the high end of the market. Also, independently owned chocolate makers are opening stores in major metropolitan areas and are educating affluent consumers about the appeals of premium chocolate. (We intend to concentrate our retail distribution in big cities because research indicates that many consumers who live or work in metropolitan areas are interested in and have the income to afford premium snacks.)

Because our snacks will be peanut- and gluten-free, we'll also be competing against firms that specialize in such products. For example, Gilbert's Gourmet Goodies, a niche marketer, offers gluten- and peanut-free sweets, but no premium snacks. Similarly, Glutino produces gluten-free pretzels, chocolate-coated cookies, and other snacks, but not premium snacks. Packaged foods giants such as General Mills and Kellogg's have been introducing gluten-free foods, but they don't compete in the premium end of the snack market.

SWOT Analysis

We have identified the eight key strengths, weaknesses, opportunities, and threats summarized in Table A.1.

Our major strength is the exclusive cobranding and sourcing partnership we have with LLLC. This strength counters our major weakness, which is that we're a start-up without any brand awareness, established image, or track record. Despite having limited resources compared with our competitors, we believe that the high profile of our partner and its reputation for quality and sustainability will give us a small but solid foundation on which to build.

PLE sees significant profit potential in the market opportunity for premium chocolates as an affordable luxury, and in particular, the popularity of chocolate/salty flavor combinations. We also know that the market for peanut- and gluten-free foods is growing much faster than the overall food market. Being able to meet the dietary requirements of people who must avoid these two allergens will give us a competitive advantage because few premium snacks are geared to this part of the market.

TABLE A.1 SWOT Analysis for Artisanal Chocolate Twists

Strengths (internal capabilities that support achievement of objectives)	Weaknesses (internal factors that might prevent achievement of objectives)
1. Exclusive cobranding and chocolate sourcing deal with LLLC	1. Lack of brand awareness and image
2. Innovative recipes and processes for producing fancy-quality, peanut- and gluten-free snacks	2. More limited resources than competitors
Opportunities (external circumstances that might be exploited to achieve objectives)	**Threats (external circumstances that might interfere with achievement of objectives)**
1. High interest in and demand for the chocolate/salty flavor combination	1. Increase in premium snack introductions by larger competitors with marketing muscle
2. Growing awareness of the health dangers of food allergies	2. Public health concerns about obesity

On the other hand, our ability to establish ourselves as a premium brand might be threatened by the entrance of large competitors who can use their marketing might to introduce high-end products for the same segments we're targeting. Should this occur, we plan to fight back using the strength of our exclusive relationship with LLLC and by highlighting our allergen-free features. PLE's size may be an advantage here, because we don't need the huge quantities of chocolate and artisanal salt ingredients that larger companies require to launch products on a large scale.

Public health concerns about obesity are definitely affecting snack and chocolate companies. As an example, Mars, the mainstream chocolate marketer, has reduced the size of its candy bars to limit calories to 250 per bar. For our part, we're positioning our Artisanal Chocolate Twists as specialty treats, not everyday snacks. Also, each pretzel will be individually wrapped, which has the effect of serving as portion control. We'll be monitoring this issue over time.

Market Size, Trends, and Needs

The overall market for snacks and chocolate is large and diverse, and served by numerous multinational corporations as well as companies that operate regionally or on a local basis. Because our snacks will be peanut- and gluten-free, we have analyzed that market, as well.

DEMAND FOR SALTY SNACKS   Salty snack sales account for more than $20 billion in annual sales. The market for premium salty snacks is growing at 7% per year, while the overall market shows little if any growth. One of today's trendiest taste combinations is salty snacks with chocolate toppings or fillings. M&Ms now markets a line of pretzel nuggets covered in chocolate, and some luxury chocolatiers offer bonbons or truffles sprinkled with specialty salt. More sophisticated salty snacks are being introduced at the high end of the market, a development that works in our favor.

DEMAND FOR LUXURY CHOCOLATES   Sales of premium chocolates top $8 billion annually, and this part of the market is growing more quickly than the overall market. Even during the worst of the recent economic downturn, top-quality chocolates continued to sell well, as personal indulgences and for gifts. Research suggests that eating dark chocolate may have health benefits, another plus for our product. Companies such as Godiva are thriving and are able to command high prices for their high-quality chocolate desserts and snacks. On average, U.S. consumers buy $60 worth of chocolate candy each year, and the size of the average purchase is increasing as shoppers acquire a taste for better quality. LLLC has years of success in satisfying the needs of upscale chocolate lovers, and our cobranding partnership will give us credibility in this profitable market.

DEMAND FOR ALLERGEN-FREE SNACKS   Because our products are peanut- and gluten-free, they will appeal to individuals and families who need or want to avoid these two allergens. Research suggests that more than 3% of U.S. consumers are allergic to peanuts or other nuts, and peanut allergies are increasingly common among children. In addition, an estimated 10 million U.S. consumers need or want to avoid gluten, a protein present in wheat, barley, rye, and other grains. This number includes 3 million people with celiac disease, who require a strictly gluten-free diet to remain healthy. Estimates of the U.S. market for gluten-free foods alone range as high as $6 billion, and sales during the past five years have been growing at double-digit rates.

The market for peanut- and gluten-free foods has special needs that we are prepared to satisfy. First, we can reassure consumers that our products are safe to eat. Second, gluten-free foods don't always have the same texture or taste as foods with gluten, but we have met that challenge with unique recipes and production processes. Third, consumers with food allergies must be cautious about the snacks they buy, especially when they aren't at home or near familiar stores. Our products are individually wrapped for safe and convenient snacking at home or on the go.

TARGETED SEGMENTS AND SERVICE REQUIREMENTS

Within the overall snack market, we have identified a number of specific segments to target (see Exhibit A.1). These segments were chosen with an eye toward market growth, relatively low price sensitivity, availability of suitable distribution, relatively low competitive pressure, and other factors favorable to our marketing.

Consumers

In the consumer market, we're targeting the segment of affluent adults with high disposable income who are early adopters, who enjoy trying new gourmet salty or chocolate foods, and who view trendy gourmet treats (particularly chocolate) as affordable luxuries. Consumers in this segment are brand conscious but not price sensitive. They like being among the first to discover something new, different, and desirable. They serve as opinion leaders for their friends and colleagues, and they're active users of social media as well as mobile technology. Our cobranded treats will appeal to their preference for out-of-the-ordinary snacks for personal consumption or as gifts.

Affluent adults

- Early adopters
- Preference for novel gourmet treats
- Brand conscious
- Not price sensitive

Middle- to high-income families

- Peanut or gluten allergies
- Seek wider range of snack choices
- Seek safe snacking on the go
- Price less important than safety, quality

Businesses

- Give specialty foods as gifts
- Want customized packaging
- Prefer prestige brands
- Rarely price sensitive

Fine restaurants, inns, hotels

- Offer premium snacks as free extras
- Accommodate guests with food allergies
- Leverage prestige brand relationships
- Market with customized logo

EXHIBIT A.1 Targeted Segments.

Another key consumer target segment is middle- to high-income families where one or more members want or need to avoid gluten or peanuts. These consumers are interested in gourmet salty and chocolate treats and tell researchers that they wish they had a wider choice of premium snacks for occasional treats or family celebrations. They're already aware of competing brands and use online communities, blogs, Facebook, and other media to share information about foods that meet their dietary needs. Snacking on the go or in a group is a particular problem that our Artisanal Chocolate Twists can solve because our individual packaging prevents accidental contamination from other foods. This segment tends to regard price as less important than quality and safety.

Businesses

We'll also target businesses of any size that are interested in buying premium chocolates or snacks for internal marketing purposes or for promotions such as holiday gifts to customers. These businesses want to give prestigious food gifts that are unique yet appeal to a broad audience. Most of the time, business customers prefer that containers or food wrappers be customized with a logo or a slogan related to the gift-giving occasion. In fact, these customers are more interested in gift presentation than price. Our individually wrapped pretzels are particularly well suited to this requirement, and we are prepared to provide customized containers in a variety of sizes as needed. We can serve this segment directly via our website.

Finally, our second targeted business segment is that of fine restaurants, inns, and hotels. Many of these businesses buy gourmet snacks to give to their customers. They'll now be able to accommodate customers who can't tolerate gluten or peanuts by offering our snacks. Fine restaurants and lodgings want to be associated with prestige brands, and our cobranding arrangement with LLLC will give us an advantage here. For restaurants, inns, or hotels, we can customize individual wrappings to their individual specifications.

Service Support

Our business customers in particular will expect and receive top-quality service. Not only is this in keeping with our upscale image, it's also necessary because our perishable products require special handling, especially during hot weather. We'll have an overnight-delivery replacement policy in place for business customers who complain about orders that don't arrive or don't arrive in perfect condition. To ensure that business customers who order products with customized packaging are satisfied, we'll conduct follow-up surveys and monitor social media for reviews, complaints, and comments.

Also, we'll survey restaurant owners, hotel managers, and innkeepers on a quarterly basis to gather feedback and comments for improvements, new products, etc. Finally, we'll set aside a special section on our PLE site with information to help this targeted segment become more knowledgeable about our partnership with LLLC, our unique production process, food allergies, sustainability, ethical sourcing, and other issues.

MARKETING DIRECTION AND OBJECTIVES

As a start-up, we're aiming for strong, steady growth that will lead us to long-term success. We've set the following specific objectives:

- *Marketing objectives.* By the end of our first year, achieve brand awareness of 40% among targeted consumer segments and 50% among targeted business segments. Establish distribution relationships with selected boutiques, high-end department stores, and gourmet food stores in the 25 largest U.S. cities by midyear. Within three months of product introduction, sign 12 restaurants, inns, or hotels as customers. Participate in two specialty food trade shows before yearend to generate 20 or more leads for retail distributors in new markets.

- *Financial objectives.* Achieve total revenue of at least $400,000 by the end of our first year. Build sales to reach the breakeven production point of 800,000 oz. midway during the second year, when we project full-year total revenue will exceed $800,000 and we will become profitable.
- *Societal objectives.* Identify six nonprofit groups to support by providing PLE's products at no cost for resale as a fundraising effort. Partner with medical or research groups that study gluten and peanut allergies to reach at least 100,000 consumers through sponsorship of allergy education apps, downloadable fact sheets, and online or in-person events for managing dietary restrictions. In addition to buying 100% of our chocolate from sustainable sources, we will operate in an environmentally friendly way by installing solar panels to power our production facility.

PRODUCT STRATEGY

The key needs of the market have led us to identify specific benefits valued by consumers that relate to particular product features (see Table A.2).

Initially, our product line will have only two flavor varieties, dark chocolate and milk chocolate, both to be introduced in January. By November, we will introduce a new flavor variety and then add another new flavor the following February, timed to make the most of peak snack-shopping seasons. Consumers will see PLE's products as gifts for Valentine's Day, Mother's and Father's Days, weddings, Thanksgiving, Christmas, and other special occasions. Businesses will see PLE's products as good gifts for employee-recognition programs, loyal customers, and thank-yous to key suppliers and distributors. By refreshing our product line, we encourage consumers and businesses to try new flavors and to avoid giving the same flavor(s) as gifts year after year.

TABLE A.2   Benefits and Features of Artisanal Chocolate Twists

Benefits and Value to Customer	Features Providing the Benefit
• Satisfyingly rich snacking experience	• Appeal to all five senses through sophisticated combination of crispy pretzel twists covered in gourmet chocolate and topped with artisanal salt crystals
• Convenient one-at-a-time snack to be enjoyed anywhere, anytime	• Individually wrapped treats are easy take-alongs and allow for freshness, product purity, and portion control
• Desire for cachet and known quality of upscale brand	• Cobranding with LLLC, a prestigious chocolate brand
• Safe snack for people avoiding gluten or peanuts	• Gluten- and peanut-free ingredients reassure consumers that these twists are safe to eat; individual wrapping protects against cross-contamination

Another reason to develop new products on a regular basis is to avoid overreliance on the original flavor combinations. We plan to vary the chocolate coating and the pretzel twist recipe to create innovative and intriguing combinations, always with all-natural ingredients that contain no gluten or peanuts. Two product introductions per year is a realistic pace, given the time and expense involved in obtaining new ingredients, testing recipes, market-testing flavors, having a lab test for allergens, determining shelf life, and preparing distributors for the new items. As noted earlier, we have to monitor trends in ingredient costs and availability in order to be prepared for possible shortages or spikes in supply costs.

The PLE brand logo will be silver and black, in keeping with the "elegance" in our company name and to reinforce the luxury of products made from imported chocolate and artisanal salts. Our packaging will consist of an artistic and protective outside container and individual wrappers for each pretzel. We're currently testing alternative designs for the outside container to determine whether an international theme (linked to the imported ingredients) or artwork more closely related to the snacks will be more appealing. Each inside wrapper will have our logo printed in silver and black and a slender silver ribbon securing the opening. For custom orders, we'll add the business's logo or slogan, print in other colors, and change the ribbon color on request.

We must encourage positive brand attitudes as we build awareness among targeted customer groups. We believe consumers will have a favorable first impression of our brand because our chocolate is supplied by our partner, LLLC, a company praised for its environmentally friendly actions and its commitment to Fair Trade certification. Also, we expect to be perceived positively because of increased public interest in all-natural foods, artisanal foods, and foods without allergens such as peanuts and gluten. Finally, we want our brand to be known for its commitment to the local community. For this reason, we'll make our products available at no cost to support the fund-raising efforts of six nonprofits that serve our area, with plans to support additional nonprofits in the coming years.

(In an actual marketing plan, the product strategy section would include more detail about branding, product line changes, test-marketing, labeling, and other important elements.)

PRICING STRATEGY

Fixed and variable costs are important internal factors in pricing our products. Our ingredients are costly because they're all natural, some are imported, and all must be completely peanut- and gluten-free. Our production facility must be strictly temperature controlled to preserve quality, and we've arranged special shipping to minimize breakage and spoilage, adding to our costs. To achieve our financial objectives, we must price near or at the top of the range for premium snacks, which research indicates would be acceptable to our targeted customers.

According to marketing research, premium snacks and chocolates are perceived as affordable luxuries. When assessing the value of a product such as ours, buyers are more concerned with the sensory experience (such as good taste and appearance), brand prestige, and quality than they are with unit price. Buyers who seek out gluten- or peanut-free snacks expect to pay more for foods that they can rely on to meet their special dietary requirements. As a result, our pricing strategy will support our products' premium positioning, will reflect the high value that customers place on the combination of benefits we provide, and will allow us a reasonable profit once we achieve breakeven.

On the basis of our research, we'll set the suggested retail price of our 12-oz. package of Artisanal Chocolate Twists at $20 and the suggested retail price of the 20-oz. package at $30.

In other words, our snacks will retail for approximately $1.50 to $1.67 per oz. For comparison, the following is a sample of competitive prices:

- Godiva markets dark- and milk-chocolate covered pretzel twists in 16-oz. canisters for $25 ($1.56 per oz.).
- Ethel M's (owned by Mars) markets milk-chocolate pretzel twists in 4.5-oz. packages for $12 ($2.67 per oz.).
- Independent high-end chocolatiers market chocolate-coated pretzel sticks and twists for about $1.50 to $1.75 per oz.
- Niche food manufacturers market nut-free or gluten-free chocolate pretzel twists and sticks for about $1.25 per oz.

Our wholesale price will be $0.75 per oz., to allow for retailers' markup to the suggested selling price. This means our 12-oz. package will wholesale for $9 and our 20-oz. package will wholesale for $12. Because we'll customize wrappings and containers for businesses, restaurants, inns, and hotels, and these customers will be buying only larger-size packages, our price to those customers will be $1.25 per oz. Given our fixed and variable costs, and expenses related to start-up, we'll reach the breakeven point after selling 800,000 oz. We expect to achieve that sales level midway during our second year in business (see the financials and forecasts section later in this plan).

(In an actual marketing plan, the pricing strategy section would include more detail about fixed and variable costs, breakeven volume, pricing by channel and customer segment, in-depth competitive pricing data, promotional pricing, and other important elements.)

COMMUNICATIONS AND INFLUENCE STRATEGY

As shown in Table A.3, PLE will use a combination of push and pull strategies in the first year through activities in advertising, sales promotion, public relations, direct marketing, personal selling, and social media. Our primary objectives are to build brand awareness to target levels, encourage positive attitudes and word of mouth, generate leads and sales, stimulate product trial, and reinforce the premium positioning. All messages in all media will be coordinated to reflect our image and points of differentiation.

During our second year, we'll expand our magazine advertising to include the top 25 U.S. city magazines, specialty magazines published by our hotel and inn customers, and additional gourmet food magazines. As each new flavor is introduced, we'll create a campaign focusing on extensive sampling and social media discussion. Each fall, we'll kick off a seasonal campaign to encourage buying of PLE products as gifts. We're currently in discussions with Lexus, BMW, and other high-end automobile firms to conduct sampling at selected dealerships during new model introductions. Another campaign in the works will put PLE snacks on board private jets rented by NetJets in order to reach business decision-makers.

Our social media activities will begin two months before the first product introduction and will continue with posts every day during the launch period. We'll offer free samples to opinion leaders who have large followings on Twitter, and we'll create a designated hashtag for postings related to our new products. Finally, we'll use social and mobile media to provide marketing support to the nonprofits that resell our products for fund-raising purposes, as a way to engage with our community and to help people in need.

(In an actual marketing plan, the communications strategy section would include more detail about messages and media, development of seasonal and ongoing campaigns, timing of communications, and other important elements.)

TABLE A.3   Highlights of Communications and Influence Activities

Communication Tool	Activity
Advertising	• Plan pre-launch trade advertising campaign with LLLC to introduce brand, attract retailers (push strategy). • Target consumers with introductory campaign, including ads in *Fine Cooking, Gourmet,* and city magazines serving the top five U.S. metro markets; paid key-word search ads; and opt-in e-mail newsletter (pull strategy). • Use targeted print and online ads to reach corporate buyers, restaurant owners, hotels, and innkeepers.
Sales promotion	• Offer free samples to affluent shoppers via in-store displays; to first-class and business-class passengers on major airlines; to customers of fine restaurants, luxury hotels, and inns; and to attendees at operas, concerts, and other cultural events. • Participate in two specialty food industry events to meet retailers and monitor flavor trends; also plan sales promotions around special events such as the New York Wine Expo. • Create brand-building point-of-purchase displays and materials for shops and restaurants.
Public relations	• Generate buzz with five-city tasting tour involving local celebrity chefs and media tie-ins. • Live-stream cooking demonstrations with LLLC experts to showcase product quality, taste, and freshness and to showcase allergen-free production process. • With medical authorities, sponsor educational food allergy apps, downloadable materials, and webinars.
Personal selling	• Prior to introduction, provide in-store training and extensive sampling for salespeople in boutiques and other retailers. • Offer incentives to reward in-store sales efforts during the introductory period and at holiday times. • Prior to introduction, train staff of specialty foods broker that will represent our brand to the trade.
Direct marketing	• Use PLE site to build the brand, help consumers locate local retailers, and link to food allergy sites. • Use PLE site as primary channel for educating business customers about the brand and products, providing creative ideas for custom packaging, and accepting business orders. • Offer multiple ordering methods through the PLE site, including phone and chat.

CHANNEL STRATEGY

We'll make our snacks available to the targeted consumer segments through two channels:

- *Retail locations.* We'll sell through selected boutiques, gourmet food stores, and other retailers in the top 25 U.S. metropolitan markets. Channel members will be selected using criteria such as compatible merchandise assortments, upscale customer base, image, and availability of equipment for storing and displaying our products in temperature-controlled cases. We'll give priority to retailers that already stock chocolates made by our partner, LLLC. Retailers will receive point-of-purchase materials for training and to introduce our brand and our quality snacks to their customers.

- ***Online.*** We'll sell directly to consumers through our own website, offering three levels of delivery service and discounts for volume orders. Toll-free phone support will be available for customers who prefer to call in orders. Our site designer is currently developing a look that's consistent with our image and the signature colors of our packaging and promotional materials. In line with our peanut- and gluten-free appeal, we'll provide detailed descriptions of our ingredients and our production process to emphasize quality control. During hot weather, we'll accept orders to be fulfilled through local retailers or, if consumers prefer, we'll pack our products to arrive safely via overnight delivery for a small additional fee. In addition, we've arranged to test online sales through specialty websites that cater to consumers with food allergies, such as the Gluten Freely website.

To reach the targeted segment of fine restaurants, hotels, and inns, we'll sell through a specialty food broker who has a decade of experience selling expensive desserts and snacks to high-end food and lodging businesses. Any leads we receive through our trade efforts, such as industry meetings or advertising, will be turned over to the broker for follow-up. We'll pay a standard commission on sales made by the broker, and we've factored these fees into our profitability calculations. These customers will be able to order customized wrapping and containers, a service included in our pricing.

For corporate sales, we'll have a separate section on our website and a special toll-free number staffed by salespeople trained to handle custom orders. We'll charge a small extra fee if corporations choose to provide us with names and addresses so that we can ship packages directly to individual recipients. Corporations can provide artwork for containers and wrapping or, for an extra charge, work with our designer to create special packaging for their specific needs. All custom orders will be subject to a lead time of ten days.

(In an actual marketing plan, the channel strategy section would include more detail about channel functions, multichannel marketing, criteria for selection and evaluation, customer requirements, competitors' channel strategies, and other important elements.)

FINANCIALS AND FORECASTS

Table A.4 shows our overall sales and revenue forecasts for the first and second year. We'll achieve profitability once production exceeds 800,000 oz.—the breakeven point—early in the second year. Assuming cumulatively higher sales, and repeat business and referrals from business customers during the second year, we'll more than double revenues from year one to year two (and double the number of ounces sold during that period). Detailed month-by-month forecasts are ready for each of our first two products and for the next two to be introduced. Industry sales trends suggest that our two biggest revenue months will be December and February. To prepare for these busy periods, we've also budgeted more for ingredients, personnel and support expenses, and shipping costs during October and January.

TABLE A.4 Two-Year Sales and Revenue Forecasts

	Consumer Market (wholesale price: $0.75/oz.)	Business Market (wholesale price: $1.25/oz.)	Total Ounces Sold	Total Revenues
First year sales forecast	400,000 oz. @ $0.75 = $300,000	100,000 oz. @ $1.25 = $125,000	500,000 oz.	$425,000
Second year sales forecast	750,000 oz. @ $0.75 = $562,500	250,000 oz. @ $1.25 = $312,500	1,000,000 oz.	$875,000

Our detailed marketing budget for the coming year indicates costs for communicating with channel partners and marketing to consumers and business customers. Based on forecasts, we'll be increasing the second-year budget for advertising and special events to support new product introductions and holiday-period buying. We'll also reevaluate assumptions and forecasts monthly to identify trends and be able to revise forecasts as needed.

(In an actual marketing plan, each marketing program or campaign would carry its own financial assumptions, management assignments, and schedules. The full marketing plan would also include a detailed profit-and-loss analysis, month-by-month forecasts by product and channel, and summary and detailed budgets by program and activity, market/segment, and manager.)

IMPLEMENTATION, METRICS, AND MARKETING CONTROL

To ensure that our first two products are introduced on time, we've prepared detailed weekly schedules for production-related activities and marketing-related activities. We have a separate schedule for stocking retailers and training retail and wholesale salespeople ahead of launch dates. Our U.K. partner will be assisting us in implementation of product launch campaigns and in monitoring quality and shipments. We'll be closely monitoring customer feedback to detect any early signs of concerns or confusion.

Weekly and monthly, we'll apply metrics to control implementation and measure progress toward objectives. Among the metrics we'll follow are unit sales and revenue, segment by segment; actual fixed and variable costs versus budget; number of retailers and businesses carrying our products; channel sales and future orders; gross profit margin by product and channel; order fulfillment speed and accuracy; production productivity; and response to communications activities.

On a quarterly basis, we'll use metrics to measure brand awareness and brand image perceptions, by segment; business customer retention and profitability; and customer satisfaction levels. For our societal objectives, we'll assess relations with our chosen nonprofit groups to determine fund-raising success and need for additional support. We'll also assess the success of our outreach efforts to educate consumers about food allergies.

We have contingency plans prepared to deal with possible ingredient shortages and possible delivery disruptions due to extreme weather or other problems.

(An actual marketing plan would include detailed implementation schedules, management assignments by program and activity, explanation of metrics, and outlines of contingency plans.)

Sources

Some background information for this fictional sample plan was adapted from: Stephanie Strom, "Frito-Lay Takes New Tack on Snacks," *New York Times,* June 12, 2012, www.nytimes.com; Chris Pleasance, "Willy Wonka Goes to Davos," *The Independent (U.K.),* June 4, 2012, www.independent.co.uk; Elizabeth Holmes, "Breeding a Nation of Chocoholics," *Wall Street Journal,* November 30, 2011, www.wsj.com; Keith O'Brien, "Should We All Go Gluten-Free?" *New York Times,* November 25, 2011, www.nytimes.com; Elizabeth Olson, "A Campaign for M&Ms with a Salty Center? Sweet," *New York Times,* June 21, 2010, www.nytimes.com; Dermot Doherty, "Nestlé Bites into Chocolate's $8 Billion Premium Market: Retail," *Bloomberg,* February 12, 2012, www.bloomberg.com.

GLOSSARY

affordability budgeting Method of budgeting for marketing in which the company plans to spend what it believes it can afford.

annual plan control Type of marketing control used to assess the progress and performance of the current year's marketing plan.

attitudes An individual's lasting evaluations of and feelings toward something.

auction pricing Type of pricing in which buyers submit bids to buy goods or services.

benefits Need-satisfaction outcomes that customers desire from a product offering.

brand equity Extra value perceived in a brand that enhances long-term loyalty among customers.

brand extension Putting an established brand on a new product in a different category, aimed at a new customer segment; also known as a *category extension*.

branding Using words, designs, or symbols to give a product a distinct identity and differentiate it from competing products.

breakeven point Point at which revenues cover costs and beyond which a product becomes profitable.

budget Time-defined allocation of financial outlays for a specific function or program.

business market Companies, not-for-profit organizations, and institutions that buy products for operations or as supplies for production—also known as the *organizational market*.

business-to-business (B2B) marketing Businesses targeting other businesses for marketing purposes.

buzz marketing More intense, company-stimulated word-of-mouth communication about a product or brand, which can spread and fade quickly.

cannibalization Allowing a new product to cut into the sales of one or more existing products.

cause-related marketing Marketing a product or brand by linking it to benefiting a charitable cause.

channel The set of functions and the structure of organizations performing them outbound on the value chain that makes a particular offering available to customers; also known as the *distribution channel*.

cocreation Involving customers more deeply in collaborating with the company for product innovation and development.

competitive-parity budgeting Method in which the company creates a budget by matching what competitors spend, as a percentage of sales or as a specific dollar amount.

concentrated marketing Focusing one marketing strategy on one attractive market segment.

consumer market Individuals and families that buy products for themselves.

contingency plan Plan that's ready to implement if significant, unexpected developments or emergencies disrupt strategy or programs.

cost leadership strategy Generic competitive strategy in which a company seeks to become the lowest-cost producer in its industry.

crowdsourcing Generating new product ideas or marketing materials by having customers and others outside the organization submit concepts, designs, content, or advice.

customer churn Turnover in customers during a specific period; often expressed as a percentage of the organization's total customer base.

customer-influence strategies Strategies for engaging customers through marketing communications and for influencing how they think, feel, and act toward a brand or an offering.

customer lifetime value Total amount a customer spends with a company over the course of a long-term relationship.

derived demand In business-to-business marketing, the principle that demand for a business product is based on demand for a related consumer product.

differentiated marketing Creating a separate marketing strategy for each targeted segment.

differentiation strategy Generic competitive strategy in which the company creates a unique differentiation for itself or its product based on some factor valued by the target market.

diversification Growth strategy of offering new products to new markets through internal product-development capabilities or by starting (or buying) a business for diversification purposes.

dynamic pricing Approach to pricing in which prices vary from customer to customer or from situation to situation.

emotional appeal Message strategy that relies on feelings rather than facts to motivate audience response.

features Specific attributes that enable a product to perform its function.

financial objectives Targets for performance in managing specific financial results.

fixed pricing Approach to pricing in which prices do not vary; the customer pays the price set by the marketer.

focus strategy Generic competitive strategy in which the company narrows its competitive scope to achieve a competitive advantage in its chosen segments.

forecast Future projection of what sales and costs are likely to be in the period covered by the plan.

frequency How many times, on average, the target audience is exposed to the message during a given period.

goals Longer-term performance targets for the organization or a particular unit.

greenwashing Perception that a company's claim about its product being environmentally friendly is overblown or untrue.

integrated marketing communication Coordinating content and delivery so that all marketing messages are consistent and support the positioning and direction in the marketing plan.

internal marketing Marketing that targets managers and employees inside the organization to encourage support of the marketing plan.

key performance indicators (KPIs) Indicators about elements of performance that are vital to achieving the organization's goals and objectives.

keyword search advertising Form of online advertising in which the company pays to have its site listed in the search results for specific words or brands; also known as *paid search*.

lifestyle The pattern of living that an individual exhibits through activities and interests.

line extension Putting an established brand on a new product added to an existing product line.

logistics Managing the movement of goods, services, and related information from the point of origin to the point of sale or consumption and balancing the level of service with the cost.

macroenvironment Largely uncontrollable external elements that can potentially influence the ability to reach goals; these include economic, ecological, technological, political-legal, and social-cultural forces.

market All the potential buyers for a particular product.

market development Growth strategy in which the company identifies and taps new segments or markets for existing products.

market penetration Growth strategy in which the company sells more of its existing products to customers in existing markets or segments.

market segmentation Grouping customers within a market according to similar needs, habits, or attitudes that can be addressed through marketing.

market share The percentage of sales in a given market held by a particular company, brand, or product; can be calculated in dollars or units.

marketing The activity, set of institutions, and processes for creating, communicating, delivering, and exchanging offerings that have value for customers, clients, partners, and society at large.

marketing audit A detailed, systematic analysis of an organization's marketing capabilities and performance.

marketing control The process of setting goals and standards, measuring and diagnosing interim results, and taking corrective action when needed to keep a marketing plan's performance on track.

marketing dashboard A computerized, graphical or digital presentation enabling management to monitor marketing results by tracking important metrics over time and by spotting patterns that signal deviations from the plan.

marketing objectives Targets for performance in managing specific marketing relationships and activities.

marketing plan A document that summarizes marketplace knowledge and the strategies and steps to be taken in achieving the objectives set by marketing managers for a particular period.

marketing planning The process of determining how to provide value to customers, the organization, and key stakeholders by researching and analyzing the market and situation; developing and documenting marketing objectives, strategies, and programs; and implementing, evaluating, and controlling marketing activities to achieve the objectives.

mass customization Creating products, on a large scale, with features tailored to individual customers.

metrics Numerical measures of specific performance-related activities and outcomes.

microenvironment Groups that have a more direct effect on the organization's ability to reach its goals: customers, competitors, channel members, partners, suppliers, and employees.

mission Statement of the organization's fundamental purpose, its focus, and how it will add value for customers and other stakeholders.

mobile marketing Getting coupons, information, directions, and other messages to customers via cell phones.

motivation What drives the consumer to satisfy needs and wants.

multichannel marketing Providing a variety of distribution channels for customers to use when buying goods or services at different times.

negotiated pricing Type of pricing in which buyer and seller negotiate the price.

niche Smaller segment within a market that exhibits distinct needs or benefit requirements.

neuromarketing Using technologies such as eye-tracking and MRIs to measure consumers' physiological reactions to products and marketing.

North American Industry Classification System (NAICS) Method of classifying businesses according to industry designation; used in the United States, Canada, and Mexico.

objective-and-task budgeting Method in which the budget is determined by totaling the cost of all marketing tasks needed to achieve the marketing plan objectives.

objectives Shorter-term performance targets that support the achievement of an organization's or unit's goals.

paid search Also known as *keyword search advertising,* a form of online advertising in which the company pays to have its site listed in the search results for specific words or brands.

penetration pricing Pricing a product relatively low in order to gain market share rapidly.

percentage-of-sales budgeting Method of budgeting in which the company allocates a certain percentage of sales revenues to fund marketing programs.

perception How the individual organizes environmental inputs such as ads and derives meaning from the data.

positioning Using marketing to create a distinctive place or image for a brand or product in the mind of customers.

price elasticity of demand Percentage change in unit sales of demand divided by the percentage change in price; where customers are price sensitive and demand changes considerably due to small price changes, the demand is elastic.

primary research Research conducted specifically to address a certain situation or to answer a particular question.

product development Growth strategy in which the company sells new products to customers in existing markets or segments.

product life cycle The stages through which a product moves in the marketplace: introduction, growth, maturity, and decline.

product line Group of products made by one company that are related in some way.

product mix Assortment of all product lines marketed by one company.

productivity control Type of marketing control used to assess the organization's performance and progress in managing the efficiency of key marketing areas.

profitability control Type of marketing control used to assess the organization's progress and performance based on profitability measures.

psychographic characteristics Variables used to analyze consumer lifestyle patterns.

pull strategy Using marketing to encourage customers to ask intermediaries for a product, thereby pulling it through the channel.

push strategy Using marketing to encourage channel members to stock a product, thereby pushing it through the channel to customers.

quality How well a product satisfies customer needs.

rational appeal Message strategy that relies on facts or logic to motivate audience response.

reach How many people in the target audience are exposed to the message during a particular period.

schedule Time-defined plan for completing work that relates to a specific purpose or program.

secondary research Research data already gathered for another purpose.

segment personas Detailed but fictitious profiles representing how individual customers in a targeted segment behave, live, and buy.

segments Groups within a market having distinct needs or characteristics that can be effectively addressed by specific marketing offers and programs.

service recovery How an organization plans to recover from a service lapse and satisfy its customers.

skim pricing Pricing a new product high in order to establish an image and more quickly recover development costs in line with profitability objectives.

social media Online media designed to facilitate user interaction.

societal objectives Targets for achieving specific results in social responsibility.

stakeholders People and organizations that are influenced by or that can influence an organization's performance.

strategic control Type of marketing control used to assess the organization's performance and progress in the strategic areas of marketing effectiveness, customer relationship management, and social responsibility and ethics.

subcultures Distinct groups within a larger culture that exhibit and preserve distinct cultural identities through a common religion, nationality, ethnic background, or lifestyle.

sustainable marketing Providing customers with value while preserving natural capital and human capital, now and into the future.

SWOT analysis Summary of an organization's strengths, weaknesses, opportunities, and threats in preparation for marketing planning.

target costing Using research to determine what customers want in a product and the price they will pay, then finding ways of producing the product at a cost that will accommodate that price and return a profit.

target market Segment of the overall market that a company chooses to pursue.

targeting Decisions about which market segments to enter and in what order, and about how to use marketing in each segment.

undifferentiated marketing Targeting all market segments with the same marketing strategy.

value The difference between total benefits and total price, as perceived by customers.

value-based pricing An approach to setting prices that starts with customers' perspective of a product's value and the price they are willing to pay; marketers then work backward to make the product at a cost and a profit that meet the company's objectives.

value chain The series of interrelated, value-added functions and the structure of organizations that perform these functions to get the right product to the right markets and customers at the right time, place, and price; also known as *supply chain*.

word-of-mouth (WOM) communication People telling other people about an organization, a brand, a product, or a marketing message.

INDEX

Note: Bold locators refer to definition of key terms. Notation "b" and "ex" refers to box and exhibits cited in the text.